Anthony Masters was born in 1940, educated at King's College, Wimbledon, and worked as a journalist and in publishing, before becoming a full-time writer. His first book, a collection of short stories entitled *A Pocket Full of Rye*, was a runner-up for the John Llewellyn Rhys Prize. He then won the Prize with his novel, *The Sea Horse*. He had written several works of non-fiction, including *Bakunin: the Father of Anarchism*, *The Summer that Bled* – the biography of Israel's national heroine, Hannah Senesh, *Rosa Lewis*, and *Bedlam* – history of psychiatric hospitals. He has written for television, and is Director of Event Opera, the well-established children's music, dance and drama organization and of Adventure Unlimited, a children's adventure training project based in Sevenoaks.

Anthony Masters is married, with three children, and lives in Sussex.

Anthony Masters

Inside Marbled Halls

*Life above and below stairs
in the Hyde Park Hotel*

Futura Publications Limited

A Futura Book

First published in Great Britain by
Sidgwick and Jackson Limited in 1979

First Futura Publications edition 1980

Copyright © 1979 Anthony Masters

ISBN 0 7088 1830 7
Printed by
William Collins Sons & Co. Ltd
Glasgow

Futura Publications Limited
110 Warner Road, Camberwell,
London SE5

Acknowledgements

I would like to acknowledge the help of the following in compiling Mary's biography: Mrs John Abbott, Sir Max Aitken, Bernard Amendt, Eamonn Andrews, Lord Auckland, Sir Peter Beauchamp, Max Blouet, Billy Bone, J. J. Briggs, Elizabeth Burne, Michael Carthy, Harold Cavallo, Justin Collier, Dr H. S. Conran, Peter Crome, P. E. Crutchley, Pearse Dooley, Sir Charles Forte, Colonel Brian Franks, H. H. Georg of Denmark, Elzie Gillespie, Tony Hart, Mrs Hickey, John Insley, Tommy Kinsman, H. B. J. Lowe, Cesare Maggi, Florence Maidment, John Maroni, H. Marston Riley, Ginger Mason, Ronald Massara, Alan Montgomery, Nonzio Nestola, Eddie Osborne, Alan Parfitt, Harry Payne, Donald Perry, Gerhardt Pfeiffer, William B. Porter, Joe Redell, Brian Rix, Tom Sawyer, Dick Sheil, Mary Shiffer, Vincent Smith, Simon Spencer, Bobby Thompson, Marcel Tissot, Commander C. G. and Lady Doris Vyner, Charles Vyse, Peter Walsh, Hugh Wilbraham.

I am grateful to the following for permission to quote from, or to adapt material from their copyright material: Sir Max Aitken for *Politicians and The War, 1914–1916* by Lord Beaverbrook; George Allen & Unwin Ltd for *Queen Mary 1867–1953* by James Pope-Hennessy; Cassell & Co. for *A King's Story* by the Duke of Windsor; Collins for *Evelyn Waugh* by Christopher Sykes; David & Charles for *Later than We Thought* by René Cutforth; Hamish Hamilton for *Beaverbrook* by A. J. P. Taylor; Hutchinson for *Men and Power* by Lord Beaverbrook;

Weidenfeld & Nicolson for *The Diaries of Evelyn Waugh* edited by Michael Davie, and Orbis Publishing for *Dance Little Ladies* by Margaret Pringle. Extracts from Queen Mary's diaries are reproduced by gracious permission of Her Majesty the Queen.

Finally, I would like to thank all the nursing staff at the Edmund Allenby Ward, St Stephen's Hospital, Fulham Road, who were so helpful to Mary and me in the many interview sessions we had. On Mary's behalf, I would also like to thank them for the twice daily glass of sherry they gave her in the last few weeks of her life.

ANTHONY MASTERS
September 1978

Contents

Chapter One

༺ᘒᘒᘒ༻

The Dubliner

1889-1902

MARY was born in the centre of a dynamo – in the hub of a relentlessly seething mass of humanity who went from home to work to mass to bar in patterns that were wholly traditional. Engine Alley was narrow, dark, Brueghelian. The tenement houses seemed to lean towards each other, their walls bulging with the poverty-stricken families which went on breeding – as the Holy Father desired. This area was The Liberties, in the district of Inchicore, in the heart of Dublin. The year was 1889.

Born Mary Dooley, she was the fourth child of fourteen. She was also the eldest girl, and within the Catholic family framework of those times she was born to serve. Mary began by serving her family. Decades later she was serving the King and Queen of England. Her last words to me were: 'I helped them all – didn't I? I helped them all!' I reassured her that she had.

Mary's parents, Michael and Elizabeth Dooley, were typical of their time. Elizabeth slaved in the house and had hardly any social life. Michael slaved at work and – as was considered his right – had a full social life on a Friday evening. He would return from this conviviality to beat his wife and children. But there was little criticism of him and not even much fear. The beatings were accepted as part of life – part of the relationship between the man and his family.

All Mary's family worked for Guinness. If they had not done so, they would have worked for the railway. Everybody in Engine Alley worked either for Guinness or for the railway. There was no other choice. Both institutions were benevolent. Both believed in the policy of low wages and free health schemes as effective methods of keeping the poor in their place in the scheme of things. Both branches of the family, the McCabes, on Elizabeth's side, and the Dooleys were devout Catholics, but the McCabes were definitely socially superior to the Dooleys. Indeed, it was generally considered by the McCabes that Elizabeth had married beneath her. The vital difference between the families lay in the fact that the McCabes were smellers and the Dooleys were draymen.

The Guinness drays were a proud and familiar sight in Dublin. The sculpted barrels, the gleaming harness, the beautifully groomed horses, the aproned and bowler-hatted draymen, the rattle and clatter of the carts over the cobbles and tramlines, the spanking ring of the horses' hooves, the rank smell of stout and horsehair in summer, the clouds of steam from the horses' nostrils in winter – all served to make an event of each appearance. But despite all this, draymen were mere carriers. Smelling, however, was an art – an art that only a first-class nose could command.

Generally speaking a smeller had also served time as a cooper – the actual manufacturer of the wooden barrel. Each cooper put a cask mark and his initial on the barrel, and the smeller had his first sniff at this stage to ensure all was well with the completed job. But the smeller came into his own when the barrel was returned to Guinness for refilling, from bars not only in Ireland but from the whole of Britain and Europe. Quite often the barrels had been stored in unhygienic cellars or had become contaminated en route back to the brewery. They were in particular danger if ferried by train, for the guard would often place his paraffin lamp in or near them – causing instant contamination.

The smeller had to keep his nose in good condition and report instantly should he feel a head cold coming on. Traditionally kitted out in tall silk hats, the smellers had their own special rest-room in which to relax their nostrils and recharge their sense of smell. They only worked half an hour at a time, and they had frequent breaks. Basically contamination was on a graded scale. If the barrel had a certain aroma of sweetness, then it was considered passable. But if it smelt 'casky', which really meant sour, then it had to go through a minor decontamination process. A 'single foul' would mean more serious treatment was necessary, whilst a 'double foul' would mean an even longer period of decontamination. For this work the average smeller would get between £2 and £2 10s. a week, compared with the more lowly wage of about £1 a week for the draymen. So the McCabes looked down on the Dooleys, with their insensitive nostrils and their artisan calling. But at least the Dooleys could crack through the streets of Dublin in any kind of weather, little fearing for the condition of their noses. To the McCabes, their noses were their livelihood, and they treated the delicate mechanisms with the same zeal as they protected their Catholic souls. There was every need for this, as each month they were tested on their sense of smell. If they failed the test social disaster was imminent.

The Liberties, the area in which Engine Alley existed, means tenements and markets and cathedrals to the Dubliner. It is roughly bounded by the Quays, the Castle, St James's Gate and Blackpitts. In the time of Mary's childhood it was an area of considerable poverty, and child mortality was very high. The Liberties' most famous figure was Jonathan Swift, who was Dean of St Patrick's Cathedral from 1713 to 1745. Its most famous streets, and those most familiar to the young Mary Dooley, were Castle Street, with its notorious tenements, which were demolished as a result of public outcry when she was ten, and Bride Street, with its bird market and the secondhand clothes stalls of Iveagh Buildings. Other landmarks were St Patrick's Cathedral, Kevin Street Garda Station, Blackpitts and the remnants of the old tannery, South Brown Street and its weavers, Tenterfields and the bleaching green used by the linen trade, the Coombe, the old Weavers' Hall and the shop that sold toffee apples. Then there was Crosspoddle, where the women washed the clothes in the River Poddle, the Marshalsea Barracks, Christchurch Cathedral, Tailors' Hall and Monniger's pawnshop. All familiar limbs of the only world that she knew.

Dubliners say that there were three kinds of tenements in The Liberties during Mary's early childhood – those where the doors were kept shut all the time, those where the doors were kept open all the time, and those with no doors at all. The Dooley household came into the first category. Respectability was everything – even if Michael Dooley did spend too large a proportion of his week's wages on drink. But as he never told Elizabeth how much he earned she could only guess at the difference between the silver he left on the mantelpiece on Friday night, and the amount he had been given by his employers earlier in the evening. Guessing at her husband's wage was an intriguing game for Elizabeth, largely because the amount differed from week to week.

As the eldest girl Mary was expected to remain illiterate. By the time she was of school age she already had three older brothers, all of whom were educated at the Christian Brothers School, which cost the Dooleys 6s. a month for each boy. The Christian Brothers, a celibate lay Catholic order, were considered superior to the less academic National Schools with their Protestant pupils. The Christian Brothers taught the Three R's with reasonable precision amidst an aura of religious grace and the ready use of the strap. But there was no money left over for Mary to attend school, and her illiteracy hung like a dead weight around her neck for the rest of her life.

As much as it was considered unnecessary to send Mary to school, it was considered necessary to teach her the whole range of domestic drudgery. By the time she was ten she was running messages, doing the washing and helping her mother to bake bread. She was a high-spirited child and she soon developed a dominating personality, which was not only useful for keeping her brothers in order but also a vital strength in the battle between her love for her mother and her hatred for her father.

It is unlikely that Michael Dooley behaved any worse than many men of that time. Every Friday evening he would leave approximately 16s. on the mantelpiece. The rest he spent on drink. After the bars closed on Friday night, he was at his traditional worst. With grim regularity he would arrive home drunk, and if a mug of tea was not instantly available to soak up the drink he would overturn the table, showering its contents about the room. Even if the tea *was* ready, a typical evening would end in a beating for Elizabeth and probably one for Mary and her sister Esta. It was a predictable and monotonous conclusion to a week of striving. But it was a style of life to which Mary knew no alternative. And despite her growing hatred for her father, there were joys as well as miseries.

Every so often Michael, in a better frame of mind, would play the melodeon (concertina) or the penny whistle. The family would dance to it, either jigs or tap, and the revelry would blend with similar spontaneous parties throughout the network of The Liberties. Tap dancing on the table, a wild jig on the floor, the tiny rooms echoing to the music – the whole of Engine Alley vibrated to the Dooleys' good-timing. It was instinctively necessary to the family – an outlet without which there would have been only apathy and more violence. The girls hurled themselves into the dancing with the same physical force and abandon as the boys. Eventually they stopped, exhausted, the spontaneity, uninduced by alcohol, over. They had pumped the grinding routine out of their systems, and were at peace with each other.

In Mary's old age, one memory, its bitterness softened by irony, was of the first and last piece of carpentry that she could remember her father doing in the house. With considerable care Michael Dooley made a small stool for her, which gave her the added height required to reach up to the kitchen sink.

The Dooley family had no holidays, and Mary was continuously sent out to buy stale bread to 'make do'. There was no oven in the house – simply a stove which was used for boiling and an open fire for cooking. They could afford only the cheapest of meats, and mutton stew featured regularly in their monotonous diet. Rice with raisins, cooked over the fire in the three-legged pots known as skillets, was another staple.

At eleven, Mary was confirmed. She was an attractive girl, small with strong features, long fair hair and a manner that was both personable and rhetorical. Her personality was strong and the dominating quality was evolving, but there was also a certain defensiveness, arising out of the awareness that her brothers were being educated while she was marking time. This awareness was instinctive, for there was nothing in her background to make her conscious of rights – and it manifested itself as a growing restlessness that eventually drove her to leave her mother unprotected, and to force her sisters to assume her arduous domestic mantle.

After her confirmation, Mary regularly attended a kind of domestic night school at a local convent. There, Sister Josephine taught her to cook and wash clothes properly. As a result Mary was privileged to attend more fully not only to the growing family wash but also to the washing which her mother 'took in' from other women.

Michael Dooley may have been a difficult man but he was not ungenerous. By Mary's eleventh birthday the family had grown considerably. There were her three older brothers, Michael, Jim and Sean, and now she had three younger brothers, John, Paddy and William. There was also Esta and a new baby girl, Bridie. But despite the ever-increasing family, each child received a farthing on Friday evening and a farthing on Saturday evening. This they spent mainly on broken biscuits or sweets. Once Mary picked up a half-sovereign by mistake and spent it on sweets. Little realizing she had received a surprising amount for a farthing, she returned home to discover her awful mistake. Luckily the shopkeeper was honest enough to rectify the situation, but Michael Dooley made sure that Mary would be deterred from making the same careless mistake again by giving her a sound thrashing and sending her straight to bed.

Mary remembered her mother as having 'lovely black hair and always a black eye to match'. But the continuous beatings did little to make Elizabeth Dooley think of leaving her husband. Her devout Catholicism prevented this, and she bore the monstrous drudgery of her life with passivity and determined teetotalism. She bore her husband's children with fortitude and serviced their proliferating needs with humility. There were many women in Engine Alley like Elizabeth – just as there were many men like her husband. The Dooleys' was the accepted way of life, and it had its compensations. The major compensation was the community, rough and chauvinistic as it was.

A small further income came from the pawn shops, and Mary pawned her father's best Sunday suit at Monnigers in Dominic Street every week without fail – though woe betide her if she forgot to get it back. This sum was supplemented by the arrival of Elizabeth's mother into the family, and the small contribution from her pension. These two subsidiary incomes might buy a few treats for the family, such as roller skates (singly or in pairs), toffee apples (a farthing each), and liquorice and fizz bags from the dozens of little huckster shops, with their minute counters and latticed panes, which littered The Liberties. Buttermilk could be bought from the dairies at a penny a tilly (a miniature churn), and Mary loved going into the cool, spotless parlours with their wooden churns, milk in earthenware crocks and marble counters. She would also buy lace from the huckster shops, as well as paraffin oil and Reckitt's blue.

At St Patrick's Park and in the Beno play-centre there were free treats. Mary and Esta and their brothers would get a bun and a mug of 'shell cocoa', a chocolate drink made from a shell-like shape of cocoa essence plunged into water. There were also other forms of entertainment which were completely free: running after the puncheons, horses towing back carts of washed grain for cattle feed, so that on a bright, raw, winter's day the children could feel the heat of the steam; watching the fighting cocks, whippets and brindle terriers bred by the pipe-smoking, cap-wearing old women in Blackpitts; watching the prize-fighting that went on in Engine Alley, as a result of pub challenges – the bare-knuckle fight would go to the man who stood up longest; and making spadgers – a singularly cruel but eventually profitable pastime. A sparrow was caught with a bit of twig with bird-lime on the end. The bird would jump on to the twig and stick fast, then becoming known as a spadger. The Dooleys would take the spadger up to Bride Street bird market, where an old man would put a few spots of paint on the spadger – which would then be passed off as a goldfinch.

And there were other joys to compensate for the hardship of the children's lives. In Patrick Street they could buy Dublin Bay herrings at a halfpenny each. The boys swam naked in the mill-race at the back of Sweeney's Lane in Talbot's Yard. And if nothing else presented itself, the children could always watch the religious statue-makers in Whitefriars Street, or the drunks being wheeled back to the Garda Station in Chancery Street on stretchers after a series of fights, or the fortune-telling budgies which for a penny would hop to the back of their cage and return with a card saying 'You are about to embark on a long journey' or 'A tragedy will soon overtake you'. Then there were the marches of the Boys' Brigade (the Catholics from South Street and the·Protestants from Lord Edward Street), or the fun of jumping on to the back axles of cabs and getting a ride up as far as Constitution Hill before the angry cabbie discovered their presence.

Then there were always the street games which the Dooley children played up and down Engine Alley, avoiding the big, box-like bakers' carts with their shelves of steaming bread and their tempting soda squares and currant squares, and the jingling milk-carts with their gleaming churns and the huge brass taps sticking out of the holes in the tail-board.

The boys often played separate games, such as Ball in the Decker, where they rolled balls into caps and then, on success, flung the ball at the boy who was nearest and easiest to hit. If the throw missed, a pebble was placed in the cap of the boy who had thrown. But if he scored, then a pebble would be placed in the cap of the boy who had been hit. When six pebbles had accumulated, the victim was stood up against a wall and ordered to place his hand against the bricks. Then each boy would take six shots at his hand with a half-solid ball. Another game, Duck on the Grawnshee, involved a marble being placed in a small depression so that it looked like a sitting duck. A chalk circle was then drawn around it. The owner of the 'duck' stood with one foot inside the circle. The other boys then aimed their marbles from the kerb at the 'duck'. If any boy failed to knock it off the Grawnshee then he had to pick up his marble without being touched by the boy with his foot inside the circle. There were other complexities to the game, and it was entirely engrossing. So was hurley, which was played in Engine Alley with all manner of implements – and many were the cracking blows taken on bloodied shins.

But despite the roughness of the boys' games, they were often anxious to join in with Mary, Esta and their friends as they played their skipping games – with a variety of different chants and songs. The dust clouds would billow up Engine Alley as the boys and girls skipped. Then they would play ring games, including 'Jennie is a-Weeping', with a girl pretending to be weeping in the centre of the ring, or 'In and Out the Window', with someone running in and out of the ring whilst the others sang:

> *In and out the window, in and out the window,*
> *   in and out the window,*
> *As you have done before.*
> *Stand and face your lover, stand and face your lover,*
> *   stand and face your lover,*
> *As you have done before.*
> *Chase him all round Dublin, chase him all round Dublin,*
> *   chase him all round Dublin,*
> *As you have done before.*

And there were other games, with names like Taw in the Hole, Up to the Mottle, Combo, or the more familiar Kick the Can.

At nightfall the gangs of children dispersed, running up the streets of The Liberties with their strange, unique names – Jamboland, Tommoland, Forty Steps, Watey Lane, Rowsertown and Pigtown – and home for their tea. Around them, as they ran through the darkening streets, the gas-lamps would be lit by the lamplighter with his long pole, and the shops would be illuminated by paraffin lamps, or the poorer ones by candlelight.

Sometimes Mary would be sent out in the dim chasms of the blue and green glowing streets, past the beggars huddling in the dark porches of the cathedrals, past the men filing into the pallid, stout-scented bars, past the clattering cabs and trams, running an errand – for a little tea, or some sugar. Or she would climb up to Meath Street or St Patrick's Hill for split loaves and a cat's lick – the cheap bread made for the poor. She would hurry back home, weary, with the prospect of an evening with Sister Josephine or round the wash-tub with her mother, while the boys lazed, argued and fought the time away. But if it was Christmas time, Mary would pause to window-shop, taking in the iced cakes and candied peel, the spices and Christmas cakes with cherries, the long red candles, the turkeys and the geese hanging while the men and women of The Liberties bargained fiercely over them.

The sound of The Liberties was its most individual characteristic. For the rest of her life, in London, Mary was to have this sound imprinted on her mind, overlaying the discreet murmur of voices in the banqueting suites of the Hyde Park Hotel, or the clatter of voices in its kitchens.

> *Coal blocks, coal blocks,*
> *Fresh fish, fresh fish,*
> *Éralamail, éralamail,*
> *Apples and oranges, apples and oranges.*

Knit together with the street cries were the clatter of hooves on the cobblestones, the iron wheels of the trams grating over the iron tracks, the babies crying and the barefoot boys and girls splashing in the pools of rainwater. This was the essence of The Liberties, the hurly-burly sound that made poverty not bearable but acceptable, the beatings not acceptable but an unalterable part of life.

There were the ballads, too, sung at the street corners by the blind and the maimed, hoping for a few pence in return for their throaty talents:

> *St Patrick was a gentleman*
> *His mother was a Brady*
> *His aunt an O'Shaughnessy*
> *And his uncle an O'Grady*
> *Then success to bold St Patrick first*
> *He was a Saint so clever*
> *He gave the snakes a toe to twist*
> *And banished them forever.*
> *St Patrick was a gentleman*
> *He came from decent people*
> *And in this town he built a church*
> *And on it put a steeple*
> *Oh stony, stony*
> *Don't let the sack-em-ups get me.**
> *Send around the hat*
> *And buy me a grave.*

And the hat was duly sent around, thus allowing the ballad-singer to avoid the dreaded pauper's funeral. Mary almost always

* Grave-robbers.

made a donation, for to her, even at that age, the very idea of not having a decent funeral was sacrilege. Amidst all this mêlée it was difficult to think of death, and Mary would hurry past the elaborate funeral processions for those who could afford them as well as the pathetic wooden boxes bundled out of the poor-houses or the night refuges en route to a pauper's grave.

When Mary was twelve, a crisis came. With it she hardened – and much of the hectic innocence of her childhood disappeared overnight. From then on she realized far more how death and hardship were connected, and the realities of life made her increasingly restless. The crisis was Spanish 'flu.

Spanish 'flu is of little importance now, but in 1901, in Dublin, it was a killer. Like most unpleasantnesses in Dublin, the 'flu was suspected to have come from England, and at its worst it was assumed to be typhoid, or at least scarlet fever. A medieval atmosphere overtook The Liberties, and the streets ran with disinfectant. As the deaths increased, the grim clatter of the funeral carriages intensified and a feeling of plague infested the silent streets and markets. No street games were played now, for fear of infection. Whole families squatted indoors, as terrified of catching the disease as people in the North nowadays are of a knock on the door from a terrorist.

In desperation the authorities went from house to house, taking away clothing, furniture and bed-linen. Only the furniture was returned. Like thousands of other families in Dublin, all the Dooleys' clothing and bed-linen was burned. Institutionalized clothing was issued, and sacks of straw and straw pillows distributed. These lay on the Dooley beds for two years before the family could afford to buy new bed-linen.

Engine Alley, though very poor, was not as bad as the worst slums. A typical breeding ground for the disease is described in this report on a classic Dublin slum, Patrick Street, in 1890. This sort of slum existed well into the twentieth century. Patrick Street consisted of

.two rows of tumble-down, mouldy-looking houses, reeking of dirt, and oozing with the disgusting smell of accumulated filth of many generations, with old petticoats hung up instead of curtains, and very often instead of glass in the dilapidated

windows. On each ground floor shops, with over-hanging
roofs, and resembling dirty cellars, expose for sale sides of
rancid bacon, bundles of candles, and jars of treacle – a
delicacy as much sought after as soap is neglected – greens,
cauliflowers, musty things and bad potatoes; while at every
three doors is a tavern, which in the midst of these hovels
resembles a palace. Every other house is an old clothes shop
where the sale of rags is combined with money-lending at large
interest. Shoes taken out of pawn there on Saturday night for
Sunday mass are pledged there again on Monday morning.

But all these ragged and vermin covered people are most
affable. . . . Far from being ashamed of their rags, they are
proud of being looked at; pretty, fair or red-haired girls whose
freshness has not yet been spoilt by bad air, insufficient food
or drinking to excess, nudge each other laughing and blushing;
cheeky children come and stare at you under your very nose,
and vanish like a flock of sparrows if you pretend to be angry;
mothers smile at you gratefully if you glance tenderly at the
baby. It is a question, as to how far these people are responsible
for the abject state of misery in which they are plunged; but it
touches one to see the good temper, sociableness, and even
politeness that survive such degradation.*

Because of the conditions, the 'flu continued to spread. Three
of Mary's brothers were taken to hospital, and recovered
miraculously. Then Mary herself went into the fever hospital,
suspected of having the much dreaded disease. Ludicrously, she
was put amongst those who definitely had it, and for days she
lay watching the last writhings of the women who were strapped
into the beds around her. Nevertheless, she also survived and
returned home. The rejoicing was short-lived. A few days later
her baby sister, Bridie, contracted the disease and died. All the
family were shattered, broken-hearted.

Sitting in one of the cathedrals, Mary reflected upon the way
the disease, with its attendant misery and stark reality of death,
had disrupted what was already a hard life. Around her in the
cathedral was a full complement of the homeless, alcoholics and
the insane. But in addition to these normal residents there were

* Anne Marie de Bovet, *Three Months' Tour in Ireland,* 1891.

many hundreds of others, of all different age groups. There was no mass being said at that moment. But it sounded as if there was, for a low muttering persisted throughout the incense-scented interior, broken now and again by a keening that often seemed to soar up to the great domed ceiling, the keening of those who had lost loved ones to the disease which was sweeping the city. The tears of the congregation mingled with their intercessions as they prayed, either desperately for the still living, or in grief for the dead.

The candles burned around Mary like stars in a clear night sky. She looked up towards her virgin namesake, staring at the painted plaster figure, wondering why she had taken Bridie so savagely. She thought of the pathetically small coffin being lowered into the grave, and her family weeping hopelessly around her. Her mother had sobbed desperately for her lost child, but her father had merely looked bemused. The tragedy was too much for him. Later Michael Dooley would find consolation in alcohol, but not so Elizabeth. She had to return to Engine Alley, already pregnant with her tenth child. Her only solace would be to apply herself to her many duties.

Mary was twelve, and there was no question of her assessing the plight of her family in this way. But as she looked around the cathedral, and at the examples of human suffering inside it, she knew instinctively that this suffering was in many ways reflected in the microcosm of her own family. Mary loved her family dearly, but even at twelve she was quite clear about one thing. She couldn't grow up like Elizabeth, condemned to marry, to breed and to be beaten. She didn't want a life of taking in washing and regular trips to the pawn shop to make ends meet, a life of daily domestic slavery.

She looked again around the cathedral, at the packed, huddled, supplicating forms. She knew that however much she loved The Liberties and the squalid, loving clamour, she would not let it take her over.

Chapter Two

෯෯෯෯෯෯෯෯෯෯෯෯෯෯෯෯෯෯෯෯෯෯෯෯෯෯෯෯෯෯෯෯෯

Two Kinds of Rebellion

෯෯෯෯෯෯෯෯෯෯෯෯෯෯෯෯෯෯෯෯෯෯෯෯෯෯෯෯෯෯෯෯෯

1916

THE man lay on the rooftop of the house next door to the Dooleys in Engine Alley. Below the search continued. Inside, Michael and Elizabeth Dooley sat totally still, so did the children. They knew he was up there, had known for hours, for he had been shifting from rooftop to rooftop all the morning. None of them knew anything about him, except that he was a Volunteer – and they didn't want to know even that. Michael had closed the big, heavy shutters in front of the windows and now they sat in their all too vulnerable fortress, waiting for something to happen. There were thirteen children now. The older children had taken the younger ones in their arms and lay huddled, with the furniture piled up around them.

Elizabeth, with her two older daughters, Mary and Esta, cautiously kept the family fed during the hours of waiting, while the three older boys, Michael, Jim and Sean, tried haltingly to keep morale up. Their father tried too, despite the fact that he cursed every inch of haphazard progress that the hunted Volunteer had made towards Engine Alley.

The Easter Rising of 1916 had started. Throughout the day the Dooleys had heard bursts of gunfire, sometimes coming from the direction of O'Connell Street (as it was then unofficially known) and at other times from neighbouring streets. Like many others, the Dooleys were completely confused by the suddenness and the sporadic siting of the rebellion. That the rebels had now managed to hold out for two days in the General Post Office was something of an achievement – yet many of the women in Engine Alley considered that they should be shot. The men viewed them more romantically. At the same time there was also a muddled worry about civil war.

The day before, Sean Dooley had spelt out to Mary the wording of the proclamation from the Provisional Government. Now, as she made what seemed to be the hundredth pot of tea of the day, the words returned to her in fragments. But they seemed to have a personal meaning – as if the revolution, like the Spanish 'flu before it, was a warning. Just as Padraic Pearse, the leader of the I.R.B., was trying to liberate the Irish people, Mary knew she must now liberate herself. Bridie's death, her thoughts in the cathedral, and her realization of what a claustrophobic future lay ahead, had not been enough. Oddly, the rebellion was.

In the name of God and of the dead generations from which she receives her old traditions of nationhood, Ireland, through us, summons her children to her flag and strikes for her freedom.

Mary was now twenty-seven and her life had been much as she feared. She retained her dominating vivacity, her archetypal Irish wit and the good looks that she had had as a young girl. Her pale blue eyes, clear skin, fair hair and diminutive neatness seemed to classify her as a typical 'colleen'. In fact, she was rapidly developing a hardened outer shell as a defence against the drudgery of family life. The swarms of children and her role as second mother had driven her, since she was twenty, to find a number of temporary escape routes. She had even been as far as Belfast, working as a waitress in a hotel. Closer to home, she had worked in a similar position in Jurys Hotel in Dublin, where a first fleeting and unhappy infatuation had returned her once again to Engine Alley.

The Republic guarantees religious and civil liberty, equal rights and equal opportunities to all its citizens.

But how could it? What would change? Certainly not her own predicament or that of anyone in Engine Alley. Their life would be the same, the poverty the same, the hopelessness of it all the same. As she passed round the tea to the crouching shapes in the darkened room, Mary knew that the rebellion was not just theirs – it was hers too, but in reverse. For as much as Padraic Pearse and James Connolly and their friends were calling on the nation, 'by its valour and discipline and by the readiness of its children to sacrifice themselves for the common good, [to] prove itself worthy of the august destiny to which it is called', Mary was preparing to leave the country. Despite her love for her family, and particularly her mother, she knew she had to go. Soon it would be too late and she would be tied to the house, and to the demands of her father and brothers, for ever. If Dubliners could be taught rebellion in such a haphazard manner, then she must teach herself to rebel, to leave Dublin and to find a life where she would not be completely taken over by Engine Alley.

The plan came to her slowly as she heard the troops marching up the street. She would, on some pretext, go to England. It would take considerable courage for she knew not a soul there. But it would be a clean break – and that was what she needed. She realized in advance the desperation of it all and the isolation and loneliness that was to come. But she knew there was only one course left to her. It was England or Engine Alley.

The noise outside was tremendous and the younger children cried out in fear. Michael Dooley cursed, flattening himself on to the floor as if he were convinced he could burrow his way into it. Elizabeth dropped her tea cup and Mary instinctively flung her arms around her mother. Bullets penetrated the wooden shutters and front door of the Dooley house, thudding into furniture and walls, spraying the interior with a sharp, deadly shower. Miraculously no-one inside was hit. Then they heard shouting and the drumming of feet as the soldiers ran across the cobbles.

Still holding her now sobbing mother, Mary had no idea whether the man on the roof had been killed or had merely moved to a less dangerous rooftop. She realized that the soldiers had probably shot up the house either out of malice or out of frustration at not getting their man, but it really didn't matter what their motives were now; everyone, except the younger ones, realized that the same thing could happen again at any time. And next time perhaps they wouldn't be so lucky.

The Dooleys stayed indoors for the first three days of the rebellion. Then, on the third night, Michael Dooley crept out for a much needed bender. He returned in declamatory but non-violent mood as he relayed to his family a highly coloured account of the Volunteers' botched raid on the ammunition dump at the Magazine Fort in Phoenix Park and their failure to ignite the bulk of the explosive (no one could find the key to the main ammunition dump). He also told them of the raid on Dublin Castle and its easy capture. What he didn't tell them were the less creditable ventures, discussed *sotto voce* by the more thoughtful in The Liberties' bars: the shooting of the seventeen-year-old son of the fort's commandant as he ran to give the alarm; or the earlier shooting of the unarmed constable of the Dublin Metropolitan Police as he tried to prevent the Irish Citizen Army getting into Dublin Castle.

The next day, Mary ventured out of Engine Alley, as determined as ever to leave The Liberties. All she had to do was to polish her plan. As she hurried amongst the huckster shops, Mary noticed a strange atmosphere in the entire area. Crowds stood around aimlessly waiting and watching – and looters had taken advantage of the situation to work over some of the larger shops. There was much talk of uprisings elsewhere in the country, and one shopkeeper told Mary that German help was on the way and that there was even a possibility that a German prince would be appointed King of Ireland after the war. This was all based on the optimistically wild despatches emerging from the General Post Office from such figures as Pearse and Connolly. She was also told that two flags were flying from the building. One was the traditional gold harp on the green background under which the words 'Irish Republic' were now picked out in gold. The other was a new flag, a tricolour of orange, white and green.

But none of this, apart from the feeling of imminent danger, aroused any excitement, romance or republican sentiment in Mary's heart. There was only one feeling emblazoned there – the desire for escape. For the next few days, however, there was no question of any immediate action.

The rebellion continued, although to its perpetrators success or failure was quite irrelevant. They felt that they were kindling the flames of nationalism throughout Ireland and that the rebellion was merely the initiation of a nationwide movement. Wisdom, considered Padraic Pearse, was quite irrelevant; in one of his plays, written in 1915, his ancient Gaelic hero says in protest: 'We thought it a foolish thing for four score to go into battle against four thousand, or maybe forty thousand.' But the idealistic reply came back: 'And so it is a foolish thing. Do you want us to be wise?'

Indeed Connolly had said to his fellow-revolutionary William O'Brien, as he grouped his men for the march on the General Post Office, that they were going out to be slaughtered. When O'Brien asked Connolly if they had no chance of success, Connolly replied, 'None whatever.'

The Dooley family remained inside their bullet-marked house for another two days, rarely venturing outside. Meanwhile the most unpleasant part of the rebellion continued – the shooting down by the rebels of fellow Irishmen. For instance, on the day of the uprising a detachment of the Irish Volunteer Defence Corps (a reserve training group of British forces staffed by middle-aged Irishmen who were over military age) was returning to the Beggars Bush Barracks at about four in the afternoon. Although they carried rifles, they had no ammunition for them. The rebels, who were sniping around the barracks, saw them coming, and poured volleys of rifle fire into the helpless, unarmed ranks. Five were killed immediately and nine were wounded.

During the course of the week there was a tendency for opinion to harden against the rebels, and in the Dooley household it was only the boys who glorified the Volunteers. Michael and Elizabeth, for their own different reasons, were tired of being housebound – and Mary, her decision to leave already made, was desperately bored. She decided to take the risk of going down O'Connell Street to see for herself the results of the fighting. The day before, Wednesday 26 April, had seen the Volunteers' greatest military success; by this time their military deployment was more effective. The British reinforcements, the Sherwood Foresters (seen as rescuers by the majority of Dubliners), had marched that morning towards the city centre. They were inexperienced troops (few had been in the army for more than three months), and as they advanced towards Mount Street Bridge to cross the canal they came under heavy fire from various outposts. The fighting was intense, and it took the Foresters many hours to cross the canal. Their losses were enormous: four officers killed and fourteen wounded, and 216 other ranks killed or wounded.

But this success was to be the beginning of the end. As Mary fearfully but curiously walked up O'Connell Street she saw the Post Office in flames and the green flag scorched brown. Despite her need to get away from Dublin she was profoundly moved. Pearse and Connolly were the last to leave the building, eventually finding temporary shelter in a fishmonger's shop in Great Britain Street.

Days later Mary returned, wandering along the masonry-strewn pavement beneath the Post Office, staring at the bullet-marked pillars, the shattered glass, the charred woodwork – reminders of the truth of Connolly's prediction, 'We are going out to be slaughtered.' The idealism of the Volunteers, their belief that they had sacrificed their lives to be initiators of a movement, and their sheer courage, lived with Mary for many years afterwards. True, they were not respectable. Equally true, their patriotism was infinitely superior to Mary's. But then they were not condemned to live in Engine Alley for the rest of their lives – they were condemned to die.

On Saturday 29 April, at 3.30 p.m., Padriac Pearse surrendered to Brigadier-General Lowe. The surrender took place on the steps of the burnt-out General Post Office. Both he and Connolly had given orders to the rebels to surrender, and by Sunday afternoon the last group gave in.

On Wednesday 20 May the Dooley family, now back in everyday harness, heard that Pearse, with two other revolutionaries, MacDonagh and Clarke, had been executed at Kilmainham Jail. What particularly upset Mary was the manner of their execution. Although the British authorities had allowed them to be given Holy Communion (Pearse was as devout a Roman Catholic as Mary), they had refused to allow the priest to remain close to them during the last few seconds before execution. Later Mary was to find a greater bond with Pearse when someone read her snatches from one of his last poems, written to his mother on 1 May 1916, in Arbour Hill Detention Barracks, two days before his execution. To Mary, the poem represented much that she felt about her own mother, particularly now that she was about to leave her to her workaday plight.

My gift to you hath been the gift of sorrow,
My one return for your rich gifts to me,
Your gift of life, your gift of love and pity,
Your gift of sanity, your gift of faith.
(For who hath had such faith as yours
Since the old time, and what were my poor faith
Without your strong belief to found upon?)
For all these precious things my gift to you
Is sorrow. For I have seen
Your dear face line, your face soft to my touch,
Familiar to my hands, and to my lips
Since I was little
I have seen
How you battled with your tears for me
And with a proud glad look, although your heart
Was breaking. O Mother (for you know me)
You must have known, when I was silent,
That some strange deep thing, when I should shout my love?
I have sobbed in secret
For that reserve which yet I could not master
I would have brought royal gifts, and I have brought you
Sorrow and tears: and yet, it may be
That I have brought you something else beside –
The memory of my deed and of my name,
A splendid thing which shall not pass away.
When men speak of me, in praise or in dispraise,
You will not heed, but treasure your own memory
Of your first son.

Mary's gift to Elizabeth was also sorrow. But she wished to alleviate it, and when she broke the news to her mother and the rest of the family that she was going away to England she softened it with a lie. She told them that she would be sailing with a friend who was a nurse and that together they would be going to assured jobs. Money would be sent back, regular visits to Dublin would be paid, and the family's financial plight would be helped considerably. In fact there was no friend who was a nurse – nor was there any job.

The family was considerably taken aback by the news. Michael, however, saw the money as a plus factor, while the boys saw the journey as a mysterious adventure and the other girls were jealous. The most extreme and profound emotion came from Elizabeth, who was heartbroken. Yet, she realized Mary's mind was made up. She knew her daughter's determined ways all too well. She knew there was nothing she could do to stop her. All she could do was to pray for her safety.

The next day, at dusk, Mary walked around The Liberties. Though she knew she would come back, she also knew it would somehow be different. This was a leavetaking, and she wanted to carry away as exact a mental portrait as she could. For she was afraid, and throughout that stroll on the spring evening the fear tore at her, trying to break her resolution. But her mind was made up – and her resolution was stronger than her fear.

It was a warm May evening. She was going down to the pawnbroker for the last time. Looking back, an old market street trader in Dublin remembered exactly how the pawn shops operated in Mary's time:

> If they were on the beer, the dealers used to pawn their bundles. And they could get £4 on a fawn shawl; pure wool, they were, beautiful and with big borders, about £8–£9 new, but you could pay the Jewman by the week. There'd be a pawnbroker on nearly every street corner; and very good they were too, they were: they never sent for people. I seen people taking down their pots and pans off the fire, anything at all.

En route to the pawn shop, Mary collected the ingredients for coddle – a very cheap but fairly nourishing stew. She bought a large bag of bacon bits, half a pound of sausages (both for 6d.), tuppenceworth of tripe, a portion of cow-heel, a couple of onions, split peas, lentils and a few potatoes. She was spending her own money, for she was determined that she would make a good supper for them all before she went away. She also bought some coal blocks for a farthing each, and then, with a sudden desire for luxury, she bought a pound of Danish butter for 8d.

On the way back, clutching her goodies, Mary went to sit in St Patrick's for a while. The cathedral was crowded and the mutter of prayer surrounded her as she tried to visualize England.

But it was impossible – she could see no further than The Liberties. A priest walked slowly past her, guiding a blind man. A few pews away sat an old man. He had his head in bandages – and a sleeve hung loosely by his side. Somebody had placed a wreath for Padraic Pearse just inside the front entrance. Others, more traditionally, had lighted candles for him. And although Mary tried very hard to picture England, all she could see were the bullet-peppered columns of the Post Office. What would Pearse have thought of her? What did her mother *really* think? Was she a traitor to go? – a traitor to her country with its new revolutionary zeal? – to her mother who needed her so desperately as daughter and companion?

Her mind confused, filled with a vague guilt, Mary left the cathedral and began to walk back to Engine Alley. On the way back she looked into the windows of slum buildings which were far worse than her own home. The children lay in the beds in waxy poverty, their hunger eloquent in their sleeping faces. She saw that many of them were ill, one of them close to death. Mary stared in almost angrily at the dying child, her feelings very similar to those expressed by Sean O'Casey in his autobiography,* when he wrote:

Such things as smallpox, typhoid fever, diphtheria and scarlet fever were the only blights that stimulated the doctors to rush about, hair-tossed and coatless, to blow on the bugles of alarm, forcing the people to close up their houses, seal themselves away from the fresh air, and burn sulphur in their rooms, filling the place with fumes, like incense rising from an altar in hell.

It was a time when every infant on some day in each passing week had to be filled with castor-oil, and dosed with syrup of squills, first having their chafed buttocks rubbed with stuff that had the grittiness of powdered steel.

Dismissing sudden and torturing thoughts of Bridie, Mary carried on through the bustling twilight towards Engine Alley. Then, as she walked into the narrow, dark street, she saw a flash

* *I Knock at the Door, Autobiography*, Vol. 1.

of colour. A fair-haired girl, about twelve years old, was dancing in the centre of a ring, under a gaslight, the blue tint picking out her pale features. The others were featureless in the gathering night. A few boys leaned up against the shuttered tenements, occasionally catcalling, occasionally throwing the odd pebble.

> *Poor Jennie is a'weeping, a'weeping, a'weeping,*
> *Poor Jennie is a'weeping on a bright summer day.*

The darkening spring evening made the sight suddenly eerie, and Mary's sense of uneasiness increased when she found herself identifying with the scruffy twelve-year-old as she twisted and turned to the lament:

> *Pray tell us what you're weeping for, a'weeping for,*
> *a'weeping for*
> *Pray tell us what you're weeping for on a bright summer day.*

Suddenly the children blocked her path, and all Mary could see in the gloom was the dead pattern of their faces. Then a boy jeered and the girl broke through the circle, running and clutching at Mary. She insisted that she joined them in their game. Almost hypnotically Mary joined in. She put her food down to one side, and all at once she was in the middle and they were whirling about her. The faster they went, the faster she danced, and the whole dim chasm of a street seemed to dance with her. She heard the boys shouting and saw that they, too, were dancing about her in a second, boisterous, jumping ring.

> *I'm weeping for my lover, my lover, my lover,*
> *I'm weeping for my lover on a bright summer day.*

And the faster she danced, the faster the tears ran down Mary's face. But she wasn't weeping for her lover. She was weeping for a childhood that was lost and a future of which she was afraid.

Only her mother came down to see her off. After the strained farewells, Mary stood on the deck of the ferry, about to begin the interminable waving that the boat's slow progress away from the pier dictated. She saw her mother looking up and down the deck, searching suspiciously for the nurse. Then an amazing thing happened. Turning to look around her, Mary saw a nurse standing alone a few feet away. Hurriedly she moved along and stood by her side. Then Mary saw her mother's expression change to one of relief. The sadness was still there, but so was reassurance. Mary relaxed. The past was taking care of itself. Only the future yawned in front of her – alien, terrifying and utterly insecure. With a final wave to the receding figure of her mother, and leaving her unknown 'companion', Mary went below. She had no wish to gaze on the calm, empty chill of the Irish Sea. Through more tears, she hoped to gain a little strength for what lay on the other shore.

Chapter Three

ᴏᴘ

Into Slavery

ᴏᴘᴏᴘᴏᴘᴏᴘᴏᴘᴏᴘᴏᴘᴏᴘᴏᴘᴏᴘᴏᴘᴏᴘᴏᴘᴏᴘᴏᴘᴏᴘᴏᴘᴏᴘᴏᴘ

1916-1917

Mᴀʀʏ's arrival in England coincided with dramatic events both at home and abroad. The battles of Verdun, the Somme and Ancre had already been fought, Kitchener had been drowned, Sir Roger Casement had been executed and General Smuts, later to use Mary Dooley as a sounding board, had been placed in command of German East Africa. Asquith's coalition government had resigned and Lloyd George was now Prime Minister. There had been Zeppelin raids all over Britain, and the musical comedy *Chu Chin Chow* had just begun its run of 2,238 shows. Liverpool Street Station was a seething mass of civilians and soldiers when she arrived. To Mary the crowd seemed immensely hostile; each person or group in it appeared totally isolated from the rest. No one cared for anyone – least of all herself. This was very different from the lounging crowds in The Liberties, who often had nowhere to go and little to do. All these people were so busy. They had set, purposeful faces and brisk, impatient strides. There was no time for idle conversation here, nor was there any glimmer of hope.

It was at this stage that Mary realized not only what a complete fool she had been, but also how grossly irresponsible. If only her beloved mother could see her now. It was lunacy to come on instinct to a great, uncaring city like this, knowing nobody, with no job. She stared around miserably, standing alone by the barrier.

Ten minutes later she was still there. For some time she had been conscious of a man watching her, the only other idler in the crowd. He was middle-aged, well-dressed in a businessman's way. He seemed to be mentally undressing her and a sudden shame burned over her. Surely she could expect little less as a result of the stupid risk she had taken. A few minutes later, predictably, he was by her side. The conversation was much as she expected.

'Hallo, little stranger.'

She made no reply.

'On your own?'

Still Mary maintained the silence that was her only defence.

'Looking for a job?'

Almost imperceptibly Mary nodded her head.

'Well . . .' His eyes seemed to consume her. 'I'm sure we can fix something for a nice trim little colleen like you. Where do you come from?'

'Dublin, sir.'

'Where the girls are so pretty?'

Mary made no reply. Then she asked, 'What kind of job, sir?'

'Oh – something in the secretarial line.'

'I wouldn't be up to that, sir.'

'Then – something in the catering line?'

'Yes, sir. I could do that. I've been—'

She broke off because the man was no longer looking at her. He was looking over his shoulder. Then he walked hurriedly away. Mary stared after him in bewilderment. She turned back to see a tall woman in the uniform she recognized from The Liberties, where it was much in evidence – the 'Sallies', the Salvation Army. The woman seemed to resemble a great crow with her sharp features, dark eyes, and bonnet almost like a ruffle of feathers.

'Can I help you?' She wore black horn-rimmed spectacles and there was an air of moral threat in her voice.

'No thank you, madam.'

'Are you alone?'

'Yes, madam.'

'Do you realize who you were talking to?'

'No, madam.'

'You were talking to a man of ill repute.'

Mary said nothing. There seemed nothing *to* say.

'Where are you from, girl?'

'Dublin, madam.'

'You're here to find work?'

Mary nodded.

'Do you realize,' the Salvation Army worker's voice trembled with emotion, 'that you were almost sold?'

'Sold? Who to, madam?'

'You silly girl. Into white slavery, of course.'

From that moment the woman took control. She told Mary that her name was Captain Allen and that Mary was more than foolish to arrive without work. She also implied that she was less than morally perfect to do so.

'What is your religion, dear?'

'I'm a Catholic, madam.'

'I thought as much,' Captain Allen observed darkly. She then took Mary for a cup of tea for which she was grateful, and a long lecture on white slavery for which she wasn't. After a while Captain Allen drew out a sombre little notebook and consulted a list. After running a steely eye down the list she closed the book with a vigorous snap and turned to Mary, her eyes alight with zeal. She told an acquiescent and by now exhausted Mary that she would be given overnight accommodation and the opportunity of a job. With genuine gratitude Mary thanked her, but she was cut short by a commanding wave of a black-gloved hand.

'It is God's wish.'

'His name be praised,' said Mary obediently, falling in with the general tenor of the conversation. They then marched to a bus-stop and eventually boarded a bus. Mary noticed that Captain Allen even asked for the tickets as if she was negotiating a country full of white slavers. Mary imagined them everywhere, waiting in dark corners or travelling in buses, luring millions of young girls to a lustful doom.

'Where are we?' asked Mary when they disembarked.

'Knightsbridge,' was the brisk rejoinder.

'Where are we going?'

'In there.'

'Holy Mother. Not in there.'

'They'll give you shelter. You've worked as a waitress. If God wills it, they may give you a job.'

Mary hesitated, but Captain Allen placed a muscular hand on her arm. They crossed the road, Mary dodging the traffic unhappily, but Captain Allen striding across Knightsbridge as if re-enacting the parting of the waters. For a moment they stood outside, gazing up at the building. To Mary the hotel looked like a fairy-tale palace. It was half past nine in the evening and each window was lit. Through a canopy over the steps which led from the pavement up to the entrance swarmed an endless procession of dinner jackets and evening dresses. Double parked at the roadside were cabs and huge, black, gleaming limousines – the likes of which Mary had never seen before. The whole sight both terrified and enthralled her. So these were the 'rich trash that had bled Ireland dry', as the English were so often referred to by her father – the lords and ladies of the land. There was a carpet covering the steps and a man in a long coat and top hat was calling cabs and opening doors.

'I can't go in there, madam.'

'Of course you can,' barked Captain Allen, looking more soldierly than ever. 'The staff entrance is round the back.'

Walking ahead, as if about to strike the colours, Captain Allen led Mary past the splendid spectacle. Mary looked up at the sign above her. It read Hyde Park Hotel. Little did Mary realize that this quite alien environment was to become more of a home to her than The Liberties had ever been. The Hyde Park Hotel was built in 1889 as a highly exclusive apartment block. On one side there were sweeping views of the park, and on the other the busy thoroughfares of Knightsbridge. The walls of the entrance halls, corridors and main rooms were lined with marble and the coffered ceilings were gilded. The apartments were inhabited by what was then described as the cream of society. In 1904 the apartments were partly burned out, and the building was reopened as a hotel in 1908. The marble and the ceilings had survived the fire and the refurbished building was even more opulent than before. Period fireplaces in the style of Louis XV and XVI were installed, while the furniture echoed the eighteenth-century theme with reproduction French and Sheraton and Hepplewhite.

Queen Victoria had insisted that no advertising signs should appear anywhere in Hyde Park, so the original main entrance, facing the Park, was closed; the rear entrance, facing Knightsbridge, had become the main entrance. The hotel was unique in that it retained the atmosphere of an exclusive apartment block as well as having a restaurant, a grill room, lounges, bars, seven banqueting suites and a ballroom. In all, there were 205 bedrooms and nineteen suites, frequented both by London society and by European nobility and royalty, either still reigning or in exile.

The British royal family used the hotel regularly, and had their own private entrance in Hyde Park (the original front entrance) which was opened only for their use. Many of the suites were occupied by long-term residents, and there was an enormous staff, including dozens of valets, who catered for the every need of their pampered clients. Apart from the 'apartment' atmosphere, the Hyde Park was also like a club – and a highly exclusive club at that. No guest was accepted without first having references checked; it was preferable to have a title and only barely acceptable to be an 'Hon'. It was downright cheapjack to be a plain Mr or Mrs. Politicians were an exception to this élitist ruling, and such figures as Beaverbrook were favoured clients because they were important and influential and gave 'style' to the hotel.

The Hyde Park was owned by the Bennetts, a benevolent family of property dealers who had bought the building after the fire and opened a hotel run in a genteel but feudal manner. This was why Captain Allen was able to bring Mary to shelter there, for the Bennetts were on the Salvation Army list as good Christian employers who were able to use a battery of servant girls. They owned various other properties in London and were known as the most generous hotel-owning family in the city. Nevertheless they had little day-to-day contact with the running of the Hyde Park, this being left to a number of managers, who were often tyrannical. They also observed the normal standards of the age regarding servant quarters, which meant that the staff lived in some squalor.

The first night of Mary's sixty-one years at the hotel began gloomily. She was desperately homesick and the dormitory space was so small that she had to sit on the bed to change her clothes – or to perform any major movement whatsoever. A towel rack stood between each bed and there was a battered locker with an insecure-looking lock for her personal possessions. The long dormitory, one of many situated below stairs, just beneath the entrance hall, was dark, dirty and noisy. One of the most alarming sounds was the machine-gun-like footsteps of the pedestrians on the pavement above.

The staff were roughly kind to her that night, and there were a number of her own countrymen among them, but this did not prevent her having a fairly sleepless night. In the morning she was taken up to see the manager. He was a Belgian named Cornu, a man obsessed by order and timekeeping. There was something of the Hercule Poirot in him, but the extent to which he exercised his little grey cells was limited to worrying about any break in the routine of the hotel. And certainly Mary represented a break in that routine.

Cursing the Bennetts' benevolence, Cornu asked Mary what she intended to do next. Tired and on edge, she told him that she did not know. He then grudgingly asked her if she would like a lowly job in the hotel – an offer she accepted with alacrity. Nevertheless, there were complications. To Cornu's considerable agitation he discovered that Mary possessed no references from anywhere. After some discussion he agreed to accept a letter from her father, vouchsafing her identity, in lieu of anything more positive. But there was no way in which she could start work without the letter from Michael Dooley. She could, however, stay in the staff quarters until such time as the vital document arrived.

Mary saw nothing of the great hotel above stairs. She spent most of her time sitting in the staff lounge thinking of The Liberties and the warm contrast it made to this great soulless cavern of a building. Once or twice she ventured into the London streets but she was quickly beaten back by their alien feeling. Once or twice she passed the ornate hotel entrance, staring into the hallway, wondering at the pomp of the doorman and his leisurely, opulent clients.

Then the letter came, and Cornu, or Creeping Jesus, as Mary was later to know him, gave her a job in an area known as the still-room. It was in this room that Mary was to spend much of her working life. It was here, too, that she soon met the first of the hotel's most celebrated guests.

The still-room has now been replaced in hotels by a system known as Central Floor Service. In fact it was the equivalent of a butler's pantry. Tea, coffee and bread and butter were prepared there at any time and the work was both demanding and exhausting. Tea and coffee seemed to be required in every bedroom and in every public room at all hours of the day and part of the night. Her shifts were long and hard – 5.30 a.m. to 3.00 p.m. and 3.00 p.m. to 9.30 p.m. – and the pay was £2 a month. All the staff had to sign in on time or they would soon feel the effects of Cornu's neurosis.

But despite Cornu's double-checking, there were many perks. Tea, sugar, coffee, milk, every kind of foodstuff, linen, blankets, cutlery and table mats regularly disappeared into the staff quarters or went home with those who lived outside. To steal was customary, and it was not only the more lowly staff who indulged. The managers were no exception, except that they smuggled things out of the front door rather than the back. This continuous stream of pilfering cost the hotel a fortune, but despite the vigilance of Cornu and the senior management the stuff continued to go. So although wages were low, no one went hungry.

Gradually the edge of Mary's homesickness disappeared, leaving only a gnawing ache. Mary adapted to the below-stairs situation at the Hyde Park with surprising ease. She also got used to the still-room and its rigours. She made and served literally hundreds of cups of tea and coffee each shift and lost count of the dozens of loaves cut up and buttered. Unable to write home, she sent money instead, though she could ill afford to do so. But it was a necessary duty and so each week a small sum was posted off to The Liberties, the address arduously printed out each time from her pocket-book. She found it more difficult to get used to the élite atmosphere of the hotel. The discreet diners in the grill room, the sudden bursts of gaiety from the ballroom, the uniforms and forced humour of the officers in the banqueting suites or restaurants, the gossiping charity ladies over tea, the regimental dinners which went on so late in the evenings – all seemed like a world apart which she serviced but with which she had no connection.

Then, with a surprising and unpleasant jolt, Mary came up against her first critic. Max Aitken, later Lord Beaverbrook, always claimed to his biographer, A. J. P. Taylor, that he had bought controlling shares in the Hyde Park Hotel so that his comfort would be assured. In fact there is no record in his papers of his doing this, and Taylor writes:

Maybe he mistook the Hyde Park Hotel for the Grand Babylon. (Perhaps Arnold Bennett's novel, *The Grand Babylon Hotel*, is no longer read. In it an American millionaire buys the hotel because his daughter cannot otherwise get steak and a bottle of beer.) Beaverbrook did acquire some shares in the hotel at a later date. He became friendly with the manager and in 1924, when there was some talk of changing the management, bought 10,000 shares. These, though only 6.6% of the hotel, presumably enabled him to defend his friend's interest. When the manager retired in 1946 Beaverbrook sold his shares.

Aitken stayed at the Hyde Park to be near the Colonial Bank in which he was involved, to survey his various business interests and to be close to Bonar Law, who was then Colonial Secretary and an efficient string-puller. At the time of Mary's arrival, Aitken was going through a crisis. He was determined to become President of the Board of Trade and expected Lloyd George to give him the post. 'In fact,' Aitken wrote, 'I had been promised the place.' The appointment would involve a by-election as at that time a newly appointed minister had to be re-elected. He had already warned the Unionist chairman at Ashton-under-Lyme and he had sent his wife there to begin campaigning. But to Aitken's horror no word was received from Lloyd George. On 6 December Aitken left the Hyde Park and wandered miserably to the War Office, where he assumed Lloyd George was allocating offices. However, his pride prevented him going in and whilst wandering about he discovered from a Member of Parliament that he had been over-looked and that Albert Stanley was to become President. Aitken returned to the Hyde Park in an ugly mood.

Three days later, on Saturday 9 December, Lloyd George and Bonar Law called on Aitken in his suite at the Hyde Park. They offered him a lesser post which Aitken refused. In the middle of this frustrating scene, Aitken rang down for some coffee. Mary sent it up, but as the system of service lifts was operated by a whistle at each floor, room service timing tended to be inadequate, and the coffee arrived cold, the final straw to Aitken. He was furious and, ignoring the Prime Minister and the Colonial Secretary, he called Cornu and practically blasted the manager out of the hotel with the force of his wrath. Wild with anxiety, Cornu dashed to the still-room, discovered that the miscreant was Mary, and threatened to sack her on the spot. Try as she would to explain the slowness of the lifts, she got nowhere at all. Hysterically Cornu repeated that there had been a complaint – a serious complaint – from the important Mr Aitken, and that if it ever happened again she would be sacked.

In punishment Mary was sent up to Aitken's suite with another tray of hot coffee. Trembling, she knocked at the door, to be confronted with the deadlocked trio – Aitken, Lloyd George and Bonar Law. In an almost unintelligible accent, she apologized and put the tray down on a table beside Aitken. The famous jowled features were flushed with anger, and he gave her a look that many were to come to know and fear. Mary fled from the room and returned weeping to the still-room, where she was given rough comfort, the staff being more interested in what the Prime Minister looked like than the coffee disaster.

Lloyd George then sent a letter to the Hyde Park. It offered Aitken a peerage, which he reluctantly took, mainly to save face at Ashton. The following extracts from his book, *Politicians and the War 1914–1916*, clarify his feelings during his stay at the Hyde Park. He wrote, 'I would much rather have stayed in the House of Commons with a suitable office. But I had been jockeyed, or had jockeyed myself, into a position in which I thought I had no choice. The Peerage was a way of escape. I took it. It would be absurd to deny that it was a very foolish way of escape.'

It would seem that Beaverbrook had deluded himself and that Lloyd George was innocent of any deception on his historic visit to the Hyde Park, but Mary received scowls from the peppery new peer for days as he paced the corridors of the Hyde Park, furious at being thwarted. At the end of his life, Beaverbrook claimed that Lloyd George had promised him the presidency under the trees at Cherkley, his country house in Surrey. However, as the actual crisis was during the winter, it is unlikely that any conversation occurred under the trees. Also, as A. J. P. Taylor points out:

> When Lloyd George read the story in Beaverbrook's proof years later, he wrote in the margin: 'I knew nothing of your desire to go to the Board of Trade. Bonar never suggested it to me.' Surely Lloyd George would not have written this, if Beaverbrook could have reminded him of his visit to the Hyde Park Hotel and so given him the lie direct. So perhaps Law made the promise? This, too, is unlikely. Law did not make such promises to his embarrassing 'intimate friend', whom he had refused to acknowledge earlier even as his parliamentary private secretary.

Beaverbrook describes his feelings on 14 November 1916, the morning after he had seen Lloyd George, and when he was ill in bed:

> Bonar Law, as was his custom on such occasions, came round to see me at the Hyde Park Hotel. I wanted, in a sense, to open the Lloyd George question to him then – but I was deterred by a variety of considerations. In the first place, I did not feel fit enough for what I knew was a vital conversation. Next, he had come round to visit an invalid friend, and it seemed rather a shame to take advantage of his kindness to bid him 'stand and deliver' politically – for I knew he would dislike the topic.

Mary remembered that 'I regularly went up to his room with coffee during the crisis, and he was always hunched in a chair.

He never spoke to me at those times. I felt sorry for him – despite his cantankerousness. He was the kind of man who was strong – but somehow had a child-like personality. He hated being thwarted. I couldn't help growing fond of him. In fact, I think I was as much fond of him as I was afraid of him.'

Beaverbrook writes: 'I went home that night to the Hyde Park Hotel and sat in my room on the fourth floor overlooking the Park. A cold north-east wind blew in from the night and the single lamp was so shaded as to give hardly a glimmer. And as I sat there alone, I thought how vastly greater were the forces ranged against Bonar Law than those ranged on his side.'

Whilst waiting for news, Beaverbrook remembered that:

A quietude like death settled on the Hyde Park Hotel. There were no more calls from politicians – no more agitated interviews. No special messengers arrived with notes. Even the telephone bell ceased to ring. The reaction was tremendous. It is said that people in a balloon do not feel any sensation of motion, but simply think the earth is drifting past them. There came to me this same curious sense of detachment – passing by degrees into boredom and then into anxiety, and finally into a kind of desperation. I had been in the centre of affairs and now I found myself translated to the extreme circumference.

I had waited in all afternoon and evening, expecting a message from the Prime Minister which never came. The dark drew down and no one came near me. There was no news of friend or foe. At last I could bear it no longer and walked out into the street.

Over the next few months Beaverbrook was to become a familiar figure to Mary in the Hyde Park. She experienced more of his wrath when he had to climb the four flights to his suite when the lift broke down, and she met him by chance in the corridor, but there were happier times when his son, Max, came into the hotel to visit his father. Mary sent tea up to the suite and on these occasions it was received without adverse comment. The boy struck up a friendship with the liftman, a West Indian and a fairly unique sight in London in those days. When the

liftman died he left his autograph book to the young Max. It
contained the autographs of most of the leading politicians of
the day, including his father's. Looking back on those days, Sir
Max Aitken told me: 'I'm not terribly sure if Father bought the
hotel or not. But he told me he did. He certainly had his suite
there because of the war – the fire-risk and the fact that he was
terrified of fire. For some reason he thought that being four
storeys off the ground made him safer.'

Sir Max remembered the Bennetts and their benevolent
hotel-keeping and pointed out that, even as a boy, he was well
aware that the clientele of the hotel during the war was almost
entirely political or military. It was one of the great political
rendezvous of the First World War and the setting for many of
his father's aspirations. It was because of this – and because of
its special atmosphere – that Sir Max used the hotel himself for
many decades afterwards.

Meanwhile, Mary's below stairs life continued to be rigorous. So
self-contained was the world at the Hyde Park that she began to
lose track of both time and the world outside her. It all seemed
irrelevant compared with the grinding bustle of the day. A
typical shift would be as follows:

4.00 a.m.	Rise and dress in the cramped conditions of the staff dormitory.
4.30	Servants' breakfast consisting of restaurant leftovers.
5.00	Into still-room to prepare tea, coffee, porridge, cream, and bread and butter for early breakfasts. This could mean preparing over 300 breakfasts to be eaten in bedrooms and dining room.
10.00	Short break.
10.30	Help clear trays from rooms.
11.30	Back to still-room to prepare for lunch, involving the cutting of mounds of brown bread and butter for the smoked salmon as well as the usual tea and coffee supplies.
3.00 p.m.	End of shift and lunch.

In the early days, before she had hardened up, Mary walked around in a daze of exhaustion. This led her into one very embarrassing situation. More exhausted than usual after a row with Cornu over the mysterious 'disappearance' of some cream from the still-room (she had palmed it through to the staff dining room), Mary dozed off at lunchtime. She was woken by the harassed waitresses who were desperate for the vital brown bread and butter that was to accompany the smoked salmon. But she had not even started. In wild panic, she desperately began to cut and butter bread, knowing all the time that she had no chance of being able to cope.

Then, as a grand finale to her plight, Cornu entered, gliding across the still-room with soundless feet. Determined not to burst into floods of tears, Mary told him the truth. She was exhausted, had nodded off to sleep, and the sacred ritual of the brown bread and butter was hardly under way. To her surprise Cornu paused, looked at her closely, and then went outside. He swiftly returned with one of the Bennett brothers. They took off their coats, rolled up their sleeves, and attacked the bread. Mary worked with them, becoming clumsier and clumsier as she worked. They made no criticism of her, and when they had won the battle against time and sufficient mounds of bread and butter were ready they went away as swiftly as they had come.

So, though life below stairs at the Hyde Park in 1916 may have been arduous and conditions may have been bad, the feudalism was strong. While the hotel buzzed with exclusivity in its public rooms, the servants busied themselves with the twenty-four hour job of cossetting them. Everything had to be perfect, from the cold buffet to the temperature of the champagne, from the vichysoisse to the mayonnaise. But if a servant fell ill or, like Mary, became exhausted, then help would come. However, woe betide anyone who fell down on the job through laziness, indifference or skulduggery. They would instantly be dismissed – and each one of the 28 valets, 42 chefs, 69 waiters, 30 launderers, 112 domestics, 12 French polishers, 14 seamstresses, 12 cellarmen, 18 barmen, 6 doormen and 12 hall-porters feared dismissal more than they feared anything else in their lives.

Above stairs, the standard of food in both the dining room and the grill room was the finest of its kind in Europe. Included in a typical 1916 dinner menu would be quails, caviar, game, oysters, trout, sole, the very best joints and fowl, fresh fruit in season, mature cheeses and exotic trifles. The Hyde Park's menu was very British, and its resources were the aristocratic lands of its clients. The Bennetts set the highest standards in traditional, beautifully cooked, beautifully served food. Despite the fact that the menu was in French and that there were some Continental dishes, everything was very much in the clubby, British aristocratic tradition. The county families expected the Hyde Park to surround them with a certain style. So did the dukes and peers, lords and marquesses, businessmen and politicians who also filtered through the hotel's bland corridors.

Gradually Mary became used to the work, and rather than going to sleep on her rare nights off she went out with the Irish contingent to cheap Irish pubs where they would two-step, quadrille and reel the night away. The tarnished gaiety reminded Mary a little of The Liberties – but only a little. She was beginning to miss her family desperately and the homesickness seemed to worsen. Cornu had 'promoted' her to work as a waitress in the stewards room (canteen) as well as using her in a variety of odd-job positions.

Meanwhile, as the war went on and the appalling death toll rose, soldiers on leave with nowhere else to go occupied the ballroom and lounge. Queen Mary regularly visited them, fighting her insularity and trying, in her quiet, passive way, to mother them. It was Mary's odd-job position that first drew her into contact with the Queen. It was to be a long and lasting relationship. At first she could hardly believe it. A few months earlier she had been sharing a poverty-stricken existence in The Liberties, now she was a servant to the Queen. She started, however, as a servant in a strange situation – as Keeper of the Royal Commode. For some reason the lavatory arrangements were few and far between around the royal entrance, and although there was a retiring room nearby there was no actual water closet. Instead, there was a commode, which apparently the Royal Personage accepted with dignity albeit perhaps with discomfort. Mary's job was to ensure that Queen Mary's 'retiring arrangements' went off smoothly. She had to clear the room, open the door, curtsey and then withdraw while the

Queen used the commode. Then, Queen Mary would wash and return to her soldiers, and Mary would deal with the commode.

Mary was as much in awe of Queen Mary at the end of her life as she had been in her twenties – despite the Queen's human needs. The charity bazaars, the relief committees, the continuous visits to the soldiers billeted in the hotel – all were carried out with the introverted sense of duty that was so typical of Queen Mary's style. Her untouchable reserve seemed to Mary to be absolutely right for a queen; any slight erring towards humanity would have been quite inappropriate. 'She was a *proper* queen,' Mary told me firmly. As ever the arch-conservative, Mary had her standards: kings and queens behaved with impeccable reserve; politicians and statesmen were allowed to be drunks; servants were humble; trade unions were the height of poor taste; wars were caused by men; the priest was her Holy Father. But, despite the black and white of Mary's standards, her sense of fun and desire for a good time caused her to make many exceptions to her firm rules on social behaviour. The drunken behaviour of Queen Mary's eldest son, the Prince of Wales, for instance, was easily tolerated – although the crisis over his abdication considerably upset her. But any slip by a woman from the 'standards' would be strongly disapproved of, its perpetrator being regarded as a tart or 'up to no good' or 'not what she seemed' or 'a fine lady'. In Mary's book men could be rakes, but women had to be dutiful drones.

Gradually an unspoken relationship grew up between Queen Mary and her servant namesake. Many society people tended to look on the war as a novelty but this casual attitude disappeared as the casualty list grew more horrendous and the great families began to grieve over their own losses – and to fear for those who still survived. The cause and progress of the war were no more than a blur to Mary.

The Queen told her that originally there had only been two ways the women of England could help the war effort. The first was by knitting socks and sewing shirts for the soldiers. The second was by collecting money and clothing for those made unemployed, and in some cases destitute, by the outbreak of war. Mary found the former rather vague, but could appreciate the significance of the latter, and told her something of the poverty in The Liberties; it was clear that the Queen was horrified.

One of the other factors which drew Mary towards the Queen was her mundaneness – an aspect of her personality much derided by her critics. Her continuous references to the weather in her diaries and letters, 'Very wet day', or, 'Poured all day. Very busy seeing people . . .', and her cosy style of description. 'We saw Captain Brough who had lost both arms – but he seemed wonderfully cheery', certainly never showed a great deal of insight, just a kind of royal homeliness. But it was this very quality that made Mary feel safe with the austere, unimaginative queen who would sit and rise with comforting regularity in the very private throne-room over which Mary presided. Mary served her Queen in the most functional manner possible, and it was because of these circumstances that she was able to learn so much about her.

Gradually Mary came to realize that one driving force the Queen had was her sense of duty, and her biographer, James Pope-Hennessy, backs this up:

> Severally or together, day after day, week after week, month after month, year after year, the King and Queen continued to perform their duties – inspecting the men of the New Armies who were going out to be killed or blinded or crippled or gassed in the trenches, encouraging those who had returned wounded or with missing limbs, trying to comfort some of the tens of thousands who would never return, touring munition plants, calling at food centres, for ever smiling and bowing and waving, never showing the exhaustion or the dull despair which filled their souls.

The Queen also told Mary about the entertainments given to thousands of soldiers, sailors and airmen at Buckingham Palace. They were given tea in the Coach House with members of the royal family serving at each table. Afterwards there were acrobats, conjurors and, most popular of all, a choir which sang the war songs. Queen Mary wrote to her Aunt Augusta saying, '. . . the men knew the choruses and sang them most lustily.

How you would have liked being present, it was all so informal, friendly and nice – we are much pleased at the success of our entertainments.'

But even so, Queen Mary became more and more depressed as the war went on. In the year of Mary Dooley's arrival in England, she wrote to Lady Mount Stephen saying: 'The length of this horrible war is most depressing. I really think it gets worse the longer it lasts.' Mary sensed the desperate weariness and the reserves of strength the Queen was having to call upon as she came into the cloakroom with that famous, set, but now strained smile. She seemed incredibly tired and anxious about the King's health (he had had an accident the previous year on the Western Front, during an inspection of the Royal Flying Corps at Hesdigneul, when his horse had reared and fallen back on top of him). Mary also knew that, despite his poor health, the King carried on but relied more and more heavily on his wife. Writing from Scapa Flow, George V said: 'I can't ever sufficiently express my deep gratitude to you darling May for the splendid way in which you are helping me during these terrible, strenuous and anxious times. Very often I feel in deep despair and if it wasn't for you I should break down.'

'She was a wonderful strong woman,' Mary told me, 'and she knew her duty.' This sense of duty Mary shared with her queen. Mary's duty was to pray, confess her sins and attend mass every Sunday, to send money home, to support her family in Engine Alley, and to keep making tea and coffee and cutting bread. She had an eye for the men and enjoyed flirting with them, but she regarded them as children and treated them accordingly.

By 1917 Queen Mary was studying the use of artificial limbs for the permanently disabled and had already given her name to the celebrated hospital at Roehampton where they were made and fitted. Still coming to the hotel for the endless charity bazaars, she told Mary enthusiastically about the construction of the limbs, how they worked, and how the disabled could cope with them. In her diary Queen Mary wrote: 'Very warm fine day. At 2.40 we motored down to Roehampton to see the hospital for limbless soldiers. . . . We saw the newest arms and legs and the men showed us what they were able to do. We visited the workshops and talked to the officers from Dover House. A nice afternoon.'

But suddenly Mary's sense of duty deserted her. Her homesickness increased and the battered, war-racked London streets seemed ever more alien. She had to get away. Every night she saw in her dreams familiar images – the Boys' Brigade coming over Thomas Hill with their bugles and their little pillbox hats:

> *Root toot root toot root toot*
> *We are the Boys' Brigade*
> *And we're eating marmalade*
> *Left right, left right . . .*

Sometimes she would hear the cries of The Liberties:

> *Coal blocks, coal blocks.*
> *Eralamail, éralamail.*
> *Fresh fish, fresh fish.*
> *Coal blocks, coal blocks.*

And sometimes the men and women bargaining in the streets at Christmas – the season that she loved best in The Liberties.

'I'll give yer ten bob for the big bird.'

'Oh no. Sorry. That one is seventeen and sixpence.'

'You can have the small one in the centre for eleven shillings.'

'Merciful God, yer wouldn't call that a turkey, that's an overgrown chicken.'

And then there were the dark canyons of the streets, with their lighted windows, bursting at the seams with their occupants. Engine Alley, with her mother sewing, her sisters washing, her brothers playing and fighting, and her father, conveniently remembered in a good humour, on the melodeon.

She would wake every morning unwilling to face the day. Somehow she had to get back, if only for a while. But with no money it seemed impossible. Then, suddenly, a glorious opportunity presented itself. Esta's husband turned up in London (she had married during the last year) and said that he would pay Mary's fare home for a fortnight's holiday. Overjoyed, but terrified that Cornu would refuse to let her go, Mary begged her brother-in-law to explain the situation to the manager and to plead her cause. This he promised to do, and Mary went off optimistically to pack. She was going back. Away from this grand hotel and the bustling, uncaring streets of London.

Presently, her brother-in-law returned and told Mary that the manager had agreed to her going. So in blissful joy and equally blissful ignorance, Mary Dooley accompanied her brother-in-law to the station on the first leg of the journey back to The Liberties, which she had decided so resolutely to leave – and to which she was now overjoyed to return. As to her blissful ignorance, this would be kept in abeyance until she returned. Then she would receive quite a shock. For, rather than seeing the manager, Mary's brother-in-law had seen nobody.

It is not clear whether this was a primitive family plot to force Mary to return or whether her brother-in-law was simply particularly stupid. What is clear is that Mary returned delightedly to her family – and then, after a few days in The Liberties, began to be reminded of all the things that had made her leave Dublin a few months before.

In 1917, when Mary returned to Dublin, the Irish separatist movement had become scattered and impotent. The central core had been destroyed in the rebellion and many cells in country districts, although possessing arms, had no organization. Most of the key personnel were in prison, which resulted in neither the Irish Republican Brotherhood nor the Volunteers being able to reorganize the movement. The only hope lay in the fact that the British were now releasing internees from Frongoch; soon the I.R.B. and the Volunteers were to regroup, with Michael Collins as a prominent member of the latter.

The atmosphere was tense. There were continuous police raids, a number of Republican figures were arrested for making seditious speeches, and in August Tomás Ashe died while on hunger strike. The British were not handling matters well. On 25 October 1916, 2,000 delegates had met at the Sinn Féin Ard Fheis, where a political separatist wing was created with De Valera as president and Cathal Brugha as chief of staff. I.R.B. men were prominent with Michael Collins as director of organization and Séan McGarry as general secretary. The Volunteers then went into the remote countryside for military training – and the Sinn Féin delegates prepared themselves for the next by-election.

In April 1917 America came into the war, and this meant that there could be no more effective support for the Irish cause from that quarter. Germany's interest in Ireland had also been shattered by the Roger Casement disaster. In the same month Lloyd George found himself facing the fact that he would have to conscript the Irish. As a result a general strike was called, and many of Mary's childhood friends flocked to the Volunteers – now called the I.R.A. Under cover of exposing a 'German plot', a harder British administration moved into Dublin Castle, and a large number of prominent Sinn Féiners were arrested. The movement went underground, raids continued, and the party became stronger.

When Mary arrived in Dublin there was considerable tension and The Liberties were a hotbed of political unrest. Her parents, however, were the same as ever – her mother still skivvying, her father still drinking – and her older brothers and sisters working either for Guinness or for small local businesses. Towards the end of her stay, Mary met Sean Macinley. He was in his early twenties, unmarried and a staunch Republican. He and Mary had been friends since the Macinleys had moved in opposite the Dooleys in 1898. Theirs had never been a sexual relationship and had lasted as the easy companionship of old friends. It came as a great shock to Mary to find that Sean was such a staunch member of the I.R.A. None of her family was political, and she had deliberately turned her back on Irish politics by leaving the country. Sean, however, was anxious to convert her. She proved a difficult case. Sitting in one of the innumerable small bars in The Liberties, Sean put his arguments to her. The more he enthused, the more Mary told him it 'was all talk' and 'would come to nothing'. Then, looking at her watch, Mary saw that it was late. She had to go. But Sean was not prepared to let the unconverted depart so easily. Somehow he persuaded her to go back to his house. There he took her to an upstairs room. Nervous of sudden amorous advances by Sean, Mary hesitated – and then slowly she went through the door.

The room was full of the clutter of half a century – a lumber room, not needed by Sean's comparatively small family. Then he showed her his cache – two rifles, some grenades and some jelly-like substance which he said was explosive. Hidden insecurely behind a wardrobe, the arms could be discovered at any time by even the most superficial search. Mary was instantly afraid, both for this naive young man and for everybody who lived in the road. She asked Sean who owned the cache and he told her, mysteriously, that he was holding them for 'the movement'. She asked him if he knew how to use the weapons and he replied that he had been 'shown how at a place in the country'.

Desperately Mary tried to make Sean get rid of them – for his sake, for everyone's sake. Sean merely laughed at her, picking up a grenade with bravado and waving it in her face. Seeing she would get nowhere, Mary went home. The next day she called at the Macinley house with a large bag, knowing everybody would be out except Sean's mentally deficient sister, who opened the door. Pushing past her, Mary firmly reassured the sister that she had come 'to collect something'. She then went straight up to the lumber room, moved the wardrobe, and put the rifles, grenades and explosive in the bag. Terrified at the danger of what she was doing, Mary then hurried downstairs and out of the door.

The contents of the bag were very heavy as Mary struggled through the crowded, bustling streets of The Liberties. Her greatest fear was that somebody would bump into her and the contents of the bag would explode. This alarming prospect was superseded only by the thought of what would happen if she was stopped by the Garda and searched. The bag, normally used for laundry, looked horribly suspicious, and the barrels of the rifles were outlined against its folds. Any moment now she would be stopped, or the bag's contents would explode. The streets seemed ludicrously full of people, all of whom appeared to be staring at her. She tried to remember the sentence for concealing arms – or would they consider this gun-running? She saw herself never returning to the marbled halls of the Hyde Park. Instead she would join the heroes of the rebellion at Frongoch. Or she might face a firing squad.

With the bag getting heavier and guilt overwhelming her,

Mary hurried on towards the Poddle. The Poddle was an underground river that ran under the Coombe in The Liberties. Legend had it that an old woman had not been told that a trap-door in her hall had been lifted to expose the dark-flowing Poddle beneath. She fell in, was swept away, and was never seen again. The truth of the story is in some doubt, but certainly older residents of the Coombe rarely say 'Run down the Coombe for a loaf' but almost always say 'Run down the Poddle for a loaf'. Mary knew of a derelict house where there was not a trap-door, but a cellar below which the Poddle flowed. As children they had found the broken flagstones and beneath them sinister black water – and they had excavated further. The house, beyond repair and derelict for years, was in a back street, more like an alley. Cobbled, dark and decayed, it always reminded Mary of the entrance to hell that she had once seen in a Victorian Protestant tract.

But whether the cellar was accessible now was another matter, and she would look very suspicious going into a derelict house with a bulging laundry bag. She arrived at the alley and walked past it several times. The house was still there – and unboarded. Waiting until there were few people around (and certainly no Garda), Mary darted into the alley and then round the back of the house. She was sweating with fear and almost tripped as she crossed the broken paving of the weed-grown backyard. The back door gaped open – a dark maw in which she was all too anxious to lose herself. Once inside she walked catiously down the broken stone steps to the cellar. There were scurrying sounds as rats darted for cover, and for a moment she felt acute nausea. The scurrying sounds, the acrid smell of disuse and the river like a velvet band beneath her feet – it was all peculiarly demonic.

She had brought a torch and shone this around the cellar. Yes – the paving stones were still raised. She knelt down and saw the dark movement below her. With great haste she opened the bag. One by one, she slipped the rifles, grenades and explosives down into the water, then the bag. They made dull splashes, followed by silence.

Hurriedly Mary left the cellar and walked up the steps, out of the house and into the alley. She could hardly breathe. Then, walking quickly, she went out into the street and straight into the arms of a Garda. She screamed, and he laughed. He told her to look where she was going, and stop bumping into strange men. Then he went on his way and she went on hers. Mary was laughing now – hysterically.

As she waited for the boat train at the station next morning, Sean arrived. He was furious but could say nothing because Mary's mother was with her. To Mary's dismay, however, Elizabeth went to buy her some sweets and in her absence Sean accused her of 'stealing his property'. But she denied everything and Sean could do nothing but rage. Some months later Mary heard that he had been arrested for possessing arms, and she realized that her mission had been in vain.

Although she had no idea of the angry welcome she would receive at the Hyde Park, Mary had mixed feelings about returning. Homesickness engulfed her most of the way back and she thought longingly of The Liberties. But as she neared London, Mary remembered her father, Friday nights, and Sean and the Troubles. She began to feel more positive. She was going back to her new life – and however hard it was, Mary was determined to make it work.

Chapter Four

❧❧❧❧❧❧❧❧❧❧❧❧❧❧❧❧❧❧❧❧❧❧❧❧❧❧❧❧❧❧❧❧❧❧❧

The Great War

⚓⚓⚓⚓⚓⚓⚓⚓⚓⚓⚓⚓⚓⚓⚓⚓⚓⚓⚓⚓⚓⚓⚓⚓⚓⚓⚓⚓⚓

1917-1918

WHEN Mary returned to the Hyde Park, she found that Cornu and many of the staff had spent a fortnight hunting for her. She had not realized the concern they felt. Captain Allen had been contacted and she had gloomily predicted that Mary had finally been overtaken by the white slave market.

Mary's feelings were mixed: she felt touched by the genuine concern of her neurotic manager, guilty at having left her stupid brother-in-law to make a mess of the arrangements, and afraid of reprisal. In fact all she received was a severe admonition from a now enraged Cornu, and she was then grudgingly re-employed in her old position in the still-room.

At this stage, Mary's personality was formed. On one level she was very mature, and on another she was incredibly naive. Much of real life passed her by. She knew nothing of politics, of how London society was made up, of its leading personalities. She knew nothing about the progress of the war, its implications or its universality. Above all she was entirely illiterate. Mary Dooley shared with many others a world of total incomprehension. All she knew she picked up in snippets of gossip and information from below stairs or in similarly unreliable nuggets from above stairs. Swallowed by the cushioned unreality of the Hyde Park, Mary's experience of life was highly subjective. The contrast between the poverty in The Liberties and the opulence in The

Hyde Park ceased to amaze her and she soon accepted it as the natural order of things.

Mary Dooley was born to serve. Throughout her childhood and adolescence she had served her family. Now, in a different fashion, she was serving the pampered clients of one of Europe's grandest hotels. But there was no bitterness in her. If there had been, she would have been more ambitious about fighting her way up the hotel's career structure. Instead she accepted her lot with equanimity. But this did not mean that Mary was humble, obsequious by nature. Indeed, she was very much the opposite. She had a fiery temper and an abrasive manner. Some feared this. Others, like Cornu, tolerated it. It is impossible to say whether Mary had the traditional heart of gold underneath this sharp crust but her heart was certainly warm and she was capable of great compassion. Nevertheless Mary Dooley was a tough young woman from a harsh background, unable to accept softness or intangibility. She needed to respect those about her and she instinctively looked for strength of personality. It was rare that she found it.

Her relationship with Cornu was typical of her relationship with all her male employers and guests. She half feared him and half fought with him. In return, Cornu regarded Mary Dooley as a 'character'. In other words he found her both impossible and irreplaceable. Shrewdly, he realized that this archetypal colleen gave the hotel distinction. She added to its originality, and he loved to hear clients, particularly distinguished clients, making remarks like, 'Do go to the Hyde Park – Mary Dooley's such a character in the still-room', or 'My dear – she's *priceless* – you must meet her'. Unwittingly, Mary was gradually becoming an essential cog in the London social wheel.

To Mary, the Great War was still remote; the Troubles seemed to be the real war. Yet, back in London, she began to be more aware of the greater tragedy. The hotel was still full of soldiers, Queen Mary regularly attended charitable functions, and Mary returned on these occasions to the Queen's retiring room. The air raids were intensified, and on 13 June 1917 162 people were killed and 432 injured. That autumn the fear was so great that many Londoners, including Mary and a number of the staff at the Hyde Park, left the hotel and took to the greater security of

the Tube stations. Meanwhile many of the clients of the Hyde
Park abandoned its marble halls and moved to the safety of
Bournemouth or Bath. In the insular world below stairs at the
hotel, much discussion was given to two main topics – food and
war babies. Strangely, these two topics were to form Mary's chief
memories of the Great War.

In the hotel itself the food was still of reasonable variety.
Plovers' eggs, quail and partridge were on the menu, coming in
from country estates. Although some of the goodies were
smuggled from the restaurant into the staff dining room, the food
below stairs basically maintained the standards of the National
Food Economy League, who published such guides as *War Time
Recipes for Households where Servants are Employed* (6d.) or *Patriotic
Food Economy for the Well-to-do* (6d.). The kind of food served in
the staff dining hall is epitomized in the following dinner and
supper menus:

DINNER

Scotch Barley Broth
Greens

SUPPER

Stewed Sheep's Tongue and Rice

DINNER

Meat Stew with Dumplings
Potatoes
Parsnips or Swedes
Greens

SUPPER

Lentil Soup with Toast

DINNER

Rice and Oatmeal Pudding
Dainty Pudding

SUPPER

Haricot Beans with Dripping

From early in 1917 queues for food were a regular sight; *The Times* of 10 December 1917 listed the following as being in very short supply in London: sugar, tea, butter, margarine, lard, dripping, milk, bacon, pork, condensed milk, rice, currants, raisins, spirits and Australian wines. The next week *The Times* reported:

> The food queues continue to grow. Outside the dairy shops of certain multiple firms in some parts of London women begin to line up for margarine as early as five o'clock on a Saturday morning, some with infants in their arms, and others with children at their skirts. Over 1,000 people waited for margarine at a shop in New Broad Street in the heart of the City, and in Walworth Road on the south-eastern side of London, the queue was estimated to number about 3,000. Two hours later 1,000 of these were sent away unsupplied.

Mary was now twenty-eight and had a regular chain of boy friends, but because of the 'war babies' scare she would not go out with soldiers. The war babies problem had hit the national conscience, and the servants' quarters of the Hyde Park, as early as April 1915, with a letter from Conservative M.P. Ronald McNeill to the *Morning Post*. McNeill claimed that throughout areas in the country where troops had been billeted 'a great number of girls' were pregnant. In fact his claims were exaggerated but a nationwide scandal began – although the plight of the unmarried mother was often looked at sympathetically. In 1918 a friend of Mary's read out to her in the still-room a typical Mission of Hope pamphlet by which it was hoped to gain funds for the Mission's homes for unmarried mothers and their children. It was called 'The Story of a Girl's Soul'.

> There came an hour when the youth pleaded and the girl yielded. She does not blame him. It is part of her honesty to tell you frankly that the fault was hers as much as his. She does not say 'he tempted me'. She says that for both of them the pressure of temptation was too strong, and that in a moment of sheer unconscious tumult of mind and heart the thing happened which was to wreck her youth.

'Contagious diseases' were the other horror talked over exclusively and vicariously by the female staff at the Hyde Park. The whole question of venereal disease was shrouded in the deepest mystery, and the ignorance surrounding it was amazing. V.D. could be passed on in the most extraordinary ways – almost as if it were some kind of infectious magic. In an attempt to combat this, various pamphlets were circulated, many of them arriving in the servants' quarters of the Hyde Park (no doubt propelled there by Captain Allen). One such work was entitled 'To Women War Workers: Some Homely Advice in Regard to the Maintenance of their Health and Comfort', and was by Lilian A. Evans, Welfare Superintendent to St Helens' Cable and Rubber Company Ltd. Much of the pamphlet concerned personal hygiene. For instance: 'A fixed bath with hot and cold water, is not always to be found . . . do not be discouraged. The whole body can be washed in a bucket of warm water, using a piece of flannel and mild soap.' Then, at certain periods: 'Be careful to change frequently. Take note of the days and be pre-pared. When wearing thin garments use a small apron of mackintosh in the seat of your cloth knickers. No accidents will then occur. The use of a calico band and loops at the front and back, will be found comfortable. Sanitary towels are cheap and save washing . . .'

But it was with reference to special personal diseases that the pamphlet had its main impact at the Hyde Park:

Certain personal diseases have become more widely spread through the war. For a long time persons who became in-fected were thought to have been guilty of immoral conduct. This is not of necessity the case. Perfectly pure, innocent persons may be infected through the carelessness of sufferers from the diseases, which are extremely catching.

In a booklet of this kind it is not fitting or desirable to enter into details [much disappointment below stairs at the Hyde Park], but any woman who finds herself suffering from an unusual discharge, soreness or eruptions, should seek medical aid without delay. Years of shame and suffering may be saved by timely action.

Then the pamphlet struck a sharper, moral tone: 'Before passing, hear a hint of warning: do not allow yourself to be hail-fellow-well-met with everyone. Maintain your womanly dignity always. Be true to your sex. It may be fun to "pick up" for a time, but the after effects are, all too often, very bitter and sad.'

Apart from giggling over the wording of the pamphlet, Mary had no wish to be 'very bitter and sad'. She wanted to have 'a good time' and to be 'carefree' and, although Mary wasn't sure what these words really meant, she was determined to discover their meaning. Besides, the work in the still-room was so gruelling that she was determined to enjoy herself in her spare time. Also, as a result of her recent experiences in The Liberties, homesickness was a thing of the past. The hotel was her home now and she was gradually adjusting to its arduous routine, the friendly superficiality of the staff, and the obsessions of Cornu and the clients, who still frightened her – for she had not forgotten the Beaverbrook episode.

In fact she was disciplined again within a few weeks of her return to the hotel by the paranoid Cornu, when she was boiling an illicit egg over a stove in a corridor. The egg was for her current boy friend – a porter on one of the floors. Appalled by the sight of this totally banned activity, Cornu crept up behind her and hissed his fury in her ear. The result was that she knocked the saucepan off the stove, and the hot water and broken egg sank into the expensive pile of the carpet. Gibbering with rage, Cornu despatched a tearful Mary below stairs. Cornu could not have been entirely without consideration, however, as witness his concern over Mary's 'holiday'. In this case, too, his compassion outweighed his rage and she heard no more of the incident. But he could easily have sacked her, though the wartime shortage of staff may have deterred him.

A few months after her return from Ireland, Mary was given the doubtful promotion of working in the restaurant as a waitress. In normal circumstances, only men were allowed to serve as waiters in the restaurant and grill room, and women were considered very infradig. But the war and the shortage of male staff made inroads in the chauvinism of hotel protocol. Mary received £2 a week and a portion of the tip pool. Once again, the clients of the restaurant seemed to be mainly military

or political, and although Beaverbrook had now left the hotel a
glittering array of politicians regularly arrived for luncheon and
occasionally dinner. Members of Asquith's old coalition government (who had resigned in 1916) as well as members of the new
Prime Minister Lloyd George's government and cabinet lunched
in the grill room and dined in the restaurant. Mary served
Asquith, with his repetitive cycle of stories, Balfour, Baldwin,
Lord Cecil, Austen Chamberlain, the young Winston Churchill,
who usually used even more matches than he smoked cigars, and
who ate voraciously, Field-Marshal Haig (Commander-in-Chief
of the British Army in France) and Bonar Law. Mary noticed
that Bonar Law smoked prodigiously but never drank. His meals
at the Hyde Park were a mere gesture, as his usual order was for
vegetables, rice pudding and a glass of milk. These he ate almost
instantly. Northcliffe also lunched at the Hyde Park, and he
usually came with his own small circle. Fun-loving Rothermere
was there too, being highly sociable. Finally, she met General
Smuts, who was currently living at the Savoy and who later
came to take up residence at the Hyde Park.

Jan Christiaan Smuts had fought against the British in the Boer
War but in 1916 commanded the Imperial forces in British East
Africa. By 1917 he was Minister of Defence and Minister of
Finance in the South African government. In the same year he join-
ed Lloyd George in the War Cabinet, and he was later appointed
to be a Companion of Honour as well as a Privy Councillor.

Smuts was fast becoming a statesman whose prestige went far
beyond the borders of South Africa. It was he who suggested to
George V that when he opened the new Ulster Parliament at
Stormont in 1922 his speech should not merely be aimed at
Ulster but at the whole of Ireland, in a spirit of general recon-
ciliation. This generous but eventually unsuccessful ideal was
strongly backed by the King; indeed George asked General
Smuts to write a draft of the speech itself as a cabinet guideline.

While staying at the Hyde Park for brief periods during the
war, Smuts came to know Mary well, as she brought meals up
to his room when he was working or in conference.

He was interested in independence [said Mary], and he wanted
it for Ireland. He didn't want us to be treated like the subjects

of a colony. I told him I wasn't a political person but he said 'nonsense – everyone is'. He said – 'didn't I care for Ireland?' – and, of course, I said I dearly loved my country – trouble torn as it was. I told him I'd left the place behind – but he told me I was just an exile. He quite often used to ask me to sit down on his sofa – and I had to, although I was worrying that Cornu would discipline me. I used to be on the hop all the time while General Smuts questioned me about the rebellion. I told him all I could – which wasn't much. He didn't seem disappointed.

During the First World War the 'white' Empire was determinedly moving towards independence. In 1917 and 1918 two Imperial Conferences were held, which had as their aims Liberty, Equality and Unity. The League of Free Nations was celebrated by Jan Christiaan Smuts in 1917 when he declared, 'Yours is the only system that has ever worked in history, where a large number of nations have been living in unity. Talk about a League of Nations – you are the only league of nations that has ever existed.'

'I never realized', Mary declared, 'how General Smuts had influenced the King when he went to Belfast after the war.' The speech, based on the draft, made an impassioned plea: 'It is my earnest desire that in Southern Ireland too there may ere long take place a parallel to what is now passing in this Hall; that there a similar occasion may present itself and a similar ceremony be performed.'

Mary continued:

I didn't feel so guilty about leaving Ireland when I had all those conversations with General Smuts at the Hyde Park. He took me so seriously – and asked me so many different questions – that I thought I was really doing my bit for Ireland by sitting on his sofa – even if I was worried about Creeping Jesus all the time. I mean – not even Padraic Pearse or Michael Collins would have got the ear of General Smuts like I did. But it's a pity they didn't – because I couldn't tell him anything very interesting or important. But at least I could speak my mind about my own country. I told him we were poor and romantic and independent. I told him we wanted our freedom – but not through the Troubles and the bloodshed. We talked about Roger Casement – and I remembered a ballad they used to sing about him on the Dublin streets. I repeated some of the bits I remembered to General Smuts.

The entire ballad was as follows:

> O lordly Roger Casement,
> > you gave all a man could give.
> That justice be not mocked at
> > and that liberty might live.
> But you hurt the high and mighty ones
> > in pocket and in pride.
> And that is why they hated you,
> > and that is why you died.
>
> Aye they stripped you of your honours
> > and they hounded you to death.
> And their blood lust was not sated
> > as you gasped your dying breath.
> They tried to foul your memory
> > as they burned your corpse with lime.
> But God is not an Englishman
> > and truth will tell in time.

Although the Hyde Park still maintained a reasonable menu – and Mary was now in a better position to smuggle remnants back to the staff dining room or to her own favoured few – some adjustments had to be made. Lamb, for instance, became impossible to obtain, so goat was served instead in the restaurant. Naturally it was still billed as lamb and nobody was any the wiser – not even the most discerning. 'The taste was the same,' Mary told me, 'or as near as made no difference.' However, she could detect the difference in appearance, and when goat was passed off as lamb to her in a nearby butcher's she created a scene. 'A real damned cheek,' she described it to me, 'A real damned cheek.'

Another distraction in Mary's free time was the cinema, and her greatest idol was Valentino – who was later to send Mary nearly hysterical when he came to the Hyde Park as a guest. In 1914 there were only 3,000 cinemas in England and the number had not radically increased during the war. They were ideal places for courting couples and as a result were seen as a dire threat to public morals. Unfortunately the specially trained supervisors, who were employed to deal with indecency or sexual assault in these darkened glory holes in prewar days, were laid off during the war. The National Council of Public Morals was outraged at this, and insisted that there should be both 'sufficient light' and 'adequate supervision'. But little notice was taken of this, and Mary continued to sit in cinemas in Victoria, swathed in the hot embrace of a number of admirers.

The cinema's respectability was ensured by the Great War, however. The government used film for propaganda purposes and this, together with Chaplin's rising importance, turned the cinema from a working-class entertainment into a diversion acceptable to middle-class and upper-class audiences too.

Mary also liked a drink in the grey war evenings when she was off duty, but was alarmed by the habitual drunkenness of her colleagues – particularly her own countrymen. It seemed that this was their main leisure-time activity, and it was brought to a head by the miracle of the Armistice in 1918. There were wild celebrations below stairs at the Hyde Park as the maroons boomed out at 11 a.m. on 11 November 1918. The headlines of Beaverbrook's *Evening Standard* blazed out:

END OF THE WAR

GERMANY SIGNS OUR TERMS AND FIGHTING
STOPPED AT 11 O'CLOCK TODAY

ALLIES TRIUMPHANT. FULL ARMISTICE TERMS

A wine waiter read the good news to Mary, but Cornu tempered her joy by telling her that, as the men would soon be returning from the war, she would no longer be required as a waitress in the restaurant. However, she could keep her job as waitress in the private dining room of the directors of the Hyde Park.

But Mary's change of circumstance hardly worried her, and she went out with the rest of the staff to celebrate the Armistice. Not for them were Beaverbrook's grim words: 'They may ring their bells now; before long they will be wringing their hands.' As they danced and drank their way around the jubilant West End streets neither Mary nor her colleagues gave much thought to the future – or to the grim statistics of the immediate past. Nine per cent of all men under fifty-five were dead, 600,000 in all, with 1,600,000 severely mutilated. In his book *Men and Power*, Mary's erstwhile critic, Beaverbrook, wrote:

> The war was over. Lloyd George was now the most powerful man in Europe. His fame would endure for ever. He was admired and praised in all countries. His prestige in the United States was so high that men said he would be elected as their President if he could run for office there.
>
> He had beaten his German enemies in the war. He had scattered and destroyed his British enemies at the polls in the course of a General Election which disclosed an overwhelming popular judgement in his favour. Hardly any political opponent escaped. They had fallen like autumn leaves.

As Mary danced the reels at the Tara Ballroom in Kilburn on Armistice Night, the garish, war-weary room became for her enmeshed with The Liberties. The Irish whiskey they were consuming helped to merge the two. Then Eamonn, one of the Hyde Park's commis waiters (trainee waiters), got up on the battered stage to sing an old Dublin ballad, 'The Night Before Larry was Stretched'. As Eamonn sang, Mary saw and heard The Liberties. A feeling of yearning overcame her, not so much for home but to be loved. Back there in the huddled streets she was loved by her mother, by her brothers and sisters, even by her father. Here she was not loved by anyone. A sense of desolation filled her. She heard again the songs of her childhood and felt again the love of play and friendship.

> *The wind, the wind, the wind blows high*
> *The rain comes scattering from the sky*
> *Mary Kelly says she'll die*
> *If she doesn't get the fella with the marble eye.*

And again:

> *He is handsome, he is pretty*
> *He is the fairest in the city*
> *He is courting one, two, three*
> *O, please tell me, who is he?*

Who is he? Mary knew that he was not around her at the moment. Suddenly the drink and the hectic gaiety turned sour. The fly-blown mirrors, the peeling shamrock green of the walls, the drink-stained furniture and the sweaty crowds made her feel shut in, trapped, helpless in an uncaring, unloving world.

For no reason an image of the seaside suddenly appeared in her mind. It was a day's outing. She was on the strand with her brother Jim, building a wall against a grey, rolling sea. There was a blustery warm wind and she could still taste the sand from the sandwiches. The rest of the boys were playing hurley with driftwood sticks and her sisters were collecting shells. Their parents sat, stiff as ramrods, perched on a breakwater, sentinel-like in their discomfort. Her mother had rolled down her stockings and her father had rolled up his trousers, but this was their only concession to the strand.

The water gradually covered the beach, breaking over the wall and dashing at the pebbles. Everything seemed immense – the sea, the sky, the landscape. Was it a song she could hear in the sea? A song of lost love, of yearning, of love never reached?

In the Tara Ballroom, Eamonn sang on and Mary could see the strand so distinctly that she could almost touch it. She could see the boys at their hurley, aroused, shouting, ready to fight. And again she could see those sentinel-like figures, her parents, on their eyrie of a breakwater.

Then she recalled the return home, burdened with teapots, kettles, cups, buckets and spades, towels and costumes – home from Sandymount via trains and trams to the houses which seemed bent under the weight of their occupants, home from the fresh sea smell to the smell of wood-rot and overcrowding, home to the smells of the brewery, the malting houses and the knackers. Mary remembered the Sunday evening mass, the salt still in their skin and the strand in their shoes. Her brothers' faces, fresh and ruddy, glowed in the light of the flickering candles, the votive lamps and the shrines. They looked like the saints themselves in their theatrical piety. Then they would go back through the hushed streets with the night wind bringing in the smell of the river, the smell of decay and the smell of poverty, back to Engine Alley, and bread and dripping, and love, and being needed.

For months after that Armistice Night, Mary felt the same yearning emptiness. Nothing seemed to matter, neither London nor Dublin. She was thirty and incomplete. She wanted to love and be loved in that crowded, hugger-mugger, Engine Alley, rowdy way.

But when love came it was very different. Jimmy Shiffer was unique, alien, apart, different in every conceivable way. He was a cellarman, bottling wine from the great hogsheads that came in from the Continent. He was a popular man for the reason that in every hogshead there could be found a little excess, so the cellar was an illegal drinking rendezvous. A little tot was always being handed out, despite Cornu's vigilance.

Gradually, Jimmy began to register on Mary as she not infrequently had her little tot. He was like a beautiful child. A Czechoslovakian, Jimmy had worked in various European capital cities as a cellarman. He was small and slender, with the figure and complexion of a teenage boy. Originally an amateur jockey, he had suffered a bad fall and as a result had a deformed back. This was the only flaw in his miniature beauty. Unlike Mary, Anthony (Jimmy was a nickname) Shiffer was an introvert. She told me: 'He was a quiet one. Always a quiet one. It took me a long time to know he was for me. I was going out with a Macaroni [one of the Italian waiters] at the time. But he was too pushy – you couldn't sit through a film with him.'

Gradually Mary saw more and more of the quiet, foreign boy-man. She felt safe with him – and then loved. She found his quietness difficult at first and his vague, Continental background impossible to imagine. He came from a middle-class family in Prague. They also were quiet, and their interests – music and art – were totally at odds with the interests of Elizabeth and Michael Dooley.

Eventually Mary began to 'walk out' with Jimmy. She no longer mixed all the time with the Irish crowd, largely because the delights of the Tara began to pall on Jimmy. They went to quiet anonymous pubs and to the pictures. She found that she could easily dominate him and yet there seemed no need. He was utterly sufficient to himself. He had established his own identity so completely that there was no chance of twisting him one way or the other. Either Mary took him as he was, or not at all. He had no need ever to say this; his very personality dictated it.

Soon Mary knew that she loved him, and that he entirely answered her yearning. One summer afternoon, walking with him in Kew Gardens, they stopped and listened to a band. Amidst the flowerbeds and formal pathways, Mary looked back in her mind to the Tara a few months before, when she had first felt that dreadful isolation, when she had thought of her family and the rough love that they represented. And here was the quiet boy-man Jimmy, giving her a very different, still love that she had never experienced before. Of course, because of his reticence and his deformed back, Jimmy brought out all Mary's considerable maternal feelings, but this was not a substitute for real love. Her love for him was genuine and complete.

It was as if Jimmy inhabited a land of still lakes, elegant castles, swans, fountains, statues, arbours and regal courtyards with dove-cotes. There was a classic romanticism to both his personality and his looks which was in total contrast to the bawdy, clamorous, stinking, ramshackle streets of The Liberties – or the home in Engine Alley which was packed night and day with life. But that fervour was something she had rejected, something she had thought would drag her down. She had come to London to escape from it, and eventually had loosened those loving shackles. But having loosened them there had been only emptiness and yearning. Now Jimmy had filled her life with an unimaginable something that she loved, and had stopped the yearning. Life at the hotel was tough and exhausting, but now it was complete, and for the first time since she had escaped from Engine Alley Mary felt content.

A few months later Mary and Jimmy were married at Brompton Oratory. Her parents and a few friends came. Jimmy's parents couldn't afford the fare. The wedding was quiet but joyful. Elizabeth and Michael were awkward, out of place, but pleased that Mary had made a good match. They approved of Jimmy's

Catholicism, but not of his foreignness. However, they supposed that they couldn't have everything. They never had. It was their first trip to England and they were anxious to get home.

A few weeks later Jimmy and Mary set up home together in a rented Victorian flat in the Wandsworth–Battersea hinterland. It was a crowded, noisy, children-strewn area of rundown streets. There was a large Irish community, and in small ways it reminded Mary of The Liberties. The flat was a refuge from the hotel – an oasis of quiet, shared happiness. They rarely quarrelled, although their mutual peace was not cabbage-like. Their relationship was tranquil in the midst of a hurly-burly life.

It was not perfect, however. Jimmy's accident made it impossible for them to have children. Gradually, they faced that impossibility together. It was not easy; both had come from large families, and both had assumed they would produce children in roughly the same numbers, despite the exigencies of the hotel. But this was not to be, and as acceptance gradually sank in Mary realized that she would have to regard the hotel and its clients not only as the centre of her life, but as child substitutes too. She would mother her boy-man, the staff of the hotel and its clients. Then the frustration of the childlessness could be borne.

She did bear it – but not without pain. Fortunately the pain did little harm to the marriage, which continued on its companionable course. But the pain settled inside, mixing sentiment and longing, catching her unawares just when she felt she had successfully fought it off.

Jimmy and Mary often worked on different shifts, so it frequently happened that one or the other was alone when they made the complicated journey from Battersea via South Kensington to Knightsbridge. Mary was currently working in the directors' dining room, and she used to leave the flat at about the same time as the neighbourhood children left for school. Winter and summer, spring and autumn, she traced exactly the same route from flat to bus-stop – through the grey Battersea streets, past the park lying serenely behind its wrought iron gates and the Thames flowing muddily under the ornate bridge.

Every day she met the children at the bus-stop. There were eight Devlins, with about a year's gap between each of them.

Pat was five, Jenny six, Seamus seven, Emmett eight, Sean nine, Edna ten, Bridget eleven and Frank twelve. On Sundays they went to the same church as Mary – the Holy Saviour – and after mass they would nod to her. They were clearly very poor, and as their parents obviously both worked Mary wondered how long the children were left on their own to fend for themselves. When she had been seeing them on this fairly regular basis for about six months, she began to think about them a good deal, both consciously and unconsciously. Sometimes she dreamed about them. The eldest, Frank and Bridget, particularly appealed to Mary. As surrogate parents they were pathetically adequate. She pictured them at home, at school, playing in the park, roller-skating in the street, buying bulls-eyes and liquorice, sleeping, curled up, four to a bed.

Soon they became part of her, and they filled her mind at almost every moment. Then, by the bus-stop, one hoary, crackling, stamping January morning, she noticed that Bridget was missing. They told her she was ill. Three mornings later they told her she was dead. Mary tried to comfort them, but they drew away bewildered, withdrawn. They suddenly seemed to Mary to have formed an alliance against the world. Mary grieved desperately for Bridget, doing all she could to screen her feelings from Jimmy. She changed the time she caught her bus, going earlier so that she wouldn't see the Devlins. She went to a different mass. Gradually the pain eased, and it was as if her yearning for children of her own had been partially exorcized. The tragedy had done Mary a service. Through the suffering of the Devlins she had suffered and now the need, though still there, was blunted.

Chapter Five

Debs, Maharajahs, Valentino

1917-1930

MARY'S work in the directors' dining room at the Hyde Park was exacting but rewarding. The Bennetts and their fellow executives ate well, usually rather better than their clients. Food shortages were circumvented by the produce from country estates and rivers, and they had the pick of the wines from Jimmy's cellars. Mary was still able to smuggle out considerable quantities of goodies, and the crumbs from the directors' dining table afforded many a treat below stairs. So did their private drinks cupboard, controlled by Mary, who was also accountable for the stocks. But what she 'borrowed' she always managed to put back, and she developed a palate for good sherry which remained with her until a few days before her death.

Mary's other duties were various. One was as chambermaid to the maharajahs and sultans who were now using the hotel. Like Beaverbrook a few years earlier, they and their entourages would take over entire floors, causing problems with their specific dietary requirements. Some of them were Moslem, and their religion dictated not only that their own staff should take over in the kitchen to provide them with special dishes, but also that flocks of goats should be tethered on the landings to supply milk as conveniently as possible. Perhaps the most lavish entourage was that of the Sultan of Zanzibar, who arrived with twelve goats, a brigade of cooks and servants, a large number of advisers, acolytes and hangers-on, and a generous display of bodyguards who positioned themselves on the landings day and night.

One night, for a bet, Mary silently and fearfully ascended the stairs. She was to gather a cupful of goat's milk – and return it to a hilariously anticipatory kitchen. But on approaching one of the more isolated goats, she almost lost her nerve. The rank smell, the agitated movements of the animal and the proximity of the bodyguards made her mission absurd from the outset. Then she steeled herself and advanced. Unfortunately Mary had more or less no idea how to milk the goat, and her first fumbling attempts met with increased agitation and an angry, throaty cry. Almost at once the bodyguard appeared and with a surprising command of English asked her, 'What in Allah's name are you doing, woman?' Unable to think of any satisfactory explanation, Mary told him about the bet, begging the bodyguard not to tell Cornu. She laid on as much charm as possible, increasing her brogue and hoping that stage blarney would appease his indignation. It only worked, however, when she jerked out a few tears – and the bodyguard reluctantly let her go. The next time she passed him, carrying a tray of morning coffee, he winked at her and asked if she would like a few lessons in milking goats. For weeks after that she desperately tried to avoid the floor of the potentate, hoping against hope that the man would not take it into his head to give her away. But he didn't, and Mary breathed a sigh of relief when at last the entire entourage plus goats left London for Europe. Only the smell of goat lingered to remind her of the incident.

The twenties roared into the Hyde Park in grand style, bringing with them the great Valentino. They also brought more suffering in Ireland with Sinn Féin rejecting the offer made to them under the Fourth Irish Home Rule Bill, of two Irish parliaments, in Belfast and Dublin. Civil war engulfed the country as the Black and Tans were introduced by the British government. Mary found the thought of this suffering intolerable and tried, unsuccessfully, to shut her mind to it. One of her escape routes was Valentino, and she became an ardent fan of his films, so she could hardly believe her luck when it was announced that Valentino would be making the Hyde Park his base for his first London appearance. On the morning of his arrival, all traffic in Knightsbridge and the West End came to a stop as the hero of the silent movie screen graciously appeared on a balcony and waved decorously to the 20,000 hysterical women gathered below.

Valentino, real name Rodolpho Alfonzo Raffaelo Pierre Filibert Guglielmi di Valentino d'Antonguolla, came from a small Italian village. By the time he arrived at the Hyde Park, Mary had seen *The Four Horsemen of the Apocalypse* and had been romantically carried into a fantasy world by Valentino's non-greasy and non-caddish Latin looks. He represented an Apollo who always treated women with deference and courtesy while promising sexual adventure with his eyes – which also promised both skill and experience. Richard Griffith and Arthur Mayer summarized his allure in their book, *The Movies*: 'The strong, silent, he-man Arrow-collar heroes of the American screen were designedly awkward in their movie romancing; it was their badge of self-respect, or perhaps of virginity. The magnetic pull Valentino exerted on millions of women signalled that they were tired of awkward love-making, on screen *and* off.'

She had also seen *The Sheik*, in which a more menacingly sexual Valentino warily circled a pleading Agnes Ayres, preparing for the inevitable clinch, although it was a long time in coming. Valentino's boss, Adolph Zukor, wrote that Valentino's acting 'was largely confined to protruding his large, almost occult, eyes until the vast areas of white were visible, drawing back the lips of his wide, sensuous mouth to bare his gleaming teeth and flaring his nostrils'.

Valentino was as histrionic at the Hyde Park as he was on celluloid. Adolph Zukor had written of him: 'He was arguing with an assistant director – about what I did not know and did not enquire. His face grew pale with fury, his eyes protruded in a wider stare than any he had managed on the screen, and his whole body commenced to quiver.'

The rare and mystic bond he managed to convey with his eyes was a little spoiled for Mary, as she took in his morning coffee, by the presence of his second and bigamous wife, Winifred Shaugnessy De Wolf Hudnut, who rather obviously preferred to be called Natacha Rambova. She had originally been a successful costume designer but was now committed to managing her husband's artistic and business affairs. Largely because of Natacha's interference, Valentino had already left Paramount for a number of unsuccessful ventures with his wife. One of the most vapid of these was the publication of a book of poetry called *Day Dreams*, a copy of which Mary bought during Valentino's stay at the Hyde Park, despite the fact that she could never read it. Luckily for Mary, however, Valentino read aloud from it at a press conference in the hotel. One example of its sugary content is as follows:

> *Your kiss*
> *A Flame*
> *of Passion's fire*
> *The sensitive seal*
> *of love*
> *In the desire*
> *The fragrance*
> *of your caress*
> *Alas*
> *At times*
> *I find*
> *Exquisite bitterness*
> *In*
> *Your kiss.*

There is no doubt that Mary took the poem seriously. But the American press did not; Valentino had been receiving bad publicity ever since he left Paramount. His kitsch Hollywood home and the slave bracelet that Natacha had given him were now seen as ludicrous rather than romantic by some sections of the press, particularly the *Chicago Tribune* when it suggested the advisability of 'drowning the "Pink Powder Puff"': Rudy the beautiful gardener's boy'. The *Tribune* was anxious that this should happen before 'the younger generation of American males replaced razors with depilatories and the ancient caveman virtues of their forefathers were replaced by cosmetics, flopping pants and slave bracelets'.

Valentino and Natacha Rambova occupied a fifth floor suite at the Hyde Park. Mary remembered:

He was as good looking as he was in *The Sheik* but he was very vain. It was almost as if he was in love with himself. He didn't look such a pretty sight when I took the breakfast tray into their room in the mornings. He just looked a tousled young boy. His hair was ruffled – and, of course, I was always used to seeing it slicked down. Natacha wore her hair very tight to her scalp too – sometimes when they were lying in bed it was difficult to tell them apart.

For Valentino, the trip to England was a great triumph. Years before, he had sailed steerage from Italy to America. Now he was returning to Europe a hero. He had walked the first-class deck in a flamboyant belted raincoat and he had dined each night at the captain's table. One of his biographers, Irving Shulman, writes of him at this period: 'Valentino saw himself as a modern Maecenas returning in triumph, but always his greatest joy was Natacha, whose regal beauty won the admiration of everyone in the first class. Her poise, manner, diction and style brought a hush to every room she entered. Valentino gloried in this and the trip was a happy one. Not once did Natacha find fault with him.'

They only arrived at the Hyde Park at midnight but they were up and ready for their press conference at nine. Mary commented: 'Outside there were thousands of screaming women – and a few managed to get into the foyer before the police turfed them out. One of them clutched me and said I could have any price if I took her to Valentino. I said it would be more than my job was worth. Then she turned nasty and said I was a mercenary little cow. She tried to climb the stairs but a policeman dragged her screaming out into the street again.'

The press conference, including the poem, degenerated into a series of clichés. Valentino was asked the usual questions about his feelings on women, beauty and so on. 'It was *The Sheik* that had carried me away,' said Mary, 'but he hated it. I once went in whistling the tune 'The Sheik of Araby' and he threw a glass of wine all over the floor. He told me the song was cheap and vulgar – just like the film. I was very surprised. I loved the film – I kept imagining myself to be proud Agnes Ayres who humbled herself to the Sheik. Why – I even remember the publicity gimmicks – Shriek for the Sheik will Seek you Too.'

The publicity certainly had been of epic proportions:

SEE

the auction of beautiful girls to the
lords of Algerian harems.

SEE

the barbaric gambling fête in the
glittering Casino at Biskra.

SEE

the heroine, disguised, invade the
Bedouins' secret slave rites.

SEE

Sheik Ahmed raid her caravan
and carry her off to his tent.

SEE

her captured by bandit tribesmen and
enslaved by their chief in his stronghold.

SEE

the Sheik's vengeance, the storm in the
desert, a proud woman's heart surrendered.

SEE

matchless scenes of gorgeous color, and
wild free life and love in the year's supreme
screen thrill – 3,000 in the cast.

The book, by E. M. Hull, on which the film was based was a sensational success in both America and England. The *Book Review Digest* of 1921 presented its readers very succinctly with the bare bones of the plot:

Diana Mayo is a young English girl, self-willed and fearless. When she plans a tour into the desert, unchaperoned and with only natives in attendance, neither her friends nor her brother can dissuade her. So she starts but very shortly is captured by the Sheik, an Arab chieftain with no standards of morality save those of a caveman. His caveman treatment of her, however, wins her, for after a few months of agonizing and despair, she suddenly finds herself in love with him, and only fearful lest she may have to leave him. Incidents of her attempted rescue and return, her capture by a hostile tribe and her thrilling rescue, add to the lurid atmosphere of the story.

Mary's romantic nature seized on what was basically a rather sadistic comic-strip of a film which had its own attendant industry, such as the Tin-Pan-Alley number that Valentino found so degrading:

> *I'm the Sheik of Araby,*
> *Your heart belongs to me.*
> *At night when you're asleep,*
> *Into your tent I'll creep.*
> *The stars that shine above,*
> *Will light our way to love.*
> *You'll rule this land with me,*
> *The Sheik of Araby.*

The film was full of classic lines like these:
'Lie still, you little fool.'
'Why have you brought me here?'
'Are you not woman enough to know?'
Or later:
'I am not afraid with your arms around me, Ahmed, my desert love, MY SHEIK.'

The book had greatly appealed to the 'New Woman' of the 1920s who, daringly, smoked, danced, had her hair bobbed and wore her skirts much shorter than ever before. It was a sign of emancipation for the New Woman to have a copy of *The Sheik* tucked under her arm.

'The film was a travesty,' Valentino later told Mary when she asked him to autograph a still from the film. And Alexander Walker, in his biography *Rudolph Valentino*, confirms Valentino's hatred of the epic: 'Compared with the sensitivity Valentino had shown in that film [*The Four Horsemen of the Apocalypse*], *The Sheik* is a crude comic strip. He knew this and always detested it. He confessed he was confused about how to play the role – as a Latin, as an Arab, or as a latent English Milord.'

On the second day of Valentino's stay, Mary took tea up to him. He was alone, Natacha being in the bath. He was restless and tired. Mary put down the tray and was just about to leave when 'he got up and started going on about *The Sheik* and how awful it was. Then he asked me if I'd bought his poetry book. I said that I had. That seemed to satisfy him for a moment. Then he went to a suitcase and picked up a copy of the book. I thought he was going to give it to me, and I was just going to ask him to sign it when he began to read aloud. I remember two of them. One was to do with a baby – the other was called "You".'

In fact both were pretty dreadful – as were all Valentino's poems:

A BABY'S SKIN

Texture of a butterfly's wing,
Colored like a dawn rose,
Whose perfume is the breath of God.
Such is the web wherein is held
The treasure of the treasure chest,
The priceless gift – the Child of Love.

YOU

You are the History of Love and its Justification
The Symbol of Devotion
The Blessedness of Womanhood
The Incentive of Chivalry
The Reality of Ideals
The Verity of Joy
Idolatry's Defence
The Proof of Goodness
The Power of Greatness
Beauty's Acknowledgement
Vanity's Excuse
The Promise of Truth
The Melody of Life
The Caress of Romance
The Dream of Desire
The Sympathy of Understanding

My Heart's Home
The Proof of Faith
Sanctuary of My Soul
My Belief of Heaven
Eternity of All Happiness
My Prayers
           You.

Valentino, having finished reading this poem to Mary, some-what abruptly asked her how he could meet the Prince of Wales. It was a strange thing to ask a servant. Her unspoken thought communicated itself to him, and hesitantly he told her that no one else could arrange a meeting for him; surely working in the hotel she would know someone. But she had to disappoint him. There was no chance of her having such contacts. Little did she guess that a few years later she would have found the introduction comparatively easy.

Valentino was bitterly disappointed that he was unable to meet the Prince of Wales. His ambition was to meet all the crowned heads of Europe, and so far, in England, the crowned heads were singularly inaccessible. The aristocracy, fortunately, were not. The Guinness family gave Valentino and Natacha dinner at Ascot, they lunched at the Savoy with Lord and Lady Birkenhead, and they met Gerald du Maurier, Gladys Cooper and Artur Rubinstein: Natacha also bought three Pekinese dogs from some exclusive kennels – all of which promptly fouled the Valentino suite. Mary was summoned to clear up the mess – which no sooner cleared was repeated. 'I couldn't stand it any longer,' Mary concluded. 'It was like painting the Forth Bridge. And all he could do was to recite more bloody poetry at me as I scrubbed the carpet with disinfectant. I was pleased when they moved on to Paris and the hotel was clear of screaming women and dogs' muck.'

Despite these natural hazards, Mary went along the next week to see *The Sheik*, which was re-running yet again at a cinema in Hammersmith. Somehow the romantic stuffing seemed to have been knocked out of the Sheik by such close contact with the actor. 'All I could see was Valentino striding up and down his suite spouting poetry – and those damned dogs doing their business all over the place. It was terrible – every time he had the girl in my arms I heard the yapping of the Pekes.'

Valentino was vital to his period; as Alexander Walker writes: 'Valentino focused an emotional need shared by millions at a particular time in history and he was fortunate in finding the right role that magnified his qualities and invited participation in the myth of love as he expressed it.' He was also obviously a product of the publicity machine. The synthetic introduction to his book of poetry summarizes his self-image well:

I am not a poet or a scholar, therefore you shall find neither poems nor prose. Just dreams – *Day Dreams* – a bit of romance, a bit of sentimentalism, a bit of philosophy, not studied, but acquired by constant observation of the greatest of masters! . . . *Nature*!

When lying idle, not through choice, but because forcibly kept from my preferred and actual field of activity [he had been recently hospitalized in Baltimore for 'nervous and mental exhaustion'] I took to dreams to forget the tediousness of worldly strife and the boredom of jurisprudence's pedantic etiquette.

Happy indeed I shall be if my *Day Dreams* will bring you as much enjoyment as they brought to me in the writing.

Unfortunately, Mary's dreams of the romantic film hero were shattered by knowing the man, but she always retained a fondness for the Italian peasant who had become a legend. When she heard through the Italian staff at the hotel that Valentino had been spat upon in his own home town of Castellaneta, she was genuinely upset.

They said he was taking photographs and, not understanding cameras, his cousins thought he was trying to capture their souls with his black box. Eventually he had to run to his car as they all threw mud at him. It made him hate Italy. But it wasn't his fault – the film company had made him what he was. When I heard the story I felt very sad – and I kept thinking what it would be like if I was suddenly famous and went back to The Liberties to have rotten fruit chucked at me. It would break my heart.

For the next few years, the Hyde Park was a very curious social mix. Entire floors were still occupied by sultans and maharajahs, the ground floor suites and banqueting rooms were dominated by the royal family, in particular by the Prince of Wales, and the ballroom was taken up most nights with the first wave of the debutante parties. Mary enjoyed the glitter but felt sorry for the girls. 'It was no pleasure for them', she told me. 'But their mothers enjoyed it.' Working overtime as a waitress for these functions, Mary was able to witness the whole exhausting, nerve-racking and totally artificial spectacle.

In 1922, Lloyd George resigned as Prime Minister, the Coalition Government ended and there was a return to party politics with Bonar Law as Prime Minister. By the following year he had resigned on grounds of ill-health and Parliament was dissolved. Baldwin led the next government, only to be defeated in 1924. He was succeeded by the first British Labour Government under Ramsay Macdonald. With the exception of the latter, all the politicians continued to use the Hyde Park extensively. 'The strain showed in them all,' said Mary, 'especially in poor old Bonar Law. He was like an old grey ghost.'

Because the Hyde Park was such a 'royal' hotel, it was considered more than the done thing to have one's coming-out party there. English society was still very much centred on the Court, and coming out was essential for any young lady of note. But, despite this, many people were seriously concerned about the validity of the Season, particularly at a time when some people were 'jumped-up', or had bad blood, or were self-made, or something else equally nasty. Before the First World War, only the very well-born with some claim to Court connections could be presented. After the War, the field was considerably widened. The *Tatler* would record ball after ball at the Hyde Park and Mary would turn its pages wonderingly, seeing the glassy smiles and awkward stances frozen into identikit photographic records. What the *Tatler* didn't record were the scenes she witnessed as she went round with the trays – and described to Jimmy in the Battersea pubs. There was the most reluctant of all debutantes –

the girl who spent most of her ball cowering in the lavatory. There were the usual gate-crashers – firmly ejected by the management. There were the mothers who quarrelled with the fathers, the deb's delight who slipped an ice-cream down the back of one of the deb's younger sisters, and the society photographer who forgot himself so far as to be sick all over a deb's mother's bouquet. There was also the young son, aged about nine, of an anonymous marchioness, who idly told Mary that all the Irish were potato-diggers. Luring him into the still-room with the promise of sweets, she boxed his ears and told him what she thought about the English. On later enquiry by the marchioness, Mary denied all knowledge of the attack, and the wretched child, apparently an acknowledged liar, was admonished.

In a feature known as 'The Passing Pageant 1920–1935', written in George V's Jubilee Year, an anonymous journalist wrote: 'By 1920, the social machine, clogged and almost broken down by the long years of war and chaotic post-war hysteria, had started revolving again. By 1921, it was in top gear and going, to all appearances, smoothly. Great hostesses began entertaining and the fixtures of the London Season again filled the Social and Personal and gossip columns of the newspapers.' Later in the article the journalist asked: 'Did Society, as represented by those terms in pre-war days, suspect the presence of rivals and interlopers in the shape of people of undoubted wealth and doubtful birth? If they did, they kept their suspicions to themselves.'

The Bright Young Things, as represented by the flappers' parties where they dressed as babies, treasure hunts and cocktails, rarely penetrated the Hyde Park. It was too grand, too stately and not nearly rackety enough. They preferred the newly emerging night clubs or the naughty nursery of Rosa Lewis's famous – or infamous – Cavendish Hotel. The ghastly Eve, gossip columnist of the *Tatler*, was most displeased with the changing social times. Writing in her usual arch manner of one of the afternoon parties of the period, she said bitterly:

Difficult to decide who looked worst, the matrons and 'young marrieds' . . . or the debs, who stood in rows in muslin and things, blue and green and purple with cold. And 'part from the clothes, 'strawdin'ry people they were, some of 'em too! Stared the poor royals positively out of countenance and to see Majesty innocently sipping its tea formed into a solid phalanx of peering pushers.

But it was Eve's replacement, Evelyn, who, in 1920, summed up the worst problem that the debs had to face, not only in the Hyde Park but everywhere else, 'The lament of the debutante is the extraordinary dullness of the young men.' This was something that Mary had noticed 'Some of their young men didn't seem men at all – they were so soft.'

By 1925 Mary and Jimmy had been married for six years and were living a happy, insular and childless existence. Michael and Elizabeth Dooley had moved out of The Liberties to the other side of Dublin. Michael had changed his job and sobered up and was now driving a horse and cart, delivering goods for a pharmaceutical company. Mary and Jimmy had twice visited Dublin, and the first time she had showed her husband round parts of The Liberties. He, in turn, promised to take her to Prague. But neither of them had their heart in the other's past. It was the immediate loving present that counted.

During the General Strike, Mary and Jimmy lived in at the hotel while many of its wealthy clients gave an amateurish hand to keep the wheels of British life turning. The miners were the first to strike after negotiations with Baldwin's government had broken down, and all the other unions came out in support in May 1926. The majority of the Hyde Park's clients blamed the Bolsheviks. One such client, a stockbroker by the name of T. Brandon-Smelby, came into Mary's still-room to tell her what he thought about the situation. She listened politely to ten minutes of vitriol from the enraged gentleman as he raved on about 'damned Bolsheviks' and 'the workers not knowing their place'. Clearly Mary knew hers, but for a few seconds she felt like up-ending a vat of boiling hot coffee over Brandon-Smelby's head as she thought of the living conditions in The Liberties and the way her own people had been crushed by their desperate poverty. She didn't feel so close to the English workers, but she knew enough about hard work in the hotel to resent thoroughly the elderly, pontificating clown in front of her. Eventually he left the still-room, announcing with unbearable martyrdom, 'if these worker chaps won't do it – we'll show 'em how.' He went out every day to man a switchboard on one of the newspapers and spent hours each evening boring everybody in the lounge with his experiences.

The *Illustrated London News* echoed his sentiments in a complacent editorial:

We feel that the heart of England must be sound . . . when we read that Mr C. E. Pitman, the Oxford stroke, is driving a train on the G.W.R. from Bristol to Gloucester, the Headmaster of Eton [Dr Allington] and about fifty of his assistant masters have enrolled as special constables . . . Lord Chesham is driving a train and the Hon. Lionel Tennyson is a special [policeman].

Mary's chief memories of the strike and its atmosphere were of the armoured cars as they escorted convoys of lorries carrying food through the London streets. She had to admire the young bloods who came up from Oxford and Cambridge to run the buses, particularly when they were stoned by the more militant of the strikers. The buses were driven with their windows boarded up – and the volunteer drivers were shut into a cage of barbed wire with a Union Jack fluttering bravely from the bonnet. Going back to Wandsworth to fetch a few domestic items from home, Mary had to direct one of the volunteers along the bus's tortuous route. He waited for her at her house and then drove on, with Mary as his guide. He was considerably agitated when he dropped her at the hotel, and she watched with trepidation as he plunged into the London traffic. There seemed no guarantee that he would ever find his way out of Knightsbridge – let alone back to the depot.

Winston Churchill lunched several times at the Hyde Park during the strike, and all the staff received copies of the *British Gazette*, the single sheet newspaper which shouted Churchillian wrath to the erring workers. The strike was broken as suddenly as it had started. The upper and middle classes had won. Lamely, the workers returned to their posts, and it was only the miners who stuck out for another six months. Finally, starvation and poverty forced them back down the mines.

The strike propped up the conversations at the Hyde Park's deb balls for months, and Mary, circulating with her trays of drinks, began to realize just how boring and vacuous the conversations had always been. Now there was a new level of boredom to be added to these occasions with the numerous strike anecdotes and Mary's heart bled for the young debs as they stared woodenly into the prattling features of their escorts. The strike had certainly made no impact on the deb system. The *Tatler* had an emergency edition printed in Paris, and Evelyn, in her column, seemed to think that the canteen work many of the debs had been doing during the strike had been of some benefit: 'The new dates for the Court were promptly announced and the unusually high number of *debutantes*, who had begun to feel rather anxious about their high season, will be none the worse for the job of work they put in during the strike.'

Not only was the Hyde Park now one of the main centres for the debutante season, but it made itself responsible for their fundamental etiquette, grooming and protocol. All this was taught in the ballroom in the afternoon by Madame Vacani, a forceful woman whom Mary regarded with both awe and affection.

Madame Vacani's highly exclusive dancing classes operated from the Hyde Park between the wars.

She was an amazing woman [Mary told me]. She took the children of aristocratic families from their first minuet to that special Court curtsey they would need as debs when they were presented at Court. She taught Princess Elizabeth and Princess Margaret. I remember her in the old days during the First World War when she used to run tea dances for the wounded troops. Some of the men were blind and Madame Vacani told me she used to practise dancing in a dark room so that she knew what it felt like. She used to hire the ballroom on Thursday afternoons for the three to six-year-olds, and on Friday afternoons for the eight to ten-year-olds. The older ones used to go to her studio just down the road from the hotel. The highspot of Madame Vacani's years was the

Dancing Matinée she used to put on in various London theatres in aid of charities. I went to one. It was quite an experience. Obviously they were all very rich children and they were dressed as rainbows and stars and sunbeams and water-babies. While I watched them I kept thinking of all those scruffy, snotty-faced kids in The Liberties – I couldn't help it. It was such a contrast. Madame Vacani used to call everybody 'dear' or 'darling' in a soft voice but when it came down to teaching and organizing she was spot on. She could be very obstinate sometimes in a royal way. If she didn't want to do something she would say 'I cannot discuss it at all'.

Marguerite Vacani started her career by teaching dancing to the two young princesses of the Spanish royal family. She then returned home to begin the *thé dansant*. The now defunct *Everybody's Magazine* commented: 'When Miss Vacani was among the first London teachers to combine two-steps with tea-cups, it was considered a very daring departure from the social code. Soon she was fashionable – and was society's dancing mistress – as well as its guide to etiquette.'

Every Wednesday afternoon [remembered Mary] she used to buzz off to Buckingham Palace to teach the royal children. If anyone asked her for an appointment on a Wednesday afternoon she would always say 'I am busy on Wednesdays. Very busy.' She used to get herself up in a party dress and a very posh hat to go there. She used to teach the children to dance to nursery rhymes first – and then when they were five or six she would teach them square dances, or reels – or even the samba. But the other side to Madame Vacani's life was teaching debs how to curtsey.

In fact the Vacani School taught girls the entire process of what to do, and what not to do, when entering the Throne Room. The biggest horror in every deb's mind was that she would fall flat on her face when presented to the Royal Personage, and that the atmosphere of the Throne Room would be rent with raucous royal laughter. One debutante recalled, 'I kept having a

terrible dream before I was presented – it involved me stepping
grandly into the Throne Room – and my knickers promptly
falling down.' It is difficult to know how Madame Vacani's
etiquette would have helped this deb out of such an unfortunate
situation, but she did try to cover every other aspect. The girls
were of course taught to curtsey, and Marguerite Vacani claimed
that the curtsey brought into use muscles that were rarely used.
The correct method was to place the right foot behind the left,
to bend the knees, to hold the trunk erect and to incline the head
slightly so that the eyes were not fixed directly on the regal
countenance. Two chairs in Madame Vacani's studio would
represent royalty while Madame Vacani herself played the part
of the Lord Chamberlain. She would read a girl's name from a
card in ringing tones while the prospective debutante stepped
forward, curtsied to the first chair, took three paces to the right,
curtsied again before the second chair, and then retreated towards
the door, taking care not to turn her back on royalty.

Hundreds of debutantes were trained by Madame Vacani each
year.

All the girls that came to the Hyde Park [said Mary] had been
through the Vacani studio. I can still hear her saying, 'Hold
those darling little heads up.' She used to say it to girls of
three and girls of seventeen. Whilst the girls were being
presented Madame Vacani used to sit and watch them in the
gold and white ballroom at Buckingham Palace – so you could
see she was pretty well in. She was always in the Press, too, so
that's why the Hyde Park was keen to rent the ballroom to
her – as well as the prestige of once again being so close to the
Palace.

The press were continuously nosing around the Hyde Park,
trying to persuade Marguerite Vacani to let slip details of the
royal children's dancing activities – or of embarrassing incidents
during presentations. But she was too clever for them and refused.
It was just this kind of discretion, of course, that kept her high
in royal favour. Typical of the kind of press comment on
Madame Vacani's grooming was the gushing *Woman's Mirror*
story on one of her matinées. Although later than this period, it

is typical of the treacly journalism surrounding this royal
favourite:

> 'Ooh ... aren't they lovely!' the murmur ran again and again
> through the crowd outside London's Palace Theatre. ...
> Ageless Miss Marguerite Vacani – whose patrons, past and
> present, include two queens, two princesses, nine duchesses
> and sixty-six peeresses – beamed with justifiable pride at her
> pupils. With the exception of one jolly little water baby who
> stepped on a drawing pin, not one of the children put a foot
> wrong. ... And all the hard work expended, all the patience
> needed, are forgotten by this wonderful teacher, when a small
> child turns round, as one did the other day, to fling her arms
> around her neck and say, 'I wish God had given me two
> mummies, Miss Marguerite. Then you could have been one
> of them.'

The captions to the photographs read, 'Patsy Arton is a high-
kicker, and she loves every moment of her dancing day', and
'Twenty tiny toes have a last try out. They belong to five-year-
olds Anna Fury-Furse and Mary Stewart, who danced the parts
of water babies.'

'But,' commented Mary, 'despite all the gooey articles in the
papers, she was a marvellous old girl and I was very fond of her.
She was married to a very romantic man called Colonel Rankin
whom she met after the First World War. He was meant to be
the tallest man in London – he was about six feet seven inches.
The only problem was that he was too tall to dance with her.'

The debutante season ended in late July when the aristocracy
left London. In the *Tatler*, Evelyn wrote that they went to
'peaceful country houses, with unlimited tennis and golf and
bridge, and a little wild dancing to the gramophone, and many
opportunities for flirtations. Or up to Scotland, perhaps, where
I hear more Americans than ever have taken moors or forests, or
off to some Continental watering place with its promise of fine
weather and smart clothes and its opportunities of indulging in a
little gambling.'

One of the principal hostesses of this period was Lady Diana
Cooper. Lady Diana is the youngest daughter of the 8th Duke of

Rutland and had come out in the very restricting prewar days. To her, great liberation had come with the First World War; she told Margaret Pringle* that before the war she had no liberty. 'I was never let out of sight and I never left the house without a friend. I would know more now if the system hadn't been like that. When the war came, I went to work in a hospital, which was back-breaking work, but I was able to live away from home. Can you imagine the happiness of that?'

Mary told me: 'Lady Diana had this style. She was so different. She once rode down Bognor High Street on a grey mare, dressed as a cowboy. I went to see her in *The Miracle* at the Lyceum in 1922. At first I didn't think it was very respectable for a duke's daughter to be on the stage. Then she won me over – she looked as if she was a delicate stone statue. It was quite eerie. She knew all the new dances – like the Jog Trot and the Shimmy and the Blues and the Charleston.'

At this time the aristocracy was trying to adapt itself to the postwar world, and this was reflected strongly in the atmosphere at the Hyde Park. Democracy was all too obviously snapping at the heels of the hotel's aristocratic clients. Lady Diana Cooper, during the General Strike, thought she could hear 'the tumbrils rolling and heads sneezing into the baskets'. And, despite the defeat of the strikers, the upper and middle classes felt an un-easiness which was only unconsciously realized. Yet revolution had been averted for so long that it was unlikely to be a real threat, for, as Stella Margetson points out in her book *The Long Party*, 'Revolution was always somehow averted, partly because even the most Radical leaders of the people were ambitious to be taken for gentlemen, and also because the highest aim of the upstart industrialists and self-made bankers was to buy an estate somewhere in the shires and, by doing so, to become members of the landed gentry.' Also, despite increasing taxation, death duties and the serious state of decay into which some of the great country houses were falling, the aristocracy forged blindly on, seemingly oblivious to the changes that were taking place. Servants were hard to come by: so many thousands had died during the war that only the very old or the very young were available.

* In her book *Dance Little Lady*.

The situation in the country houses was echoed in the Hyde Park, and Mary found her tasks becoming more and more arduous as she had to 'cover' for the dead middle-rankers who had done jobs like waiting, valeting or heavy-duty cleaning. Keeping the great hotel ticking over in the state of grace to which its clients were accustomed was no easy task with such staff shortages, and Mary's shifts became longer and longer. Apart from serving in the directors' dining room, she would be detailed to clean rooms or corridors, to do extra duty in the still-room, to clean a corridor of shoes – and so on. But this rallying process, even under the eagle eye of the ageing Cornu, did not deter Mary. In fact, she rather enjoyed it. At the same time it served to weld her even further into the structure of the hotel until her life outside was indivisible from her life inside. Or, more likely, the life inside took over completely. As Jimmy also continued to work in the hotel, he raised no objection, for he was equally involved. The Hyde Park was an answer to their companionable yet childless life. The flat in Wandsworth remained a refuge, but to Mary it became more and more barren. The bustle of hotel life suited her, and gave her no time to think or yearn. Indeed, Mary would much rather slip into the wine-cellar and be with her husband when she was off-duty, than sit round the Wandsworth hearth. In addition to all the extra jobs she had to undertake, she would also help out her colleagues by providing support or helping them to finish their own work. So, while Mary was desperately needed in the Hyde Park, she was a nonentity outside. And she knew it.

Meanwhile the strange combination of traditional English and exotic French cooking was maintained in the Hyde Park kitchens. For instance, for 5s., guests could feast off the Déjeuner des Gourmets. The menu read:

Hors-d'Oeuvre de Choix
Crème Parmentier

———

Oeufs Cocotte a la Crème
Filet de Meulan au Gratin
Blanchailles Diablées au Citron

———

Steak and Kidney Pudding
Cotelette de Volaille Périgourdine
Côte de Boeuf, Yorkshire Pudding
Viandes Froides Assorties

———

Céleri Demi Glace
Pommes Purée

———

Compôte de Fruits
Patisserie Française
Jam Roll

Mary told me: 'It was the jam roll that was the most popular
pudding. A lot of people still didn't trust all the Continental
stuff. One old dowager, who used to live in the Hyde Park, had
jam roll at lunch every day for five years. I think it reminded her
of the nursery.'

Chapter Six

❦❦❦❦❦❦❦❦❦❦❦❦❦❦❦❦❦❦❦❦❦❦❦❦❦❦❦❦

The Prince of Wales and the Depression Years

❦❦❦❦❦❦❦❦❦❦❦❦❦❦❦❦❦❦❦❦❦❦❦❦❦❦❦❦

1926-1936

ONE of Mary's most important relationships was with the Prince of Wales. He used the Hyde Park constantly for both lunch and dinner, and would regularly come into the still-room to talk to Mary. He was often drunk and whether this was the reason he visited her, or whether he was escaping from his set and felt some need for her company, is not clear. Either way it was a curious, fairy-tale situation, and continued right up until his abdication. Mary told me:

> If he'd stayed there would never have been a republic in Ireland. He was worried about the poor. Always. But that didn't mean to say he wasn't a bright spark. He was always in the still-room or the pantry. Always came in for a talk. Mind you – he was often tipsy – but still a charmer. In the day he used to use the American Bar like a pub – quickly dropping in for a drink. In the evening he used to eat in the restaurant and then come to see us afterwards. He drank whisky through his meal – and afterwards. He never used to drink wine.

A year earlier, in August 1925, King George wrote to the

Queen: 'I see David continues to dance every night and most of the night too. What a pity they should telegraph it every day, people who don't know will begin to think that he is either mad or the biggest rake in Europe. Such a pity!'

But there was more to the Prince than being 'a bright spark', as Mary put .it – or 'the biggest rake in Europe', as his dour father would have it. His social conscience was considerable, and this may well be the key to his 'interest' in Mary. She was so clearly a product of her own background – in some ways almost a prototype – that she became a symbol of his social conscience. This is not as unlikely as it sounds, for it must be remembered that the Prince's arid and protected background hardly fitted him to be experienced in such matters.

Gradually Mary began to understand his dual personality: that of the Bright Young Thing and aspiring social reformer. He talked to her about the problems of poverty. 'He really understood about it,' she told me, 'which is more than you can say for the rest of them.' Slowly she learned what he had been trying to do, and the experiences he had had.

By 1926 the Prince had returned from his journeying abroad and was wondering what on earth he could do to fill the time. He was as restless as ever and quite unable to find a royal position which made him feel he was doing a worthwhile job. The sterility of his relationship with his parents, the stifling formality of George V's Court, the feeling of being cut off from the rest of society, and the protection given to him during the war, all combined to make him highly resentful of the restrictions imposed upon him – and the resultant criticism when he tried to break out.

Although Queen Mary continued to exchange mistress-servant intimacies with Mary, it was hardly likely that she would behave with the same informality as the Prince of Wales. As James Pope-Hennessy says in his biography of Queen Mary, the isolated élitism of George's Court 'was to protect the Royalty in the centre of the hive from any form of avoidable anxiety and from crude contact with the outside world, so as to preserve Him or Her healthy, serene and intact for the performance of Royal duties with the maximum of efficiency and the minimum of worry'. So the whisky-drinking prince, who would find solace with Mary in the still-room, was hardly behaving as if he were part of that system, and as a result his father breathed heavy disapproval.

The Prince was very interested in The Liberties and appalled by Mary's halting yet graphic description of the poverty there. The Prince's social conscience had been fired at the end of his tour of the British slums in 1923 when, inspecting a soup-kitchen somewhere in the provinces, he saw a man with no shirt under his coat. On later tours, he would choose to call at houses completely at random and was once again appalled by what he saw. His frustration was particularly great because he knew there was nothing he could do – and this was one of the main points he made to Mary. He was hamstrung, powerless, a mere figurehead unable to alleviate the common lot in any way. Later he wrote that he was in a position that 'at times seemed to leave me dangling futilely in space between the ceremonial make-believe, symbolizing the power of high and mighty princes, and the discouraging realities of a world that insisted upon relegating even a conscientious prince to a figurehead role'.

Mary was immensely attracted to the Prince, who still looked like a teenager – doll-like, as Jimmy was. Basically, his social conscience embarrassed her and she sometimes dreaded his drunken appearances. She preferred to see him in his fairy-tale prince role. Indeed, Mary expected her royalty to behave in the same way as George hoped his son would. But the Prince refused to conform. Deb after deb was thrust upon him at the Hyde Park balls, but the girls he liked were not 'suitable' for Court circles, and even with the 'unsuitables' he soon lost interest. His constant companion was Edward Dudley Metcalfe (known as 'Fruity' Metcalfe), who had joined the Prince on his Indian tour and was now an official equerry.

Edward naturally preferred the Kit Kat Club or the Café de Paris – London's most exclusive and rackety nightspots – to the greater formality and constraint of the Hyde Park. So, if he was not attending a banquet or a debs' ball, he would only drop in for a warm-up with Fruity Metcalfe beforehand or a nightcap afterwards if the evening had been bad, and it was then that he would often see Mary.

The Prince of Wales did not always discuss poverty and his social conscience with Mary. Once he told her about his campaign to get rid of what he afterwards described as 'the tyranny of starch'. This included the stuffiness of formal dress and its attachments, such as hard collars, cuffs, the boiled evening shirt, and spats. But in the main he pumped her about The Liberties – and it was about The Liberties that Mary increasingly spoke.

It was a curious relationship. The Prince and the young Irish woman, sitting in the muted light of the still-room in the early hours of the morning, the splendours of the hotel wilting about them. No doubt he was patronizing her, no doubt he was using her as some kind of sounding-board, no doubt if he had been politically fulfilled he would not have bothered to go into the still-room. But for some months he did, and as a result Mary became deeply attached to him. To her, he was immature, naive, anxious to learn about the world of the under-privileged. To him, she was the classic face of the poor he was unable to help. 'He kept asking me,' she said, 'and I kept telling him.' She kept whisky back in the still-room for him, and the preliminaries to his visit were clandestine, schoolboyish. He was off the hook for half an hour, having briefed Fruity Metcalfe or 'Burghie', the Earl of Westmorland, to keep the party going outside, or at least to keep it at bay.

Mary would not always talk directly to the Prince about the poverty in The Liberties, and when she did she would often exaggerate, largely because she felt that everything should be bigger and better for him. She told him about the street markets, about the brewery, and about the seaside trips. She told him about Bridie's death, but kept off the rebellion for fear of embarrassing him to such an extent that he would never come back into the still-room again. One aspect of life in The Liberties she did tell him about, and which he listened to with some amazement, was of the home cures prescribed for a variety of different conditions. She told him how doctors cost half-a-crown a visit and how this expense would be incurred only if every other cure failed. A bump on the head, she told him, was treated with a cold saucer, cuts with iodine, a burn with soap, a sprain with eel's skin, warts by spit and the sign of the cross, boils with bread and water poultice, and so on. She was too modest to mention other cures – soaking chilblains in your own urine, and sitting on a bucket of cow's dung to cure piles.

For the Prince, Mary evoked the sound and smell and clamour of a completely alien community which he would have given much to meet on its own home ground. But this was never to be; he could only experience it second-hand from Mary. So their late-night meetings continued, their atmosphere giving another perspective to his searching, restless, pre-ordained life. Within the desperate flurry of his existence, the Hyde Park still-room, Mary and the clandestine whisky represented an oasis in a frustrating world – an oasis of yearning to be involved with the common people. But she had sublimated her frustration by assuming a maternal role with the staff of the hotel and its guests. Just as she had 'potted' Queen Mary, she now provided alcohol, solace and escapism for her son.

As the last stale moments of the last dance of the ball arrived, or as the last cigar was ground out at a banquet, the Prince of Wales would appear, guilty, boyish, happy in the knowledge that he was evading his responsibilities. Other staff would scatter, and Mary would produce the whisky. He would sit down, light a cigarette and breathe a sigh of relief, always keeping one eye on the door. Mary would then sit down at the opposite end of the table and pour herself a cup of tea. She would wait until he spoke first. Then she would talk about whatever the Prince wanted to talk about. Their social positions remained the same, but both were suddenly and fleetingly off-duty.

In his book, *A King's Story*, Edward VIII wrote:

Whenever I entered a crowd it closed round me like an octopus. . . . Midnight often found me with wearied brain and dragging feet and the orchestra blaring out the by-now hackneyed tunes. If, mindful of next morning's programme, I were to suggest leaving a party early in order to make up some sleep, or if in an unguarded moment my expression betrayed the utter fatigue that possessed me, my hosts, who no doubt had spent weeks preparing an elaborate and expensive party in my honour, would disappointedly attribute my attitude to boredom, or what was worse, bad manners. And so I drove myself many a night to the edge of exhaustion, lest unfounded rumour create the suspicion that I was an Ungracious Prince.

In fact Mary realized exactly what pressure the Prince of Wales was under and why he needed the therapy of the still-room so much on the occasions he was in the Hyde Park. She thought about him a great deal, taking the memory of their meetings back to the flat in Wandsworth. Sometimes, nodding off to sleep in the rare moments when she and her husband were at home together, she saw in Jimmy's face the features of the Prince. Wearily she confused the two, and then jerked back to consciousness as she realized where she was. For a moment she had dreamed of the still-room – and the Prince moving towards her, leaning against the table, whisky glass in hand. Sometimes in the dream he grasped her hand, at other times she knelt before him.

'Be my Queen,' he would say.

'Your Honour – I'm not worthy.'

'I love you,' he would return, occasionally kneeling beside her, putting the whisky glass down on the table.

'You're making a joke of me.'

'I'm in deadly earnest, my dear.' His eyes would be clear blue and ferocious in their determination. 'I'm asking you to be Queen of England. To be my wife.'

'You'll marry a commoner?'

'I'll marry my true love.' He would bring her hand again to his lips and the dream faded for the sake of having nowhere to go.

In the late twenties Mary's brother Paddy suddenly arrived from Dublin and got employment at the hotel as a commis waiter. He was a remarkably poor one and was frequently sacked. But inevitably he was reinstated, for he was the best player in the inter-hotel league football team and the staff rose up in arms at his dismissal. Without Paddy Dooley the team would founder and the Hyde Park would no longer be in the league. Meanwhile Paddy, on a return trip to Dublin, had regaled Michael and Elizabeth with tales, heavily embellished, of how Mary was leading a fairy-tale life in London. He told them that Mary was the toast of London, that she was a friend of royalty and a prop to the aristocracy, and that she had, at one stage, been Rudolph Valentino's lover. Faced with these astonishing stories, Elizabeth was merely bewildered, while Michael had the sneaking feeling that if they were true then the money Mary sent home could be increased sixfold. Little was said about it at the time, but when Mary and Jimmy went back to Dublin for a holiday Michael was not slow in taking her up on her day-to-day life. Hesitantly, he asked her how well she knew the Queen.

'Very well,' she replied.

'And her son, the Prince of Wales?'

'Why – he's a darling.'

'You *know* him?'

'Of course I know him.'

'And the film star – Valentino – were you taking a shine to him?'

But Mary, realizing what Michael was getting at, infuriatingly changed the subject. Every day Michael Dooley gamely tried again, but it was to no avail. Then, towards the end of the holiday, he asked her how much she was earning.

'Five shillings a week.'

'And is that all they pay you for hob-nobbing with royalty?' he asked. Mary laughed and Michael went out to get drunk. He said to his cronies bitterly: 'Merciful God – me daughter's a friend of the British monarchy and they pay her 5s. a week.' What could you expect, they replied, and the conversation turned to republicanism – of a theoretical kind.

Not only did Mary travel to Dublin, but Jimmy also took her to Prague to see his family, the Schifferovás. It was an alien but interesting time, which somehow put her in mind of a living travel film. She was anxious to get back to the hotel where she was really needed. When she returned, Paddy told her that her brother Jim had left home to marry, against their parents' wishes. There was a great furore going on back in Dublin and for this, in some ways, she was grateful, for at least it turned the attention away from herself.

Back at the Hyde Park, Mary was taken out of the directors' dining room. Throughout the late twenties she did a variety of different jobs: running the visitors' lift, the staff lift or the food lift (a whistle code for every floor), working in the still-room or pantry, helping the waiters on the floors, laying up the tables in the restaurant or the grill room. By now she was such a familiar figure in the hotel that the clients regarded her as if she were a piece of furniture, incapable of indiscretion, always serving, always obliging, always there. In fact she drank in every word that was said and announced the details of each client's private life to as many members of staff as were interested – which was most of them.

At this time two men arrived who were to be Mary's colleagues at the Hyde Park throughout the rest of her life. They were also to become two of the greatest chefs in Europe. In 1928 Harold Cavallo came as a fish chef, with experience of such establishments as the House of Commons, Kettners' Restaurant and the Royal Palace Hotel in Kensington. The next year Marcel Tissot arrived from the Ritz, where he had been an apprentice under the great Escoffier. Cooking was a great tradition in the family, and his father and grandfather had been chefs at Buckingham Palace. Tissot had held a humble position as a vegetable cook but soon began to rise to great culinary heights.

It was through these two men, and through some of her more general tasks, that Mary became familiar with the charnel-house atmosphere of the Hyde Park's kitchens. For years the place terrified her. The stifling heat, the bellowed instructions, the kitchen French and the high emotions made the culinary dungeons seem like a highly-charged inferno. They reminded her of a picture of hell she had once seen in Mrs Mackinnon's front parlour in The Liberties: the vast maw, the leaping flames, the pits of brimstone, the lake of molten fire, the souls in torment. In the subterranean depths of the kitchens at the Hyde Park, Mary saw the whole gamut of human emotions, ranging from wild frustration to manic joy, from the depths of despair to the heights of ecstasy. There was even physical violence – fistfights in the steamy heat were a common enough sight, and, wild Latin temperaments abounding, knives were often flourished dramatically, though they were rarely used.

But order somehow reigned in all this hysteria, and from this factory of gourmandism came art.

Mary came to realize that Cavallo and Tissot were artists and that the dishes they prepared were celebrations of their art. Gradually she became absorbed by the kitchens, and in her off-duty moments she would try to make the chefs' lives more comfortable. The kitchens, once she became used to them, brought out her maternal instincts. She made sure there was a constant supply of iced mineral water or fruit juice, because most of the men in their sweated labour suffered from de-hydration. She would make tea, tidy up and ensure that the mounds of soiled linen were promptly despatched to the laundry. The she would return to her normal, lowly job elsewhere in the hotel.

One of the most dramatic episodes Mary witnessed in the kitchens involved the extreme temperament of one of the sous-chefs (under-chefs). Working to an impossible deadline for a banquet which the Prince of Wales was to attend, Jean Rossier burned a large dish of kidneys. With a howl of demonic rage he began to wreck the kitchens, up-ending food, equipment and some of his fellow chefs as he went on the rampage. Finally, he grabbed an enormous meat knife, holding the entire staff at bay, while he hurled imprecations and curses at them all. Then, with unerring aim, Mary brought the proceedings to a halt by throwing a bucket of slops over him. Temporarily shocked out of his rage, Rossier was quickly disarmed. But he was not dismissed. It was within the nature of the environment for such incidents to occur. The kitchens were the creative hub of the Hyde Park and artistic temperament was understood.

The food was now becoming more exotic and the 'old-fashioned' British food had slipped from grace. Tissot remembers a typical menu of the time. The guest list was equally dis-tinguished.

Huîtres Natives
Barquettes de Caviar de Beluga

———

Consommé Excelsior en Tasse
Brindilles Dorées

———

Darne de Saumon Amiral

Poularde Rose de Mai
Coeur de Romaine à l'Estragon

Caneton d'Aylesbury à l'Anglaise
Petits Pois Frais à la Menthe

Pêche de Nice Jean Granier
Coeur Flottant Aurore
Friandises

Café

As the twenties merged into the thirties, Mary's relationship
with Queen Mary and her erring son, the Prince of Wales,
remained constant. While Queen Mary now tended to use the
Hyde Park less for functions, the bored Edward used it more and
more. But he used it on the same basis as before – either for
formal engagements or for casual drinking. Slowly, and without
the benefit of reading the gossip columns, Mary became increasingly aware of the relationship between mother and son.
Queen Mary still potted in the retiring room, and would
obliquely ask Mary if she had seen 'the Prince of Wales last
night'. She seemed to want to keep a check on his movements,
and although she could not bring herself to ask, Mary was sure
she was anxious to know who he was with and how he had
behaved. But even the least withdrawn of queens was hardly
likely to ask a cloakroom attendant about the less decorous
activities of her son. For his part, the Prince remained as much
of a 'bright spark' as before, although Mary suspected that the
brightness was becoming paler and more synthetic as one
decade ended and the next began. He moved within a narrow
set of personal friends and they rarely seemed to change. To
Mary, Edward remained a perpetual adolescent, and his con-
tinuing naivety seemed to reinforce this. His visits became more
regular, and he seemed ever more anxious to make temporary
escapes from the freneticism of the jovial, young and vacuous
company around him.

Once the Prince came into the still-room with a look of dejected boredom on his face. He had been presiding over an official banquet and was barred from going on to the Kit Kat Club by the elderly company who wished to sit on in the Hyde Park. He compared the situation bitterly with Windsor, under his father's regime, where everyone went promptly to bed at eleven. He went on to tell Mary how he and George had once tried to enliven the situation. They had rolled back the carpets and forced an unwilling band to play some foxtrots. But the oppressive atmosphere was too much for everyone – including the Prince of Wales – and the evening ran down like a tired battery. 'It was too dull for him,' Mary told me. 'Everything was too dull for him.' Later he recounted the incident:

Life at Windsor for young people was a trifle over-powering to say the least. Nothing was lacking but gaiety; and the abrupt end of the evening at 11 would leave us subdued and at a loss. One evening my brothers and I were emboldened to try to enliven the atmosphere for the younger members of the party. We had arranged with the band to wait for us in the Green Drawing Room. When my parents had gone to bed, we returned; the rugs were rolled back; and the musicians, more familiar with classical music and martial airs, made an earnest attempt to cope with outmoded foxtrots, which were as close as they could come to jazz. But our efforts to be gay were a failure. The ancient walls seemed to exude disapproval. We never tried again.

The culmination of Mary's relationship with the Prince of Wales came at the beginning of the thirties – and the coming of the Depression. The Abdication Crisis, a few years later, was to end the relationship – but not without her gaining further insights into the characters of the restless Prince and his withdrawn mother.

The Depression which followed the Wall Street crash was worldwide; over the next four years world trade dropped by almost 50 per cent. In England, as industrial production slumped, so did the demand for cotton and rubber. The North of England was particularly badly hit and unemployment in Britain rose

from one million in the twenties to two million by the end of
1930, and to three million by the end of 1932. The Prince of
Wales wrote, as he toured the country:

> Throngs of idle men everywhere, with nowhere to go. In
> town after town, village after village, one would come upon
> dejected groups aimlessly milling in the streets or standing
> about outside the labour exchanges and in front of the pubs
> they lacked the means to patronise. The saddest fact of all
> was that tens of thousands of these unemployed had come to
> judge themselves useless and unwanted.

In face of the disaster Ramsay Macdonald resigned, but
George V returned him to power as Prime Minister of a National
Government, which was composed of some of Macdonald's
more senior colleagues as well as Liberals and Conservatives.
In the following emergency budget, 10 per cent went on surtax,
6d. on income tax and 1d. on a pint of beer. The weekly dole
was reduced from 17s. to 15s. 3d.

Mary witnessed the hunger march of 1931 and suddenly felt
threatened. All at once the feudal security of the Hyde Park
seemed to have been stripped away. Supposing she lost her job?
Supposing they both lost their jobs? The Prince, now less
constant a visitor to the still-room, continued to tell her about
conditions outside London – of the soup kitchens, of the
desperately poor cottages of unemployed miners, of the sullen
silence that met him before the working people began to
realize that he was genuinely anxious to be of practical help. He
became patron of the Lord Mayor's Fund for distressed miners.
He also continually appealed for recruits for the voluntary
social services.

Sitting in the frantic and noisy bustle of the Hyde Park
kitchens, Mary heard the Prince on the radio narrate the following anecdote about one such voluntary committee. It was
touching in its simplicity.

A committee meeting was in progress just before Christmas
in a small club in a very poor neighbourhood of London.
The members, mostly unemployed or casually employed,

with large families and living in two rooms on a very small weekly income, had already contributed towards a Christmas party for their own children. Further suggestions were called for by the chairman and one man got up and proposed that another subscription should be raised amongst the members for another party for the children of the people in the neighbourhood who were even poorer than themselves, and who had not the benefit of the club and its canteen. This was done.

But it was her own personal confrontation with the hunger strikers that made Mary so very desperate to keep her humble job at the Hyde Park, and aware of the worsening situation outside the confines of the hotel. She also realized that conditions must be as bad, if not worse, in The Liberties – for news from home had spoken of unemployment and often near-starvation.

She had been walking through Hyde Park to the hotel one morning in 1931 for a late shift. But progress through the royal park was difficult, for on the grass sat 2,500 unemployed. Mary remembered the trilbies, cloth caps and bulky, ill-cut clothes – a grey mass of abject, humble misery. For the most part they were silent, there were a few banners, a few orators, but in the main there reigned a great quietness over Hyde Park. This was not the raucous poverty that Mary had grown used to in The Liberties. This was the ominous stillness of a poverty that could soon mean death through starvation. Bemused, she wandered amongst them, thinking of the untrammelled luxury of the hotel a few hundred yards away, and of the comfort of its clients. But no cold anger seized her – only a bitter recognition that there were two worlds: the poor and the rich. And she served the rich. Memories of the rebellion came into her mind – and the way she herself had treacherously, if courageously, turned her back on the poverty she knew and come to England to improve her lot. And she had succeeded in doing this, despite the fact that she was a mere maid-of-all-work, and saw no reason for her circumstances to change. Mary knew she had not left The Liberties to begin a rags to riches story, but for something much less tangible.

Her feelings were mixed as she moved slowly amongst the

ranks of the unemployed. She felt both guilty and thankful: guilty that she had turned her back on Dublin; thankful that she had been taken into the marble halls of the Hyde Park; thankful too that she had met Jimmy, and that despite their childlessness they managed to live in cosy, loving companionship. But she felt fear too, fear that she might join the ranks of the unemployed. She had already seen what the unemployment crisis had done to Wandsworth. The reading room at the public library was crammed, and every chair was occupied throughout the day. With Woodbines at 2d. for a packet of five, no one could afford to smoke, let alone drink. She recalled the silence and the glassy eyes of these semi-starved men, who had resigned themselves to living in this slow limbo world. She remembered, too, the faint but unmistakable smell of unwashed clothes, the smell of despair. René Cutforth, in his book on the thirties, *Later Than we Thought*, remembers an almost identical situation:

There was a faint, sour smell of unwashed clothes (hot water cost money) and this increased as the day wore on, until by closing time at six o'clock, with the gas hissing as it poured a wash of primrose-coloured light over the dark caps and overcoats and the walls of institution-brown, the fug in the reading room was more than cosy: self-hypnosis, the one true friend of the desperate, had been achieved.

With sudden resolution Mary began to move towards the hotel, away from these hopeless, tired, sweaty hunger marchers. Then, just as she was leaving the main crowd, a man approached. Instinctively he had known she was Irish. So was he – a brick-layer from Liverpool. He had been out of work for months and he said his family were starving in The Liberties. There was no money to send back. Already two of his younger children were dead, and the rest were heading for the poor house. Mary listened to him horrified. She had become involved. He begged her to send money to them but when she asked for the address he merely cried. Eventually he stumbled away from her and she was never to know whether he had been telling the truth, trying to con her, or driven out of his mind and memory by the Depression.

Just as she walked through the staff door of the Hyde Park, Mary heard the sounds of the baton charge the police made against the hunger strikers to clear them from the park. Later Jimmy told her that their plight had been reduced to near-farce after being scattered. They had brought with them a huge petition which was to be presented to Parliament. It had been put temporarily in a left-luggage office in one of the London stations. But when they returned to claim it, the petition had strangely disappeared.

The deb balls at the Hyde Park continued, quite unaffected by the Depression. The 1929 election had been a mere inconvenience, and Evelyn wrote in the *Tatler*:

The election, of course, meant a complete cessation of social activities . . . it was the poor debutantes who suffered most, for their dances were definitely off, while those of the slightly older generation found compensation in a few on-the-spur-of-the-moment parties, in the intervals of strenuous election-eering. On second thoughts, though, the week's rest from late nights was probably for the good of the debutantes' looks.

Throughout the early thirties the Seasons continued, attended, often reluctantly, by the Prince of Wales, who was both impatient of the debs and repelled by the contrast between this high living and the surrounding poverty. Nevertheless, veteran good-timer that he was, Edward could not resist joining in. The Hyde Park ballroom pulsed to such melodies as 'Sleepy Lagoon', 'On the Sunny Side of the Street', 'Happy Days are Here Again', 'I'm Happy When I'm Hiking' (*not*, presumably, meant to be a light-hearted reference to the hunger marchers), 'Life is Just a Bowl of Cherries', and, more ironically, 'Ain't it Grand to be Blooming Well Dead', and 'Brother, Can You Spare a Dime'. At the cinema, always a popular pastime with Mary and Jimmy, people could find escape with *The Love Parade* (Maurice Chevalier and Jeanette Macdonald), *The Blue Angel* (Marlene Dietrich) and *Goodnight Vienna* (Jack Buchanan). And as the Depression worsened, and an ominous tension began to build up in the Jarrow dockyards, *Harpers Bazaar* had the gall to advise its readers on its New Year resolution page for January 1933: 'To drop from your conversation for ever the words "crisis" and "depression". In fact to be sufficiently *grande dame* to stop talking about money altogether.'

With his double standards, but also with sincerity and a grim awareness that he could only 'advise' the government, the Prince continued his tours of the worst hit areas. He was still received with suspicion, and the popular phrase, 'I danced with a man who danced with a girl who danced with the Prince of Wales', continued to dog him. But he was delighted when A. J. Cook, an anti-establishment left-winger, told him, 'I was with two Communist friends and when your name was announced they understandably scoffed. But they listened to what you had to say and when you finished, with tears in their eyes they put their hands in their pockets and gave what they had on them to the fund.'

By 1935, Ramsay Macdonald had resigned and had been succeeded by Baldwin – Prime Minister for the third time. Meanwhile, the Depression was largely ignored by the upper classes but the Prince's social conscience was twenty years ahead of its time, and he still confided much of it to Mary. One evening, after a wearying deb ball, he managed ten minutes with her before going on to a night club. Soon he was to meet Wallis Simpson and his visits to Mary were to peter out. On this occasion, one of the last, Mary once again realized how deeply he cared. He looked exhausted, and for some minutes he sat at the table without saying anything. Then he told her that he had been to the mining communities in Wales, where the Depression had probably bitten more deeply than anywhere else. The poverty he had seen there was appalling, and he had been both shocked and frustrated. He told her what he had told the press, 'Something must be done.' He also told her about Baldwin's reaction to the remark, and that Baldwin hated him going into the depressed areas in the first place. Later Baldwin wrote: 'I did not think much of it. For it was a case of a sovereign publicly expressing views on matters which were the subject of political controversy.' But the day after the Prince left South Wales *The Times* leader said that the visit would 'greatly help to concentrate attention on the distressed areas and the failure of

Engine Alley, Mary's birthplace

Cottages Mary knew as a child

The Hyde Park Hotel as Mary first saw it, looking down Knightsbridge towards Hyde Park Corner

The front foyer of the Hyde Park Hotel in 1925

The Smoking Room

The Grill Room

The American Bar

The Ballroom

The Receiving Office
and Bureau

Jimmy — Mary's boy-child husband

Battersea — shades of The Liberties

Rosa and her 'boys' —
Rosa Lewis photographed
outside the Cavendish in
1941

A plague of goats at the
Hyde Park — in the suite of
the Sultan of Zanzibar

Left :Madame Vacani —
tutor to the deb

Mary's last days. Above: Her retirement cake.
Below: Sir Charles Forte making a presentation to Mary Shiffer

the industrial revolution to penetrate the economic backwaters that are particularly affected'.

Before the Prince left Mary that night, he also spoke of the house he had bought in 1930, Fort Belvedere, and his love for it. 'My get-away-from-people-house' as he called it. He had talked about it to Mary before, but on this occasion he talked about the ugly, Gothic, fortified private house near Windsor almost as if it were a person. He seemed to want to withdraw into it – to go into a hermitage away from the endless parties, the debs who bored him, his uneasy relationship with his parents, the frustration of his political impotence, and the general feeling of lack of direction that was swamping him that night. He told Mary about the garden and the physical passion he felt working there. 'I love it,' he told her, 'I love every part of it.' He had cut down shrubs, relandscaped, and built a swimming pool. What is more, he had forced many of his weekend guests to help him, although he drily observed that many of them 'weren't used to that kind of activity'.

Lady Diana Cooper wrote of the Fort:

He had turned a royal folly near Virginia Water into a liveable house, where he could rest from his labours at the week's end. It was called Fort Belvedere and was a child's idea of a fort. Built in the eighteenth century and enlarged by Wyatville for George IV, it had battlements and cannon and cannon-balls and little furnishings of war. It stood high on a hill, and the sentries, one thought, must be of tin.

The Prince stood up and drained the last of his whisky. Then he said something that made Mary's heart give a sudden lurch, and she felt an almost physical pain, for what he told her came so close to what she wanted most. Hesitantly, almost abstractedly, he told her that he had knocked at the door of a miner's house to find that the man's wife was about to have a baby. 'If you wouldn't mind holding her hand,' the miner had said, 'She'd never forget it.' He had held her hand – and then had quickly gone away. Humanly enough, Mary wished to God that it was she who had been pregnant and her hand that the Prince had held. Then she thought of the woman's poverty and tried to dismiss the thought as unworthy. But it wouldn't go away.

1935 brought an easing of the Depression, the Silver Jubilee of George V and Queen Mary – and the arrival of Mrs Wallis Simpson in the Prince's life. Mary and Jimmy celebrated the Jubilee by going to the Hammersmith Palais the week before and joining in a street party the next afternoon. On the bandstand at the Palais was the society bandleader, Tommy Kinsman, who, after the Second World War, was to become a vital part of the Hyde Park team. The cavernous ballroom was jam-packed as Kinsman took them through 'Anything Goes', 'Red Sails in the Sunset' and, ironically, 'Why Did She Fall for the Leader of the Band'. In fact Mary didn't fall for the glamorous Kinsman, but she was later to regard him as a kind of magician who turned the staid Hyde Park dances into a world of light, rhythm, sparkle, and allowed her to escape for a time from her drudgery. Mary was exhausted by the time the street party was held, but a few drinks soon reinvigorated her as she joined in with step-dancing, reels and songs to the harmonica, led by the Irish community of the area. She was exhausted because she and Jimmy had spent the previous night sleeping in the street so as to be sure of having a good view of the royal procession. The sixth of May 1935 had been warm and sunny. But much the best thing about the day was that the Prince of Wales had seen, recognized and waved to her. It seemed a special wave, reminiscent of the late-night conversations in the still-room which, like Fort Belvedere, had been for him a get-away-from-people place. As she danced and drank, Mary could remember the procession exactly. The Mall was very crowded, lined by guards, policemen and thousands of enthusiastic royalists. The first coach carried the Speaker of the House of Commons, and he was followed by the Dominion Prime Ministers, ex-Prime Minister Ramsay Macdonald, the Lord Chancellor with his wig, minor royalty, the Yorks, the Kents – and then the Prince of Wales sitting with his elderly aunt, the Queen of Norway. Finally the King and Queen passed, George looking drawn and grey, and Mary remote and gracious.

In typically prosaic manner Queen Mary noted in her diary that 6 May was a 'lovely, warm day'. She went on to record:

'Our Silver Jubilee. Crowds in the parks and streets quite early.
At 10 we went downstairs & saw all the members of our family
who were to take part in the various carriage processions.'
No doubt she also took this opportunity to warn her eldest son
about any possible breach of behaviour or etiquette on his part.
She then went on to write:

We had a marvellous reception from the crowds of people
all the way to St Paul's Cathedral & back. The thanksgiving
service at 11.30 was beautiful – Back before 1 and we all
went on to the Balcony where the crowds cheered us. – After
luncheon we had to go on the Balcony again – Sat out in
the afternoon & read letters and ans'd telegrams – . . . I
listened to G's wonderful message to his People which was
broadcasted – most moving. After dinner we had to go out
on the balcony again – A wonderful day.

Despite her compassionate personality there was no doubt
that Queen Mary could reduce any occasion to crashing boredom by her dull prose style. But there was more to it than that.
Her reserved and introverted personality made her unable to
communicate with the Prince of Wales at all; later, as his
relationship with Mrs Wallis Simpson developed, she was
typically unapproachable. 'David dined with me this evening,'
she wrote. 'We talked of nothing very intimate.' The same
applied to George V, whose dullness and unapproachability was
far greater even than that of his wife. It is easy to imagine the
impotent despair of Harold Nicolson, the King's biographer,
when he wrote of George as Duke of York, 'for seventeen years
he did nothing at all but kill wild animals and stick in stamps'.

With the lifting of the Depression, the second half of the
thirties was the prewar heyday of the Hyde Park. The Bennetts
were still in charge, and they continued to run the hotel in a
feudal but benevolent manner. Cornu had now retired and he
was replaced by a succession of less passionate, blander personalities. 'I missed Creeping Jesus in the end,' declared Mary.
'He'd put up with a lot from me – and I from him. We were
old enemies – but, in a way, old friends too.'

In 1935 oysters were 5s. a half-dozen in the restaurant, while caviar was 5s. 6d., lobster 4s. 6d. and smoked salmon 2s. 6d. The *plat du jour* offered *Culotte de Boeuf à la Mode Velouté de Céléris* at 3s. 6d., or *Poularde du Surrey à la Broche Pommes Mignonnette* at 4s. Nursery treats like Bread and Butter Pudding featured in the *entremets* at 2s., while the more sophisticated *Coupe de Pêche Melba* could be had at 3s.

The guest list was as distinguished as ever, and the debs' balls were on the increase. The grand hotel atmosphere was at its zenith despite the changing social conditions all around it. Mary continued to fulfil a wide variety of humble jobs – and Queen Mary continued to use the banqueting rooms for charity functions. Over Christmas Mary and Jimmy went back to Dublin, while King George and Queen Mary went to Sandringham, where the Queen wrote in her diary, 'awfully cold here'. In early January, the King went out in the Sandringham grounds on his pony, Jock. James Pope-Hennessy writes:

With Queen Mary walking beside him he looked his last upon the gardens and the grounds of Sandringham, the place which he preferred above all others in the world. Light snow drifted over the bare garden beds and powdered the dark evergreens; the pond, scene of so many jovial skating parties in the long ago, was thinly coated with ice. On some mornings the east wind brought bitter rain.

On Monday 20 January King George died, with Queen Mary and the children at his bedside. With sudden vehemence and lack of restraint, the Queen wrote in her diary: '*Am brokenhearted* ... at 5 to 12 my darling husband passed peacefully away – my children were angelic.' On another page she wrote some words commemorating his death. They read: 'The sunset of his death tinged the whole world's sky.'

Mary heard the news in Dublin and cried for the Queen whom she had grown to know so well, yet so slightly. Unable to write to her, Mary determined that she would express her feelings to the Queen when she next came into the Hyde Park retiring room. But Mary herself was undergoing a period of introspection and somehow the grief of the Queen and the accession to the throne of the Prince of Wales as Edward VIII deepened further her growing feelings of unrest.

At forty-six, Mary once again felt detached and isolated. At the Hyde Park she was a servant looking in. At home she was a woman with a husband she loved and would never leave, yet he would never be a father nor she a mother. The old feelings of pain surged up in her again and increased as she went out of her way to hide her feelings from Jimmy. His quietness, his placid reassurance, his undemanding personality, made her feel all the more restless, not to be rid of him, but to bring something out of him, like the making of a child.

On the day before they were due to return for George V's funeral, Jimmy had a cold and stayed in bed. On a whim Mary went down to the sea. It was a bleak January weekday and the beach was deserted. Everything was grey – the sand, the sky and the sea which stretched to infinity. The seascape exactly matched her mood. The tide was coming in and the tiny, rippling, invading waves looked like molten slate on the chilly sands. Gulls swooped low over her, hoping for scraps, as Mary walked over the beach and out towards the curling sea. Swiftly, so as to keep other thoughts at bay, she turned to fantasy. As Mary shivered in that vast, cold arena she imagined herself not married to Jimmy, but to the Prince of Wales. She saw herself mirrored in the grey-green rock pools: their courtship, their wedding, their reign. Edward and Mary. Queen Mary. She saw herself strolling with him in The Liberties. Arm in arm they walked through The Liberties amongst the milling children. The new king handed out sweets and coins. 'Something must be done', he said, as he looked at the rackety poverty about him. On his arm Mary felt older and wiser. Nothing could be done. Not by a king. She kissed him affectionately. He was so young, so innocent. An old whore leaned out of a window in Engine Alley and shouted 'God Bless the King', just as she would have done as a young girl to his grandfather.

The fantasy deepened as the King walked into their old house. Her father, strangely jovial, was playing the melodeon and was not in the least disapproving of his daughter's rise to the monarchy. He didn't even ask her for money. Her mother was dressed in her church clothes and was dispensing stout and sandwiches. Her brothers, for some reason boys again, and dressed in the uniform of the Boys' Brigade, stood to attention and saluted as she and Edward came in the door. Later they danced a reel and then went out into the streets. It was a brilliant sunlit evening and she and Edward rode regally on the back of her father's horse and cart. Suddenly the drab streets were hung with bunting and lined with singing children. Strangely but persistently one side of the street chanted: 'Catholic, Catholic, go to Mass, riding on the Devil's ass', while the other side chanted:

> *Proddy, Proddy on the wall*
> *Proddy, Proddy, you're going to fall*
> *Hold on, by day and night,*
> *And read your Bible by candle light.*

Even more strangely, the King didn't seem to mind.

They rattled on, past St Patrick's, past Marsh's Library, past Kevin Street Garda Station with the entire Garda taking the salute, down South Brown Street past the Weavers' Hall and on past the drinking fountain in Gray Street. Emmett's Arsenal, the Marshalsea Barracks, Christchurch Cathedral, all flashed past. Behind them ran the children, the boys cheering, the girls cheering, the streets cheering. They stopped by the canal where boys were fishing and swimming and mud-throwing. The old dredge barge had dumped mud two feet high on the Devoy Road side of the canal and there was a mud-war going on between two gangs of children from rival streets. They were plastered in mud – and one mud-ball came dangerously near Edward's bowler hat. Then someone shouted from behind and one urchin on the canal bank whispered, 'Holy Mother – it's the King and Queen'. Edward bowed to Mary as they stepped out of the cart. Suddenly she was in robes. Her father struck up 'God Save the King' on the melodeon. Majestically Edward and Mary climbed the canal bank and stood amongst the mud-stained boys. All Dublin stood singing and cheering about her. The bells in the cathedrals rang out and choirboys followed Father Aidan as he walked slowly towards the canal, swinging incense and praising God.

On the way home they stopped at Irma's Bar for a snifter and then went on to St Patrick's for their first communion together. So what if she had gone and married a 'Proddy'. Her seascape fantasy could fix everything. They knelt together in the great, dust-scented gloom of the cathedral. A thousand candles burned about them. Mystic altar boys brought bread and wine. Father Aidan loomed over them, looking more pagan than Catholic. There was a wild light in his eye as he blessed Edward and gave Mary communion. She turned to kiss Edward – and saw him take a sandwich out of his bowler hat. The fantasy turned to farce – and she was back in the seascape.

She was standing far out on the sand, with the incoming wavelets slapping and playing at her. Mary suddenly realized how cold she was, standing by this sad, flat sea. In it she momentarily caught a glimpse of herself and Edward, dancing up the streets of The Liberties, the children wheeling like the gulls above her. Then she turned, and saw a shouting, waving, slender boyish figure. For a moment she was confused – Edward? – but it was Jimmy. She ran over the sands towards him.

He had come because he didn't want her to be alone. Well bundled up, his voice almost gone from the cold in his head, he must have sensed her bout of emptiness. Mary realized this as she walked with him along the sand and on to the pebbles. He was her quiet man. Not a dashing, debonair prince now to be king, but a quiet man who understood her ways, and who understood without speaking what was bothering her. They found a tiny, steamy café open by the harbour wall, and went into the stale, stuffy interior to order tea. It was the best cup she had ever had – like a restorative draught, hot and strong and heavily flavoured. Silently they watched the mist creep up over the sea, covering the beach and the breakwater. A gull mewed plaintively above them. Then Jimmy said,

'Do you want to come back?'

'Come back?'

'Do you want to live back in Dublin?'

But Mary shook her head. She had no place in Dublin any more. The hotel was her world, their world. There could be no other now.

They stood up to go, and when Jimmy was paying the weary,

apathetic old lady who had served them their tea Mary's attention was drawn to the counter. There, and on the dusty shelving above, was a commercial shrine to the Prince of Wales. His face smiled artificially at her from sweet tins, biscuit boxes, trays, mirrors, rock – even a pair of bathroom scales. Without thinking Mary turned to the old lady and said,

'I know that fellah.'

'Who?'

'That fellah there.' And she pointed to the Prince's face gleaming rosily from a biscuit tin.

The old lady took a close look at Mary, raised her eyebrows, and then stared at Jimmy, to whom she then passed the change.

'Thanking you,' she said very loudly, keeping her eyes firmly averted from Mary's face. 'Thanking you.'

As they hurried laughing from the café, Mary knew the old lady thought she was mad. But she wasn't, she really knew him. I know the King, said Mary to herself. It made her feel lucky.

Mary was in the front line of mourners as they waited for George V's coffin to be brought past. It was taken from Kings Cross to Westminster Hall. En route she witnessed an odd and rather eerie episode. The Imperial Crown had been fastened to the coffin over the top of the Royal Standard. The jolting of the carriage somehow unloosed the Maltese Cross on top of the crown – and sent it tumbling into the gutter. It was almost instantly rescued by the company sergeant-major who was bringing up the rear of two files of grenadiers. But to Mary it seemed a bad omen. She said as much to Jimmy, but he shrugged, making some remark about superstition and the Irish. But Edward shared Mary's presentiment. 'It seemed a strange thing to happen,' he wrote, 'and, although not superstitious, I wondered whether it was a bad omen.'

George V lay in state for four days in Westminster Hall while a million of his people filed past the coffin. Although he was such a reserved and introverted man, this was at least four times the number of people who had filed past his father's coffin when he lay in state. But George V had come to represent all the archetypal qualities of kingship that the British people respected – reserve, dignity, formality and duty. None of these was so strongly represented in the more rumbustious and far less conventional figure of Edward VII.

Mary came on her own to Westminster Hall after a late shift. As she queued and then slowly walked past the coffin she saw that it was midnight. Apart from the shuffling of feet and a continuous mutter of coughing, there was silence in the great hall. Then, with a shock, Mary saw the King with his three brothers standing by the coffin. Their eyes were lowered but as Mary came slowly past Edward looked up. Like his brothers, he was in full dress uniform with his sword reversed. He smiled at her and looked down again. Tears flooded down Mary's cheeks as she walked on.

Queen Mary wrote in her diary of 27 January, 'At midnight my 4 sons stood guard over their father's coffin for 20 minutes, a very touching thought.' She later commissioned F. E. Beresford to paint a portrait of the vigil and the painting, called 'The Vigil of the Princes', was given to Edward as a birthday present the following June.

At the funeral procession to St George's Chapel at Windsor, five kings marched behind the coffin. And as George V found his final resting place in the royal vault, King Edward VIII scattered the coffin with earth from a silver bowl while the priest intoned the words, 'Earth to earth, ashes to ashes, dust to dust.'

Chapter Seven

⚜⚜⚜⚜⚜⚜⚜⚜⚜⚜⚜⚜⚜⚜⚜⚜⚜⚜⚜⚜⚜⚜⚜⚜⚜⚜⚜⚜⚜

Abdication

⚜⚜⚜⚜⚜⚜⚜⚜⚜⚜⚜⚜⚜⚜⚜⚜⚜⚜⚜⚜⚜⚜⚜⚜⚜⚜⚜⚜⚜

1936-1937

THE fact that Edward VIII abdicated from the throne came as
no shock to Mary Shiffer. 'He knew what choice he was going
to make – he knew it all the time,' she told me, 'It would be her.'
Later she said, 'He was lonely – and he loved her very much.
Much more than the throne.' Yet Mary, who felt that kings
should reign, was shocked by Edward's abdication. On the
other hand, she tended to separate him into two different
people – Edward the King, and Edward the man in the Hyde
Park still-room. In fact, his visits to the hotel were few and
far between during his brief reign, and he only had one conversation of any significance with Mary and that was towards
the end.

Although Mary sensed Edward's total devotion to Mrs Wallis
Simpson, she would much rather have echoed the sentiments of
the kind of loyalist letter the press were printing in their
thousands, of which the following is a typical example. 'Isn't it
very dreadful that Edward VIII, son of our beloved King George,
should bring Hollywood ideals to Britain. Surely he could have
found a sweet British girl?' This letter was written in the early
days of 1936 – a time when the below-stairs conversation at the
Hyde Park dwelt obsessively on the whole scandalous subject of
Mrs Wallis Simpson's relationship with the King. Mary was slow
to join in. She regarded her late-night relationship with Edward

as special and private. Nevertheless she followed each develop-
ment of the slowly mounting drama with considerable alarm.
The events of the Abdication Crisis are so well known and so
well documented that there is little point in reiterating them
here. I have therefore recounted them only as Mary remembered
them – and as they affected her.

It was towards the end of October that she saw him for the
last time. Controversy was now raging around the King and Mrs
Simpson, and Mary's first reaction on seeing him again was how
much he had aged. The youthful face had a sudden strained
maturity to it, and there was a tension in him that instantly
communicated itself to her. But there was a defiance in him as
well – a doggedness that was his strength.

Edward had dropped discreetly and briefly into a private party
in one of the banqueting rooms. He was about to leave with his
retinue when he paused, made an excuse, and entered Mary's
domain. Two waitresses hurriedly left the room, curtseying
clumsily, as he came in. He had a glass of whisky in his hand as
he sat down at the table, which was stacked with dirty glasses.
He asked Mary how she was. She told him that she was well,
that her husband was well, that they had been back to Dublin,
and had returned for George V's funeral. But he hardly seemed
to be listening. Then he suddenly asked if she 'had been reading
the newspapers'. She said she had. He rose and began to pace
round the room. Mary could think of nothing to say. Then
Edward turned and walked quickly towards the door. At the
door he looked round and smiled at her. She curtsied, trying to
keep the tears out of her eyes, but failing. Edward opened the
door and Mary, desperate to say something of comfort, blurted
out, 'God bless you, sir.'

He thanked her very gravely, and walked out of the room.
She never spoke to him again, but followed the final weeks of
the Abdication Crisis as if she were following the misfortunes of
a close friend. Being a devout Catholic, Mary naturally disapproved of divorce. The sanctity of marriage was all-important
to her. The Established Church of England took the same view,
although its elders realized uneasily that their institution had
been founded on a divorce, and a famous one. As one of Mary's
fellow countrymen earthily wrote:

> *Don't talk of your alien minister*
> *Nor his Church without meaning or faith!*
> *The foundation stones of its temple*
> *Are the bollocks of Henry VIII.*

Despite her Catholicism, Mary began to be more and more obsessed with the future happiness of the beleaguered couple. She saw the romance in the affair, too, and realized that Edward was suffering from a romantic love that had become a single-minded driving force solely because of his position as King and because of Baldwin's refusal to entertain the idea of a morganatic marriage. The Bishop of Bradford had unleashed the press with his comment:

The benefit of the King's coronation depends, upon God, on two elements – first on the faith, prayer and dedication of the King himself – and on that it would be improper for me to say anything except commend him to God's grace, which he will so abundantly need, as we all need it – for the King is a man like ourselves – if he is to do his duty faithfully. We hope that he is aware of this need. Some of us wish that he gave more positive signs of his awareness.

All the bishop really meant was that he wished Edward would be more church-going, but the British press regarded the speech as public licence to join the American and European press hullabaloo.

Mary's conception of Edward's love for Wallis Simpson as 'romantic' is well borne out by René Cutforth's assessment in his book, *Later Than We Thought*:

Millions of words have been written in explanation of this worldshaking affair, and American friends of mine cling to this day to the theory that only some shared sexual deviation could explain Edward's insistence on a world well lost for love. In the thirties we thought Freud could explain everything. I don't believe it. I think the King, who had played Prince Charming to a full house with rapturous applause all over the world, had only been able to do it because he was a very ordinary young man. He had had to be a good mixer, and at the same time completely apart. He had been deprived of his birthright of ordinariness and Wallis, ordinary herself, gave it back to him. It was, in fact, a simple case of delayed adolescent romantic love, and I think Ernest Simpson, who to my mind is the graceful hero of the whole affair, knew this well enough. He used to refer to the Prince of Wales as Peter Pan.

Every day in the stewards' room, Mary studied what the papers were saying about 'her' Edward. Unfortunately she could only 'read' the picture papers and it was therefore up to Jimmy, when they got home to Wandsworth, to read out the text. Both the *Mail* and the *Express* sided with the King – although Beaverbrook's main aim was not so much to support Edward as 'to bugger Baldwin', as he succinctly put it. The *Express* said that Baldwin and his government 'do not reflect the true feelings of the British people if they base their opposition to the marriage – as their press supporters do – on the grounds that Mrs Simpson has divorced her husband'. Later the paper said, 'No government can stand in the King's way if he is resolved to walk that way . . . let the King give his decisions to the people and let him give the reasons for them too.' The *Mail* underlined the humanity of the situation: 'He is a man as well as a King and . . . being a man, he is not exempt from mortal emotions. They resent most strongly the one-sided attacks which have been made upon him by censorious critics.' The liberal *News Chronicle* also came out on the King's side. 'Neither the people of Britain and the Empire nor their representatives in Parliament have ever had the issue explained to them – much less been given the opportunity of expressing their opinions on it. If in these circumstances the King feels himself compelled to abdicate, there is danger of the growth of a feeling of grave resentment. Both parliament and the people need time for reflection.' The Conservative newspapers were against him, and went on in some detail about the danger of the King's 'private inclinations' being allowed to prevail over his 'public duty'. But the most prophetic press comment of all was one of the very earliest, by an American columnist named Arthur Brisbane. He wrote at the time of George V's death, 'The

King's life is moving peacefully towards its close. It seems to me this night that the reign of his son is moving to its close, although not peacefully.'

With Mrs Simpson hounded abroad and the King hourly contemplating his abdication, Mary dragged an embarrassed Jimmy down to the gates of Buckingham Palace where she wore a poster which read, GOD SAVE THE KING FROM BALDWIN. Jimmy wore a less emotive poster which simply read, WE WANT OUR KING. There were thousands gathered there that night. The demonstration had been organized by the 'King's Party', and other posters about them read, AFTER SOUTH WALES YOU CAN'T LET HIM DOWN, COME TO THE PALACE NOW, CHEER THE KING, or CHEER YOUR KING AT THE PALACE TONIGHT.

Edward described the King's Party as 'a rocket, not a very big rocket, but for a moment it hung brilliantly in the sky'. He might have guessed that Mary would be an ardent supporter, a faithful party member who, dragging her husband after her, could be seen noisily demonstrating in the streets and singing 'For He's a Jolly Good Fellow' outside the Palace gates. Unfortunately the non-royalists in the King's Party were merely using it for their own ends, either with an eye to getting Baldwin out and Labour in or to enable Mosley's Blackshirts to use the situation to their own power-seeking advantage. They chalked 'Stand by the King' on walls and paraded around the streets shouting the same slogan. They constituted much the greater element of the King's Party, and certainly did Edward no good.

But despite everything events moved slowly towards their inevitable conclusion. At lunchtime on 10 December 1936 life at the Hyde Park ground to a halt whilst guests and staff alike listened to an announcer reading the text of Edward's message to Parliament embodying his Instrument of Abdication. Mary heard it while waitressing at a cocktail party. The buzz of conversation faded as the wireless on the bar was turned up loudly. The announcer read the message in sepulchral B.B.C. tones, but even this was unable to eradicate the emotion that came through with every word. Mary was sobbing by the time the announcer came to the last paragraph, and there were very few dry-eyed people in the room. As the words were broadcast, she could only think of the man with whom she had fallen in love in her fantasies. She saw the delicate features, the jaunty air, the bowler hat and umbrella, the springing walk and the good-timing smile. She also saw the strain, the tiredness and the concern. Unlike other kings, he had been concerned with the plight of his subjects, and then had come to the grim realization that he was only a figurehead and politically impotent. Perhaps that was another reason for finding the throne possible to renounce. The speech ended: 'I conceive that I am not overlooking the duty that rests on me to place in the forefront the public interest when I declare that I am conscious that I can no longer discharge this heavy task with efficiency, or with satisfaction to myself.'

The previous day Queen Mary had actually found it necessary to use a number of exclamation marks in her diary: 'Bertie [the future George VI] arrived very late from Fort Belvedere and Mr W. Monckton [Edward's adviser] brought him and me the paper drawn up for David's abdication of the Throne of this Empire because he wishes to marry Mrs Simpson!!!!!! The whole affair has lasted since Novr 16th and has been very painful – It is a terrible blow to us all & particularly to poor Bertie.' The following day she wrote: 'Dark gloomy day. I saw Ld Salisbury & the P.M. [Baldwin] – at 3 to Piccadilly to see Elizabeth who was in bed with a cold, too unlucky. The P.M. made his announcement in the house about David's final decision – which was received in silence and with real regret – The more one thinks of this affair the more regrettable it becomes.'

On 11 December, fog blanketed Wandsworth as Mary and Jimmy sat in their flat, listening to Edward's final words on the radio to the British people. He was speaking from a room in Windsor Castle, overlooking the Great Park.

'*At long last I am able to say a few words of my own.*'

As she listened Mary saw again Edward in his old carefree days at the Hyde Park. Before he met Mrs Simpson and while he was still a fun-loving child with a social conscience.

'*I have never wanted to withhold anything, but until now it has not been constitutionally possible for me to speak.*'

But the loneliness, she knew, had been like a raw nerve. So many dinner parties and so few friends.

'*A few hours ago I discharged my last duty as King and Emperor, and now that I have been succeeded by my brother, the Duke of York, my first words must be to declare my allegiance to him. This I do with all my heart.'*

Mary remembered him once hurrying through the corridors of the Hyde Park. He was going to some appointment or other, a banquet, some business dinner, a cocktail party or just a grill room lunch with some stuffy dignitaries. Rarely with his few friends. He dashed past her and she had thought to herself, 'He's a man in a hurry with nowhere to go.'

'You know all the reasons which have impelled me to renounce the Throne. But I want you to understand that in making up my mind I did not forget the country or the Empire which as Prince of Wales, and later as King, I have for twenty-five years tried to serve. But you must believe me when I tell you that I have found it impossible to carry the heavy burden of responsibility and to discharge my duties as King as I would wish to do without the help and support of the woman I love.'

'Were you happy in The Liberties?' he had once asked Mary. She thought carefully before replying, 'Sometimes you never know when you're happy, sir.'

'And I want you to know that the decision I have made is mine and mine alone. This was a thing I had to judge entirely for myself. The other person most nearly concerned has tried up to the last to persuade me to take a different course. I have made this, the most serious decision of my life, upon a single thought of what would in the end be best for all.'

Best for all. There was another phrase Mary had heard in relation to that. 'You can't please everybody all of the time.' And he wasn't going to.

'This decision has been made less difficult for me by the sure knowledge that my brother, with his long training in the public affairs of this country and with his fine qualities, will be able to take my place forthwith, without interruption to the life and progress of the Empire. And he has one matchless blessing, enjoyed by so many of you and not bestowed on me – a happy home with his wife and children.'

Another memory of their still-room conversations sprang to mind. He had asked her, 'Do you have children?'

'No, sir – we're not able.'

'I'm sorry.' He had looked away from her in sudden embarrassment.

'During these hard days I have been comforted by my mother and by my family. The Ministers of the Crown, and in particular Mr Baldwin,

*the Prime Minister, have always treated me with full consideration. There
has never been any constitutional difference between me and them and
between me and Parliament. Bred in the constitutional tradition by my
father, I should never have allowed any such issue to arise.'*

Mary found herself trembling as she listened and Jimmy drew
her to him, putting his arm around her, comforting her. But still
her trembling continued.

*'Ever since I was Prince of Wales, and later on when I occupied the
Throne, I have been treated with the greatest kindness by all classes,
wherever I have lived or journeyed throughout the Empire. For that I am
very grateful.'*

'Something must be done', over and over the phrase echoed
in her mind. 'Something must be done.'

*'I now quit altogether public affairs, and I lay down my burden. It may
be some time before I return to my native land, but I shall always follow
the fortunes of the British race and Empire with profound interest, and
if at any time in the future I can be found of service to His Majesty in a
private station, I shall not fail.'*

One final memory returned to Mary, that of Edward standing
in the still-room, of him walking to the door, and of her saying
'God bless you, sir.'

*'And now we all have a new King. I wish him, and you, his people,
happiness and prosperity with all my heart. God bless you all. God save
the King.'*

After his broadcast Edward joined the rest of the royal family
at the Royal Lodge. That night he was to begin his exile by
travelling to Austria. His brothers stayed with him until midnight.
As they left Edward bowed to George, his new king. But George,
still shocked, cried out, 'It isn't possible. It isn't happening.'
But it was.

Wallis Simpson lay on a sofa in the villa at Cannes, her hands
over her eyes throughout the broadcast. The rest of the household left her on her own after it was over but it was a very long
time before she had enough self-control to go upstairs to her
bedroom. Mary Shiffer remained in her husband's arms for some
hours after the broadcast. Then he reminded her that they had
an early shift at the Hyde Park and he helped her stiffly to bed.

Meanwhile Walter Monckton drove Edward through the night
to Portsmouth. There he boarded the destroyer H.M.S. *Fury*

which was to take him across the Channel to begin one of the many journeys of a long exile. The ship was unescorted.

Mrs Simpson eventually cried herself to sleep in Cannes, while, in Wandsworth, Mary Shiffer lay awake through the long urban night, wondering how quickly Edward would grow up. She knew he would need to do so very quickly.

Chapter Eight

๛๛๛๛๛๛๛๛๛๛๛๛๛๛๛๛๛๛๛๛๛๛๛๛๛๛

Queen Mary - and the Beginning of the End

๛๛๛๛๛๛๛๛๛๛๛๛๛๛๛๛๛๛๛๛๛๛๛๛๛

1937-1940

ALTHOUGH Mary saw considerably less of the old queen during the years leading up to the Second World War, she was aware of her deep hurt over the abdication. 'Really,' she was heard to remark, 'this might be Rumania!' Her conversations with Mary, however, revolved largely around the weather, and only an occasional glimpse of what she was suffering showed through. Mary was once bold enough to ask her how the 'dear Duke of Windsor was', and Queen Mary replied courteously enough that 'he was in good health but missing England very much'. But the Queen's voice shook as she said the words and Mary immediately apologized for asking the question. The Queen frowned and Mary realized the apology had been unfortunate. She had intruded. Then she realized something else. Queen Mary was not only deeply hurt by her son's action, but also very angry. In his biography, James Pope-Hennessy tends to bear out Mary's impression. ' "The plain fact was that H.M. is still angry with the Duke & I really think that helps her to bear what she called 'the humiliation' of it all," wrote an old friend with whom the Queen Dowager "talked hard about the Duke of Windsor and all her troubles", in March 1937.'

On another occasion, a few weeks later, the Queen Dowager thanked Mary for asking after her son. 'It was most kind of you.' Tactfully, Mary did not venture any comment, firmly running hot water into a basin. But Queen Mary did not seem able to leave the subject. 'He is still well,' she said as Mary nodded her head dumbly, 'but he must be very lonely.'

Many years later Mary said to me, 'If it hadn't been for Queen Mary the country would have gone mad.' Once again Pope-Hennessy bears this out when he says:

> But, sorrowful and indignant, Queen Mary had risen magni-
> ficently to meet this crisis; the new King and Queen, and
> indeed the whole of the Royal Family, recognised how much
> the smooth transition from one monarch to the other owed to
> Queen Mary's wisdom and popularity. 'Thank God we have
> all got you as a central point, because without it [the family]
> might easily disintegrate,' one of the family wrote to her at
> this time.

But George VI, who, after the Second World War, was the third member of the royal family to feature strongly in Mary's life, was also another intelligent saviour of the status quo. Prince Albert, Duke of York ('dear Bertie'), chose the title of George VI. The two recent Edwards had had a rakish reputation — Edward VII as a reformed rake although a good constitutional king and Edward VIII as a rake with a social conscience and an immaturity which made the constitution take second place in his brief reign. It was essential to return to the conservative image of George V — the stuff of kings that the public found so reassuring. And George VI was determined to be reassuring, a stable family man with a sound wife and two pretty daughters (Elizabeth Bowes-Lyon and daughters Elizabeth and Margaret). Photographs of the time took care to underline their domestic cosiness; one such shows them all happily peeking from the children's playhouse with corgis abounding. All was domestic bliss — without the merest hint of international high living or sophisticated American divorcees.

One final conversation of importance ensued between Mary Shiffer and the Queen Dowager. Mary had been talking with

Queen Mary as she added just a dusting of powder to her nose before an afternoon charity concert in the ballroom. They had, of course, been talking about the weather. Then Queen Mary said, 'I wonder if Mrs Simpson will make David happy.' All too aware of her past blunders, Mary was determined to say nothing. The Queen Dowager smiled at her gently, 'You don't have to be afraid to speak you know.' Mary burst into hesitant speech, 'Your Majesty, I sincerely hope she will.' The Queen Dowager replied softly, 'But how are we to know?'

In the same year Walter Monckton wrote of a conversation he had had with the Duchess of Windsor:

I told her that most people in England disliked her very much because the Duke had married her and given up his throne, but that if she made him, and kept him, happy all his days, all that would change; but that if he were unhappy nothing would be too bad for her. She took it all very simply and kindly, just saying 'Walter, don't you think I have thought of all that? I think I can make him happy.'

By December 1936 preparations for the coronation were well under way and it seemed the constitutional shock was gradually easing. A few months earlier the Duke of York had written to Sir Godfrey Thomas, 'I will do my best to clear up the inevitable mess if the whole fabric does not crumble under the shock and strain of it all.' But the fabric was made of outraged British conservatism and, in face of the impending coronation and a more conventional monarch, the system licked its wounds and quickly healed them.

At the Hyde Park all was pre-coronation bustle. King Gustav of Sweden, King Rico of Denmark and a host of other European royals descended on the marbled halls that were now so synonymous with regal occasions. Queen Mary came in several times to greet these visitors, having obviously decided to banish the memories of Edward's abdication by entering fully into the coronation spirit. Mary saw she looked much calmer, and several times the Queen Dowager commented to her on the decorations in the London streets. Shortly before the coronation she told her that 'we are all going to have a pleasant family lunch'. She also entertained the Hyde Park royalty in the Palace, recording in her diary that '. . . I dined at the Palace, State Banquet to 450 people in Ball Rm & Supper Rm, Bertie in Ball Rm, E [Elizabeth] in Supper Rm. I sat opposite Bertie with Gustav of Sweden and Rico of Denmark as neighbours . . . Went off very well.'

Meanwhile Madame Vacani still taught dancing, deportment and etiquette in the Hyde Park ballroom and the debs' training school continued. She branched out, however, in these prewar days, almost making the debutante system a part of show business. 'We used to have a matinée in one of the London theatres,' she remembered, 'and one of the acts was always the debutantes in their long dresses. They would do something very simple, just with a little fan or a flower, because often they were not very adept.'

Throughout the Spanish Civil War, whilst the shadow of Hitler emerged over Europe, the debs danced on, as oblivious of the threat of a second world war as they had been of the first. 'It was still a cattle market in full swing,' Mary told me, 'You felt sorry for the girls – but you couldn't feel much for the boys. They were all dummies, God help them.' Lady Sandilands' opinion of them was even more abrasive:

The young men who did the season were so unutterably stupid you could not believe it. But you see, anyone who was doing anything interesting did not bother to do it. The young men were either army or just dull and old-fashioned. I can now see how stupid most of the regulars were. . . . By and large the ones who were the successful debs . . . were the ones who made a lot of noise. There was always a sub-conscious divide between the upper-class deb and the middle-class one, who usually tried harder. They knew all the catch phrases – 'Isn't it amusing, my dear?' – and they did the Lambeth Walk. Now they are all rather fat crippled old ladies with jerseys drooping around the edge.

In The Liberties the coronation was enthusiastically celebrated, as one of Mary's cousins, looking for work in London, later related to her. The jumbled streets were alive with bunting and in Engine Alley the flags stretched across the street, just as they

had in Mary's fantasy about Edward. Each house boasted a
picture of the royal couple in its front window and the shops
were crammed with coronation bric-à-brac. Loyalty to the
Crown was almost as strong in Dublin as it was in London –
despite the increasing presence of the Irish Republican Army.

In London, Coronation Day, 12 May 1937, was overcast and
rainy. After queueing all night, Mary and Jimmy took up their
position in front of Westminster Abbey. Cold, exhausted and
barely able to stand, Mary still managed to remain at the front
of the densely packed crowd. Unlike Edward, Queen Mary did
not acknowledge Mary, although she passed within inches of her.
She travelled in a glass coach, escorted by a troop of mounted
Horse Guards. Queen Mary was robed in purple and ermine and
had an open crown of diamonds on her head. She wore clusters
of jewels and looked majestically withdrawn – which struck just
the right note with the crowd.

No untoward incident, as in George V's funeral procession,
marred the day, and a swarm of Hyde Park clients passed Mary
as she stood shivering in the gently falling rain; some of them
acknowledged her. The Duke of Norfolk, the Marquess of
Salisbury, the Duke of Sutherland, the Marquess of Londonderry,
the Duke of Abercorn – all passed her in a welter of aristocratic
flamboyance.

A few days later Mary watched the service in Westminster
Abbey, in the comfort of the Granada Cinema, Lavender Hill.
For the first time newsreel cameras had been allowed into the
Abbey and the public was able to share in all the pomp of what
had originally been witnessed by only the privileged few. As she
sat in the packed warmth of the cinema, eating popcorn, Mary
watched the ceremony unfold in all its stage-managed, smooth-
running, medieval sumptuousness. The pageboys, the heralds,
the bishops, the peers – all combined to produce a bejewelled
canvas, whose rich colours were embossed forever on Mary's
mind. She recognized many of those involved, ranging from the
lesser members of the royal family to the leaders of the great
aristocratic families – as well as visiting European royalty. Mary
kept whispering their names to Jimmy until she was stopped by
an irate woman behind her who asked her to 'kindly refrain from
spoiling other people's enjoyment'.

Queen Mary commented in her diary that 'Maud [Queen Maud of Norway] and I processed up the Abbey to the Royal Box. I sat between Maud and Lilibet, Margaret came next, they looked too sweet in their lace dresses & robes, especially when they put on their coronets. Bertie and E looked so well when they came in & did it all too beautifully. The service was wonderful & impressive — we were all much moved. . . . A wonderful day.'

Some weeks later, Mary congratulated the Queen Dowager on her seventieth birthday, which had been celebrated exactly a fortnight after the coronation. Ironically, on 3 June, which was King George V's birthday, Edward married Wallis Simpson at the Château de Condé, in France. Queen Mary received Mary's congratulations graciously and told her, 'I am really going to enjoy myself in Coronation Year.' Less graciously, she said to Mary, 'I expect you have read that my son was married yesterday — it would have been his father's birthday.' Queen Mary confided even more bitterly to her diary, 'Alas! the wedding day in France of David and Mrs Warfield [she had reverted to her first married name]. . . . We all telegraphed to him.'

The next Saturday, Mary watched the Windsors' marriage at the Granada. 'They looked scared,' she told me, 'As if they had suddenly realized how many people they were defying. I kept wondering if she'd stay with him. Later I prayed that she would.'

Edward may well have been uneasy in his defiant marriage, but he was also extremely angry. He had naturally assumed that if he were to be His Royal Highness, the Duke of Windsor, then his wife would become Her Royal Highness, the Duchess of Windsor. But the royal decree said nothing of the kind. Only Edward was to be His Royal Highness, the Duke of Windsor, neither his wife nor his descendants would be able to use the 'Royal Highness' title. In her autobiography, she writes: 'Nothing in the aftermath of the Abdication hurt David more than that gratuitous thrust. In his eyes it was an ultimate slur upon his wife, and, therefore, upon himself.' The exile was now permanent — and there was nothing she could do to change her husband's mind. But Mary disapproved of Edward's attitude. 'He thought too much of titles. He had a wife and a fortune. Wasn't that enough?' It wasn't.

Edward was naturally anxious that his mother should eventually see his point of view – and understand why he had had to abdicate. But her sense of duty was too strong. In July 1938 she wrote to him:

> You will remember how miserable I was when you informed me of your intended marriage and abdication and how I implored you not to do so for our sake and for the sake of the country. You did not seem able to take in any point of view but your own. . . . I do not think you have ever realised the shock which the attitude you took up caused your family and the whole Nation. It seemed inconceivable to those who had made such sacrifices during the war that you, as their King, refused a lesser sacrifice. . . . All my life I have put my country before everything else, and I simply cannot change now.

To fill up her time and to stop herself from thinking, Queen Mary decided to plunge herself still further into public duty. This took her away from the Hyde Park, and she never returned. There was no reason for her to go back, particularly as the charitable functions of the old days began to be eclipsed by the shadows of a new war. Mary followed her royal progress in the picture papers and on the newsreels. She saw the Queen Dowager lend her stately presence to Court functions, the tennis at Wimbledon, the Derby, the Aldershot Tattoo, art galleries and theatres. She was also to be seen taking the two princesses, Elizabeth and Margaret, on 'educational visits' to such places as Hampton Court, Greenwich and the Tower of London. Her other main interest in the years leading up to the war seemed to be creating and unveiling as many monuments to her late husband as possible.

Apart from Edward's abdication and subsequent marriage, Queen Mary's greatest sadness was that she had outlived so many people – her husband, his brother and his three sisters as well as numerous friends. When her sister-in-law, Queen Maud of Norway, finally died, she was heartbroken; it is fitting to end Queen Mary's place in this book by quoting the diary reference to this: 'Wet day. At 9 to my consternation I received the news that darling Maud had died at 12.25 a.m. of heart failure, after the serious operation on Wed last – I felt stunned at the tragic news as we had hoped she was improving.' Mary Shiffer summed up her relationship with Queen Mary well: 'In the cloakroom she was an ordinary woman talking to another ordinary woman about her troubles. Outside the cloakroom she was Queen Mary – an old-fashioned Queen. She always did her duty and knew she had to do it. There was no escape. She was just what everyone wanted – a storybook Queen.' Pope-Hennessy echoes Mary's sentiments in the concluding paragraphs of his biography of Queen Mary. Writing about her funeral in 1953 he says:

> Most of those in the crowd could scarcely recall a period in which Queen Mary had not seemed an essential part of life in London, personifying for them all that was noblest in the country's tradition. They were conscious – some sharply, others dimly – that on that chilling afternoon they were mourning the unique. For it was Queen Mary's crowning reward, as it is the fundamental lesson to be drawn from any contemplation of her life, that, by undeviating service to her own highest ideals, she had ended by becoming for millions an ideal in herself.

Mary had one most poignant memory of her:

> She never said anything that wasn't ordinary – and that made her a comfortable woman. When the troops were in Hyde Park it was her being ordinary that counted most with them. She would go up to a man with half his limbs shot away and talk about the weather. That might sound crazy – but it put them at their ease. They could see by her eyes she cared very much. She would ask them about their families – and their children. She often said the same things to every man. But they didn't mind. She was ordinary to them. Like she was to me. And it was so surprising when she was also a Queen.

Slowly the thirties dwindled and the threat of war came closer. Below stairs there were considerable feelings of insecurity. Call-up was preying on the minds of the younger men, while the older men were straining at the leash. Talk of war was obsessional, and the Bennetts were already trying to reorganize the kitchens. The older style of Hyde Park client – mainly the crotchety bachelor businessmen who were residents – decided that they would ignore the atmosphere of expectancy. They were an extraordinary breed, those long-term residents, and most of them took a highly idiosyncratic approach to their day-to-day lives in the hotel. They all had their own solitary tables in the grill room and they would be most affronted if a less permanent guest strayed incautiously to their eyrie. All their clothes were valeted daily, their shoes shone to a glossy brilliance, taxis waited at the door for them; and they were treated like royalty. The very thought of having to leave the Hyde Park was anathema to them. It would have been like leaving a deep, luxuriant, super-protective womb. Mary remembered one such client, who for obvious reasons must remain nameless:

He had lived in the Hyde Park for over twenty years and he completely ignored all the warnings of war. He was a stock-broker or a banker – I can't remember which. But he was old and sad and lonely and very dependent on the hotel and us. I expect a lot of hotels were full of people like him – but we certainly had our fair share. Every year the old boy used to throw a staff party for us – and regularly every year he used to get drunk. I remember him prancing through the kitchens with a bottle of champagne in one hand and a string of sausages in the other. He tried to get into one of the fridges one night – and I remember hauling him out. They were good times – I think the best times he ever had. He was always in a filthy temper the next morning and would send his breakfast back downstairs with some piffling complaint. But we were very fond of him. I think we knew that we were all he had. He left the Hyde Park when the bombing started – and went to a hotel on the coast. I expect he died there – the poor old soul.

To Mary the war threat was reflected in London and Dublin, and both experiences were very vivid to her. In London gas masks were being issued, sandbags stacked and Anderson shelters delivered. Meanwhile children ran in Battersea Park singing the popular rhyme of that uneasy time:

Under the spreading chestnut tree,.
Neville Chamberlain said to me:
If you want to get your gas mask free,
Join the blinking A.R.P.

Jimmy was too old for military service and so both he and Mary, despite the complexities of their shifts at the Hyde Park, joined the A.R.P. Systematic recruiting for the Air Raid Precautions volunteers had begun on 14 March 1938 when the Home Secretary, Sir Samuel Hoare, broadcast for 'at least a million men and women . . . for work that in an emergency would be exciting and dangerous'. Mary joined the A.R.P. largely as a result of one of the Hyde Park clients, Lady Reading, appealing for the new Women's Voluntary Services for Civil Defence. She did not join Lady Reading's organization but she saw the force of her emotive clarion-call. Lady Reading wanted 'every kind of woman in every kind of sphere of life . . . to prepare patiently and thoroughly . . . a protection . . . for our loved ones and our homes'.

A flood of leaflets suddenly appeared through the Shiffer door, beginning with the thirty-six page booklet, 'The Protection of Your Home Against Air-raids', according to which the head of the house was to consider himself 'Captain of the ship'. Other leaflets included 'Masking your Windows' and 'Your Gas Mask'.

Mary's strong sense of humour did not always allow her to take the A.R.P. very seriously; typical of the black farce of the situation was the 'Operation Casualty' held one evening in a local Catholic day nursery in Wandsworth. The walls were covered in a frieze of Beatrix Potter characters as well as holy pictures showing Christ sauntering in a garden strewn with children and Mary embracing the infant Jesus. The chairs and tables were minute and toys, modelling clay and picture books covered the table space. Superimposed over all this, however, were more macabre artifacts. There were charts showing the human body burned, wounded and paralysed, pictures showing broken bones and torn skin, and a lurid poster detailing how to treat patients suffering from mustard gas burns.

Ranged about the floor were twelve 'patients', all of whom were suffering from the effects of bombing or gassing. They were, in fact, the leading lights of a local amateur dramatics company. One of their members was also feigning the second stage of labour, and a flustered woman was making preparations for the makeshift delivery of the 'baby', simulated by a mature-looking doll. Blankets, first-aid boxes, dressings and first-aid manuals littered the miniature tables.

Each patient was being dealt with by two women. The population of the room was socially mixed – working-class women who were coping well enough and making up the bits they didn't know, and middle-class women who were largely panicking. Wives of white collar workers did not go out to work – it was an unwritten rule – so when it came to the workaday yet traumatic business of the A.R.P. they were extremely flustered.

Making tea at the back of the room, Mary had a sudden moment of objectivity. The scene before her was incredible. Twelve dramatically writhing patients lay on the stretchers. Hysterically 'tending' them were dozens of women, some as feverish as the simulated patients themselves. One 'patient' was feigning hysteria anyway, which added still further to the confusion. It was when a furious argument developed between two women over a roll of lint dressing that Mary finally lost her temper. As they tugged at the dressing while the 'patient' moaned melodramatically on the floor, Mary bore down upon them. 'For the Lord's sake – you're fit for no bloody war!' she yelled at them, her brogue thickening in her fury. Both women immediately united, differences forgotten, in their mutual condemnation of Mary's insolence. They 'well really'd' and 'How dared she' together. Mary turned on her heels and went back to her kettle.

Another presage of war came when Mary made a last pre-war visit home in 1939. Dublin was tense when she arrived. With the I.R.A. declaration of war on London, its subsequent bombing campaign, and De Valera's conviction that Ireland should remain neutral, an uneasy foreboding was in the air. Sitting in a bar in The Liberties Mary and Jimmy were surprised by the sudden silence that had enveloped them. They turned, to see a number of men standing at the door. They stood on the threshold, quietly dressed with their hands in their pockets. The group had their eyes riveted on an ordinary-looking man, sitting with his friends in a corner. In turn, his eyes were firmly fixed on the intruders. Mary could see despair and hopeless pleading in his face. He slowly rose to his feet, nodded dumbly a couple of times, then walked over to them. His hands were half raised. They took him away.

Gradually normal conversation resumed. Jimmy took Mary's hand as they both stole a glance at the empty chair and the men sitting staring at it. Mary thought of the man's family, and the grieving that would soon begin. There was a war in her own country — let alone the war outside, that might, as she often thought, end the world. So many men were going to die, so many families would be left bereft.

The next morning they went out to Booterstown to collect cockles. They would eat them raw, with fresh bread, butter and salt. It was a calm, still spring day. Three years before, Mary had been sitting on the rocks, dreaming of the King. Now she was thinking of war. Thank God Jimmy would never be involved. And as they had no children there was nobody to lose. Yet a sadness settled over her, and Mary fell to thinking about the man who had been taken from the bar. No doubt he was in the mortuary now, with a hole in his head.

They returned to Dublin by train and then took a tram from the station. It was as they rattled along the superior Merrion Road with its trees and large houses that Jimmy again suggested that they stay in Dublin to avoid the air-raid dangers of London. Mary refused. She wanted to go home, to the Hyde Park. There's war everywhere, she told Jimmy. There was no way they could avoid it.

Back at the Hyde Park there was a feeling of urgency in the air. The hotel, like the country, was preparing for war. Indeed, it was this war which brought together the team that was eventually to save the fortunes of the Hyde Park, and to raise it to even greater heights of social grace than ever before. Already three members of the team — Mary, Tissot and Cavallo — were well established. Brian Franks, an ex-Etonian with a military background, formerly manager of the Mayfair Hotel, had just joined the Hyde Park board of directors. Franks had employed at the Mayfair a restaurant manager called Ronald Massara, who was also to act as a catalyst to the Hyde Park's postwar fortunes.

Massara had previously worked at the Savoy with Santarelli, at the Paris Ritz with Madame Ritz and at the Berkeley with Cavadini. Tommy Kinsman and Maroni, another top restaurateur, were to complete the team.

Ronald Massara's single-minded devotion to his career had ensured his rapid rise to success in the hotel business. He grew up in Alice Castello, a tiny, primitive village near Turin: he had a Scots mother and an Italian father. In fact he was born in London but was sent to Italy at two because his parents, who had one other child, found they could no longer afford to keep him in their minute rooms in Blackfriars. Massara (as he came to be known, Ron being too unexotic for such a fiery personality) was brought up by his grandparents on their farm, which was little bigger than the average smallholding, and on which he worked from an early age.

In later life Mary returned to Dublin more or less every year, and so did Massara to Alice Castello. Yet, once Mary had left The Liberties she refused to regard them as home any more. The hotel was her home, and Dublin receded more and more into the background. This was not the case with Massara. Alice Castello is still his spiritual home and he loves it with a possessive ardour that is unshakable. He once said to me, 'The best part of me is the village.'

At twelve, Massara was shattered by having to return to London. His English was virtually non-existent, his parents were strangers, his brother an instantly hated rival. He was desperately homesick for Alice Castello.

After a year of misery at home and at the local school, Massara realized that he wanted to be a survivor. Aggression became his weapon, and gradually it gave him the assertion which was to turn him from a bewildered peasant boy into one of the greatest restaurateurs in Europe. He once said to me, 'I think of every new day as a new fight.'

At school he worked obsessively, mastered the language and became the darling of his teachers. Naturally gregarious and aggressive, he got on well with the other boys, learned to play football and became a leader. This was partly because of his 'foreignness' and partly because he was 'colourful'. In other words, Massara had developed charisma, something that was to

be a big mainstay in his life. His 'foreignness', originally considered a drawback, was now a distinct advantage.

When Massara was fourteen, his father took him away from
school and brought him into the Hotel Cecil, a Gothic sugar-
cake of a building on the Embankment opposite Cleopatra's
Needle. He started work as a waiter, an invaluable wage-earner
for his family. The plush hotel world overawed him, as did the
grand personages of the managers of this world of luxury. For
some time Massara dreamed of joining them. Then he remon-
strated with himself. There was no point in dreaming. Waiters
had been known to rise; here was a real world of ambition. If he
couldn't go back, Massara determined to go forward. And as he
waited on the rich clients of the Cecil, Massara pledged himself
to playing the system, and to rising higher than even he could
conceive. Power beckoned, and Massara began to fight his way
towards it.

At the Mayfair, Massara was suave, debonair and aggressively
foreign. He had become a character, and when he married, the
Daily Express further established him with a report headlined
EX-WAITER WILL MARRY HEIRESS. Massara had arrived. He also
genuinely loved his wife. The impending war, however, was to
prove an interruption to the consolidating of his experience.

It was ironic that Massara should have risen to such heights
and Mary remained in such a lowly position, particularly as they
came from such similar backgrounds. But it was not necessarily
just an example of the chauvinism of the times. Massara was
extrovert, self-taught and ambitious. Mary was extrovert, still
illiterate and quite unambitious. When Massara revisited Alice
Castello, although accepted back into the community, he remained apart from it. Mary revisited The Liberties and merged
back into it. Yet she thanked God every time she went back that
she was no longer part of the grinding poverty she saw around
her. Perhaps it was being released from this that made her unambitious, or perhaps it was just being ordinary, like her namesake the Queen Dowager. Yet Mary's personality was vivid and
strong and warm enough for people to confide in her, and for
people to trust her. And there is no doubt that these people were
very far from ordinary.

Amongst the last functions at the Hyde Park before the outbreak of war was the annual dinner of the Chelsea Arts Club. Mary served the members a menu that was, for the Hyde Park plain and straightforward, reflecting the coming of war economies. They ate:

Soup St Julien

Mousse of Lobster

Roast Turkey and Chipolatas

Cold Roast Loin Veal and Ham
Salad
New Potatoes
Green Peas

Neapolitan Cream

Diana Savoury

Cheese Straws

Dessert, Coffee

It was the last dinner of quality that Mary remembered serving before the war began to reduce the Hyde Park menu to a very rudimentary form. Amongst the guests at this dinner were Sir James Agate, Sir Edwin Lutyens and J. B. Priestley. Mary noticed that Priestley was sunk in gloom and that there was a feeling of false gaiety to the dinner.

Mary was in the hotel when Neville Chamberlain made his famous broadcast to the nation on 3 September 1939. She was cleaning a grandiose suite that overlooked Knightsbridge. Surreptitiously, Mary had turned on the radio and sat down in one of the Louis Quinze chairs. It was 11.15 a.m. and Chamberlain's voice was that of an old and broken man.

I am speaking to you from the Cabinet Room at No. 10 Downing Street. This morning, the British Ambassador handed the German Government a final note, stating that unless the British Government heard from them by 11 o'clock that they were prepared at once to withdraw their troops from Poland, a state of war would exist between us. I have to tell you now that no such undertaking has been received, and that, consequently, this country is at war with Germany.

Eight minutes later Mary was looking out of the window down at the street below, through which little traffic circulated. Then the sirens went, and policemen cycled through the streets with 'Take Cover' notices pinned on the front and back of their uniforms. The few people in the streets filed towards the trenches in the park in an orderly manner. She could imagine them, at another time, obeying other instructions and filing in an equally orderly manner to the park – not to enter the protective trenches, but to face a firing squad. Suddenly she saw Knightsbridge peopled with German soldiers and a great swastika draped over the front of the hotel. She imagined herself taking breakfast up to the Führer. 'Irish scum' he called her through a mouthful of buttered toast. Then, casting her fears aside, Mary hurried down the stairs to the shelter. But she went instead to the wine-cellar.

Jimmy was in there, and when she asked him why he wasn't in the shelter he shrugged and poured them both a glass of wine from the hogshead. He said it was probably a false alarm. (It was.) Then he insisted she drank the wine. They raised their glasses to each other as the sirens wailed overhead. Jimmy asked her if she wasn't glad that they didn't have children to worry about during the war. Mary said nothing. She stared into her wine. In it she saw the Duke of Windsor. He was tied to a post and his eyes were blindfolded. Then shots rang out. Mary looked up at Jimmy. 'I love you,' she said. He smiled at her gently.

'We'll need luck to get through this,' he said. 'Irish luck.'

'We never had any,' replied Mary. She put down her glass and urged her husband into the shelter.

Chapter Nine

෯෯෯෯෯෯෯෯෯෯෯෯෯෯෯෯෯෯෯෯෯෯෯෯෯෯෯෯෯෯෯

The Interruption

෯෯෯෯෯෯෯෯෯෯෯෯෯෯෯෯෯෯෯෯෯෯෯෯෯෯෯෯෯෯

1940-1945

FOR Mary the war years were dominated by three people: Jimmy, and his miraculous escape from death; Rosa Lewis, and her traumatic arrival at the Hyde Park; and Evelyn Waugh and his idiosyncrasies.

At the outbreak of war Mary Shiffer was forty-nine. With the men conscripted, she once again returned to full-time waitressing in both the grill room and the restaurant. Then, as the hotel emptied and the war tightened its grip, the restaurant, like the banqueting rooms and ballrooms, closed. The once glamorous hotel was silenced, reduced to a shell. The debs no longer fluttered anxiously down its corridors, nor did their chinless escorts accompany them. No royalty graced the marble halls of the Hyde Park and distinguished foreign visitors no longer arrived.

During the summer of 1940 the bombing crept closer to London. In mid-August an attack on Croydon resulted in sixty-two people dead within half an hour, and on Saturday, 7 September, London 'bought' it. The Blitz began with the wailing of the sirens on a beautiful early autumn afternoon with a cloudless blue sky – out of which came death. From then on there was hardly a peaceful night in London until Sunday, 11 May 1941, when the last heavy raid of the war proclaimed the end of the Blitz. During the Blitz both Mary and the Hyde Park suffered – the former rather more than the latter. But had it not been for an alert A.R.P. warden the Hyde Park would have been razed to the ground.

After a particularly heavy raid, Mary and Jimmy emerged from the shelter and returned to the hotel. As Mary passed the grill room entrance, she saw a hole in the road. Beside it, lying on a pile of debris, was a metal ring. Deciding to keep it as a war souvenir, Mary pocketed it. Meanwhile the area was roped off, and the staff of the Hyde Park were sent home. The general feeling of the authorities was that there was a bomb somewhere in the area and a search was carried out, but to no avail. A later newspaper account took up the story: 'There was a hole in the road which caused a certain amount of debate but an authority, after making a thorough inspection, claimed that it was a hole caused by a bomb that must have exploded. The incident was closed for the night, and some of the wardens slept quite close, in one of the posts.'

Back in Wandsworth, Mary showed the ring to an Irish friend, Shamus, who was also an A.R.P. warden. He looked at it idly, without comment. Then he said he could not think what on earth it could be, but the next morning he was going along to a Royal Engineers lecture. Why didn't Mary come too, and learn more about the objects an A.R.P. warden should look out for. Reluctantly, as she had the next morning off, Mary agreed to go.

The next morning, in the dull grey-green atmosphere of the lecture hall, Mary received one of the greatest shocks of her life. Shamus had risen somewhat pompously to his feet during question time and held the ring up for the lecturer to see.

'Where did you find that?'

'A friend picked it up – in the street.'

'Recently?'

'A day or so ago to be precise. Why – is it important?'

Suddenly Mary's scalp felt as if it were about to rise off the back of her head. The lecturer's expression was both smug and reproving.

'You – or your friend – ought to have reported it at once.'

Shamus's voice rose in anger at the complacency in the man's voice.

'Then what in God's name is it?'

'It's a kops ring.'

'So—?'

'It's part of a high explosive bomb – and if you find a kops ring lying about then you can guarantee there's a 2,000-lb. bomb lying pretty close to it.'

Shamus turned to Mary.

'There's your—'

But she was already standing up, mouthing wordlessly.

'What's the matter? Have you lost your wits?'

'Merciful Mother of God!' Mary grabbed the kops ring out of Shamus's hand and pushed her way out of the lecture hall. Seizing the nearest phone, she called the manager of the Hyde Park. With some difficulty she at last managed to convince him of the significance of the ring and the urgency of the situation. The newspaper account relates the panic that immediately began.

Back to the 'incident' went the wardens in haste and in a very short time digging began by the R.E.s around the hole in the road. They dug for a week. Then, sure enough, deep down under the Hyde Park Hotel they found an unexploded 2,000 lb. bomb. It was brought up, not without difficulty, rendered harmless and used as a collecting box for several months to raise £250 for the dependants of demolition and rescue workers who had been killed in the 'blitz'.

A few years after the war the event was celebrated in the hotel and a lavish party was held for the air raid wardens in the Hyde Park, and as Mary helped to serve them drinks and food she thanked God that the now rather worn luxury of the hotel had been saved. The press, on Friday, 23 January 1948, went to town on the occasion. One headline read:

THEY DANCED IN HOTEL OF DEATH
A 2,000 LB. BOMB THAT WAS 'MISSED'
WESTMINSTER WARDENS MAKE MERRY

Part of the account read: 'Five hundred ex-air raid wardens from all over Westminster – members of the Westminster Wardens

Association – went to the Hyde Park on Tuesday night for their grand reunion and New Year's party. They took pride in going to the hotel because it is one of the hotels they rightly claim to have helped save from destruction during the war.'

It was only a few weeks after this trauma that the bomb hit Mary and Jimmy's small flat. The Anderson shelter was the Shiffers' only protection, and during air-raids at home Mary dutifully went into it. But Jimmy was stubborn. As the Blitz continued he became more and more loath to use the claustro-phobic shelter. At first Mary nagged him but this only made him more stubborn. Then she gave up. Nowadays Jimmy's attitude seems extraordinarily foolhardy – though the Anderson shelters were extremely unpleasant.

The shelters were supplied free to those earning less than £250 a year (as were the Shiffers), and erecting them was a complex business. A hole had to be dug 7 feet 6 inches by 6 feet wide to a depth of 4 feet. Into this pit were inserted six curved steel sheets, bolted together at the top to form an arch. Flat steel plates were positioned at either end, and one of these contained a section which could be unbolted and used as an emergency exit. The other end was the normal entrance – a hole at ground level through which they climbed down into the shelter.

Being inside an Anderson shelter was like being locked in a damp bicycle shed. Outside Andersons had to be covered in fifteen inches of earth, and Mary's landlord had surmounted this with a hideous combination of rockery and marbled tiles. It gave every appearance of being some ancient Troglodyte palace and emanated a sinister, earthy atmosphere day and night. Slugs and snails readily found their way into it, and once Mary and her fellow tenants were held, shrieking, at bay by an enormous rat, while bombs fell with monstrous noise around them.

That September night Jimmy had refused to leave the warmth of their bed, and cursing him for his obstinacy Mary repaired to the dreaded Anderson. 'I could hear the bomb coming,' she said, 'and I knew it was for us.' The whine, silence and eventual impact seemed to take an eternity.

There was no question of caution as Mary tore her way into the house. At first sight it seemed impossible for anyone to have

survived in the totally collapsed structure. Water ran over her
shoes from broken pipes and there was an ominous smell of gas.
Praying aloud Mary struggled into the wreckage. Please God,
don't let him be dead. As she tore at the broken woodwork and
bricks in the hall, she promised God that she would be a better
Catholic, would be more detailed in her confession, would attend
every office on Sunday, would stop pinching from the Hyde Park
kitchens, would return all the linen and serviettes she had removed from the laundry, would— Suddenly she realized that
she was surrounded by others, toiling away in the seemingly
impenetrable debris.

Eventually firemen and wardens found him. For some reason,
perhaps a last-minute attempt to reach the shelter, Jimmy had
been coming down the stairs when the bomb hit the house. He
had fallen with the bannisters on top of him and it was all this
Victorian woodwork that had taken the main load of debris and
kept him intact. Gently they lifted the bannisters away and a
shaken, bruised and battered Jimmy crawled out from underneath them. Above him the bedroom was completely flattened;
if he had stayed in bed there is no doubt that he would have been
killed instantly.

Jimmy was taken to hospital but not detained. In the cold light
of day Mary discovered they had lost everything; practically
nothing was salvaged from the building. As no other accommodation was immediately forthcoming, Mary and Jimmy spent
the next part of the Blitz sleeping in Underground stations. But
they found it almost impossible to sleep and, because of this,
equally impossible to get their work done at the hotel. The
trains ran through till twelve and there were no lavatories.
Originally the government had banned sleeping in the Tubes but
most people bought a 1½d. ticket and refused to surface again.
By late September 1940, 177,000 men, women and children were
using the Tubes. Eventually bucket lavatories were set up on
every station and 22,000 bunks were installed on the platforms.
But these were inadequate, and Mary and Jimmy quite often
found themselves sleeping on the ground.

Eventually they were given permission to sleep in the hotel,
and they both slept for months in the telephone room. Despite
what had happened in Wandsworth, both the Shiffers doggedly

refused to go to the park shelters during the air raids, preferring
to huddle under the telephone exchange. Whatever the dangers,
at least they got more sleep. This 'temporary accommodation'
was to continue for two years until eventually they were rehoused
a few streets away from their blitzed flat.

During the first few months of the war, the Hyde Park was
still serving a lavish menu in the grill room, although all public
diners were ostentatiously economic. Much of the food came
from the same sources as in the First World War – from the
estates, grouse moors and trout streams of its rich clients. For
instance, in early 1940, Mary was serving smoked salmon at
2s. 9d., fillets of sole at 3s. 6d., poached turbot at 4s. and trout
at 4s. A mixed grill was 3s. 6d., lamb cutlets 1s. 6d. and entrecôte
steak 3s. But there was considerable public criticism of this
privileged menu, and in July 1940 it was made illegal to serve
more than one course at any restaurant meal. The restricted
dishes were marked with a star. By June 1942 this system had
been even further tightened up with the introduction of a 5s.
maximum for all meals. The Hyde Park and other luxury hotels
were, however, allowed to demand an extra 7s. 6d. cover charge
for their decaying environment and decreasing service. And
certain foods, like oysters and caviar, could still be served at an
extra charge. By 9.30 p.m. the grill room at the Hyde Park was
closed – sometimes it was even earlier – for by then the kitchen
would have used up its nightly food allocation. Then Mary would
descend to the wine cellar, which was rapidly becoming a wartime social club, and later to the bleak stillness of the telephone
room. By 1943 a Hyde Park wartime menu read as follows:

DINNER
9s. 6d.

Hors d'oeuvre

Hors d'Oeuvre Variés

Potages

Consommé en Gelée
Potage Garbure

and only one of the following dishes:—

Poissons

Coquille de Saumon Mornay

or

Entrées

Côte de Volaille Pojarsky
Filet de Boeuf Richelieu
Cold Veal Pie

Legumes

Haricots Verts   Pommes Rissolées
Vegetable Marrow   Pommes Nouvelles

or

Salades

Laitue   Mixed

Entremets

Coupe Normande

Towards the end of the Blitz the indomitable and unforgettable Rosa Lewis arrived to spend a brief period in the Hyde Park, while her own hotel, the Cavendish, was being repaired after bombing. Mary and Rosa Lewis did *not* get on; Mary described her as that 'God-awful woman'. Rose spent most of her time at the Hyde Park in a dreadful rage at being unable to continue in the unique atmosphere of her own premises – and therefore criticized everything she could around her. Admittedly her companion, Edith, tried to calm her down – but to no avail.

Rosa Lewis was, even at that time, almost a legendary figure. Starting from a lower middle-class background in Leyton, she had risen from kitchen maid to a cook in the house of the Comte de Paris. She was then cook in turn for the Prince of Wales (later to become Edward VII), Lady Randolph Churchill, Margot Asquith, the Astors and the Kaiser. After an 'arranged marriage' for respectability's sake, she became the *concièrge* of a suite of private apartments at 55 Eaton Terrace in which the Prince of Wales could disport himself with his mistresses in privacy. From the kitchen of 55 Eaton Terrace, Rosa Lewis ran a unique catering service for Edwardian house parties, the Foreign Office and state occasions. She had close relationships with Sir Anthony Eden's father, Sir William Eden, and Lord Ribblesdale, which caused considerable comment.

When Edward VII was crowned, he dropped Rosa Lewis instantly as he strove for greater respectability. Soured by this rejection, Rosa got rid of her now unnecessary husband, expanded the catering service and then bought the Cavendish Hotel. In its ageless Edwardian atmosphere, Rosa Lewis played decadent hostess to the doomed young men of the First World War and, later, the frenetic Bright Young Things of the thirties. Much to her annoyance Evelyn Waugh immortalized her as Lottie Crump in *Vile Bodies*.

By the time she came to the Hyde Park, Rosa Lewis, at seventy-four, was something of an Edwardian relic. She was also considerably embittered and spoiling for a fight. Rosa felt antiquated, rejected by modern society, the confidante of drunks, lonely, and, like Mary, childless. She tended to dwell in the past, reliving her heyday of Edwardian dinner parties, the young officers of the First World War whom she regarded as her children, and the Bright Young Things whom she regarded as her grandchildren. Worse still, her memento-hung parlour in the Cavendish had suffered as a result of the bomb damage and much of its nostalgic content was lost forever.

The Hyde Park with its élitist atmosphere and regal dignity was a far cry from the dusty, champagne and cigar-sodden atmosphere of the promiscuous Cavendish, and Rosa set out to take it by its heels. But she had not reckoned on having such a tough adversary as Mary Shiffer.

Rosa Lewis had originally come to the Hyde Park to use its air-raid shelters; a former Hyde Park receptionist remembers her first visit: 'She came in there one Sunday evening, and asked to see the manager (Mr L. Burdet, a Frenchman who soon after joined the Free French Resistance forces). He was not available, and so she took her departure.' Later, the receptionist remembered: 'I was told by a member of the staff that, when the Blitz in London was at its height ... Mrs Lewis used to come into the Hyde Park Hotel to go to the air-raid shelter, which was in the lower basement there.'

But in residence Mrs Lewis was a holy terror. She had two favourite ways of causing embarrassment. The first was the reason why the Ritz refused to take her in. She would walk into the bar or the grill room and there spot some aristocratic roué, peer or cabinet minister who was known to have 'dropped in' at the Cavendish. Then, much to the consternation of her faithful companion Edith, she would launch into a tirade of personal abuse. 'Hallo mutton chops,' she said to one ageing marquess, 'still fancy a nice clean whore?' Or to a duke, 'How's the old water works? Still as unreliable as ever?' She had cause to say to one old soldier, 'Hallo droopy drawers. When're you coming round the Cavendish to bounce a cheque?' while she nearly finished off a senior officer in the Guards by asking if he still got the 'lover's droop'. The staid Hyde Park, like the Ritz, found it all too much. The manager tried, ineffectually, to remove her from the public rooms, but she refused to budge. She was even worse in the restaurant.

When Mrs Lewis came in to dine everybody knew about it. She insisted on ordering a vast amount of champagne and talking to the people at all the other tables. She was unmerciful if she recognized them and unbearably rude if she didn't. If a waitress annoyed her, the language was very colourful. Mary considerably annoyed Mrs Lewis by treading on Kippy – one of a long line of West Highland terriers which were all called by the same name. They came everywhere with Mrs Lewis and no restaurateur had so far dared to evict them. 'Mind my bleeding dog!' The caution was mild enough coming from Rosa Lewis but it was the breaking point for Mary. She was over-tired from sleeping in the telephone room and she was damned if she was going to have this soured old woman queening it over her. She tried to be polite.

'I'm sorry madam but—'

'All right – just get on with your job, for heaven's sake, woman.'

Mary dumped a plate of tomato soup in front of her with such force that some of it slopped over on to the tablecloth. Even Edith's eyebrows rose. Mrs Lewis hit the ceiling.

'You careless bitch.'

'I won't be spoken to like that, madam!'

'You'll be spoken to any way I like!'

Then Mary's temper finally broke in full and fiery display. The grill room paused agog, sniffing blood.

'Holy Mother,' said Mary. 'You're a real crackpot!'

'I beg your pardon—'

'Who do you think you are coming into a respectable hotel like this—'

'What?'

'And behaving like an old whore!'

Mrs Lewis half rose, hand to withered neck. Edith stared aghast. No one had ever stood up to Rosa like this before. Rosa had never been spoken to like this.

'You ought to be ashamed of yourself!'

'I'll have you sacked for this,' hissed Rosa.

'They won't sack me that easy!' shouted Mary at the top of her voice, her brogue thickening as she grew more emotional. 'You come in here, calling people names, making dirty cracks, embarrassing our gentlemen—'

'Gentlemen! There are no bloody gentlemen here!' said Rosa Lewis, looking round triumphantly. She was back in control.

'And you're no lady. Why don't you go back to your – to your tarts' paradise—'

'If I did I'd take half your clients with me. The lot probably.'

Mary shook her fist at Mrs Lewis and for a moment it looked as if she would strike her. Then she was saved by the air-raid siren, as it suddenly wailed forth, and the battle was forgotten by the diners as they hurried towards the shelters. At the same moment the grill room manager came up and took the trembling Mary quietly away. She began to cry, complaining that 'the old bitch' would get her the sack. The manager shook his head and told her he was sure there was no chance of that.

Back at the table Rosa Lewis remained seated. Then, slowly, she rose, and leaning on Edith she limped out of the room. She looked a very old lady. But this was not the end of the incident. That evening Rosa Lewis was moving back to the Cavendish and, true to form, she was standing in the foyer giving abrasive instructions to the staff about her baggage and commenting on the length of time the taxi was taking to arrive at the front door. In the midst of all the confusion she slipped away.

Mrs Lewis found Mary in the still-room. She walked straight in and dumped a £5 note in front of her.

'I don't want your money,' said Mary stolidly.

'Take it.'

'I said I don't—'

'And I said take it, woman!' Then Mrs Lewis's voice lost something of its harshness. 'Take the bloody stuff – it's all I can give anybody nowadays.' Before Mary could say anything, Rosa Lewis had disappeared. She never saw her again.

The war dragged wearily on and the Hyde Park grew shabbier every hour. The carpets became threadbare, the gilt lost its sheen, the ceilings darkened, the mirrors blurred; even the marble seemed to have lost its lustre. Sometimes Mary would wander about the great, dusty, empty ballroom and the equally deteriorating banqueting suites, where the Prince of Wales had held court. She even sat in the still-room for a while trying to recall the old atmosphere. But it would not return; it remained obstinately distant. She could not even hear the ghostly chatter of debs' conversation or the baying voices of their escorts. There was nothing. Much of the hotel was dead, perhaps never to breathe life again.

Mary was such a permanent symbol of the hotel that she viewed its structural deterioration with alarm. Determined to maintain standards she saw to it that she was dressed as smartly as she could be each day. On her small salary, she went to endless trouble with new clothes, most of which she made herself. Whatever happened she was determined not to become as war-weary and decayed as the Hyde Park. But despite Mary's efforts the deterioration continued, until the hotel was no more than a fading shadow of its former elegance.

The grill room, equally shabby, was at least alive and packed out both at lunchtime and in the evening. The *Tatler*, meanwhile, recorded how society was dealing with the blackout and praised the Queen for maintaining 'a happy medium in the clothes she is wearing; not too bright and painfully *chic*, nor dreary and un-feminine. Women who made the war an excuse to wear their shabbiest blacks, unrelieved by even a clean white collar, are asking to be run-over.... The small proportion of Mayfair which has not gone to the country (Mrs Charles Sweeny is still rolling bandages) has got an attack of "uniformitis" with blacks as the only alternative.'

The *Tatler* was also interested in the capital's remaining night life:

> Though London's streets are still black, restaurants and the places where they dance are (behind light traps reminiscent of the older sort of nightclub) turning up their lights to shine 'o'er fair women and brave men'. The main change from pre-war days is sartorial; uniforms and the lounge-suits of the civil defence workers (with uniforms of khaki and navy and air-force blue predominant) having invaded the strongholds of the white tie. Quaglinos and the Café de Paris were among the first to adjust themselves to war conditions and are now nightly gathering to themselves people temporarily 'off-parade'.

Various tips were given about dress, even in the air-raid shelter, and Mary saw some of the Hyde Park clients wearing Marshall and Snelgrove's specially designed hat, 'felt reinforced with a lightweight steel cap . . . fitted with rubber round the edge to prevent undue pressure'. *Harpers* had a suggestion for a fashionable gas-mask holder: 'Elizabeth Arden makes cases in velvet, all shades, with a silk-lined pocket fitted up with beauty preparations on top; also in waterproof satin and in waterproofed snow leopard velvet – very good in a blackout.'

As 1942 passed into 1943 war shortages increased and many of the suites in the Hyde Park were closed. In the remaining few each bathroom carried the following notice.

THE BATTLE FOR FUEL:

> As part of your personal share in the Battle for
> Fuel you are asked NOT to exceed 5 inches of water
> in this bath. . . . Make it a point of honour
> not to fill the bath above this level.

Alas, not all the Hyde Park guests were that honourable, and the cleaners reported back to Mary that they had found some bath tide-marks that were well above five inches.

Another shortage in the Hyde Park, most apparent in 1944, was the paper shortage, and this particularly affected toilet rolls. Various subtle (sometimes too subtle) notices were posted in the lavatories imploring guests to 'be sparing' with the 'toilet facilities'. In the staff ladies' lavatory the paper was rationed to four sheets each, and newspaper was banned in case it blocked the cistern. Mary noticed that a good number of guests brought their own toilet paper and often wondered what black market source it came from. Once the hotel completely ran out and even more discreet (and very distressed) notices were posted pointing out that 'Under circumstances beyond our control you are warned that the facilities in these toilets are diminished'. Such notices were just as obscure as the message by which one Croydon housewife let her neighbour know that toilet paper had returned to the shops: 'Boots have stationery in.' One family in the suburbs were so affected by the shortage that they pinned up this poem in their bathroom:

> *When this cruel war is over*
> *And once more we live in clover*
> *We will have a Victory Roll –*
> *Meaning no death-taking toll,*
> *Merely that the Bowrings have*
> *Proper paper in the lav.*

In 1943 Mary and Jimmy moved into a new flat in Battersea, in a Victorian terrace house almost identical to the one they had lived in before. For entertainment – and for the necessary escapism – they went to the cinemas, which were packed. Flashes would be shown on the film when the sirens sounded, and the manager would arrive on the stage to make it clear that there was an impending air raid. But few moved, and Mary and Jimmy watched Clark Gable and Bing Crosby in happy abandon, oblivious to what would happen if the cinema was hit. Eventually the cinema managers gave up and instead a slide with a red light was put up. It read: 'An air-raid warning has just been sounded. If you wish to leave the cinema please do so as quickly as possible. Those who wish to remain may do so at their own risk. The film now continues.' Quite often they would go to the Granada at

Clapham where the management sometimes put on five films a night, although most of the audience was asleep by the early hours of the morning. To give the projectionists a break, the organists played, an amateur talent contest was held or community singing was led by the usherettes. Inevitably the most popular song was 'The White Cliffs of Dover'. One night Mary summoned up her courage and volunteered for the amateur talent contest. A diminutive figure on the Granada stage, she belted out 'If You're Irish Come into the Parlour' with some vigour. The audience joined in the chorus, and as there was a large contingent of her countrymen there there were few dry eyes amongst them.

Evelyn Waugh came into the Hyde Park entirely as a result of his association with Brian Franks, who was having a highly distinguished war. Waugh was not good soldier or officer material – although he desperately wanted to be. Franks started out with the Commandos in the Middle East and eventually became a high-ranking member of the S.A.S. Waugh was disillusioned with army life; as his biographer Christopher Sykes points out: 'He admired the tradition of the officer and gentleman, but then he admired the tradition of the country squire living as a benevolent sovereign on his acres, but found in practice that the life was rather boring. So, I think, he felt about army life.'

Waugh was an officer in the Royal Marines from December 1939 to November 1940. He was then transferred to Combined Operations and in 1941 went with No. 8 Commandos, whose commanding officer was a friend of Franks named Colonel Laycock, to Egypt and to the Middle East Command. He fought courageously in the battle for Crete, during which he was Laycock's personal assistant. At the end of 1941 No. 8 Commandos returned to Dorset where Waugh remained during most of that year, with several assignments to Combined Operations H.Q. in London as an intelligence officer. While in the Middle East Waugh had met Brian Franks, and as a result, in September 1942, he stayed at the Hyde Park with his wife Laura. In his diary there is a mysterious reference to the suite in which he stayed. Nobody, including Mary, has been able to shed any light on which suite this might be. 'On 14th we went to London by the night train and we spent the night at the Hyde Park hotel in the suite where the "Mayfair men" attacked M. Bellinger.'

Basil Bennett, son of the founder of the Hyde Park, had also become very friendly with Waugh since the time when they shared digs in 1942 when they were both stationed at Shipbourne in Dorset. Basil Bennett became chairman of the Hyde Park in 1943, and it was he who appointed his ex-Commando brother officer, Colonel Brian Franks, to be managing director of the hotel. Waugh makes a number of affectionate references to Bennett in his diaries, such as, 'Basil Bennett brought large quantities of liquor for us. I think we are the only mess in Europe which constantly drinks claret, port and brandy at dinner.'

But sharing digs with Waugh was not a calming influence on Bennett, and Waugh records him as saying, 'I must chuck it. We can't go on here. I have become a marionette. You make me do the most extraordinary things. I have never twiddled clocks anywhere else. I am going mad. Why should I pay that ridiculous woman for telephone calls [a reference to their difficult landlady]? I am going to leave the army. You want to go to the snake-house. I shall live at Weymouth. It's all over with us here.'

In July 1943 Laycock took No. 8 Commandos to Italy, but to Waugh's chagrin he was not included. No amount of pushing in the right places could alter the decision, and he was then put under instruction to join the S.A.S. in North Africa in November. But the order was cancelled. Waugh was then posted to the regimental H.Q. of the Royal Horse Guards at Windsor, but he managed to extricate himself from this by persuading Brendan Bracken, currently Minister of Information, to give him time off to write a book. The Military Secretary, much taken aback, eventually agreed, and in January 1944 Evelyn Waugh went to Chagford to begin to write *Brideshead Revisited*.

Just before this, Waugh injured a leg in a parachute jump, and he and Laura spent a fortnight at the Hyde Park. He writes, 'I spent a happy two weeks there (£71 exclusive of wine) entertaining continuously. I thought my friends would have been less attentive if I'd been in Millbank Hospital.'

'He wasn't an easy patient,' said Mary, who took the Waughs' meals up to their rooms. 'He was moody. Sometimes he's ask me how I was. Sometimes he'd tell me to "hurry up and get the hell

out of here". Maybe his leg was more painful than he let on. He
liked a lot of luxury – and he liked servants in their place.'

In April 1944 Waugh, having completed most of *Brideshead*,
returned to the Hyde Park. He writes, 'Came to London to the
Hyde Park Hotel, and spent two weeks idle in London waiting
for an appointment to conduct journalists round the Second
Front. Most of my day at White's. Saw a number of friends, drank
a great deal of wine which is getting scarcer daily but still
procurable by those who take the trouble.'

Certainly the Hyde Park was still prepared to take trouble with
wine, and Jimmy's cellar held some of the best wine in Europe.
Meanwhile, Waugh's 'literary leave' was further extended as sick
leave because of his leg injury – though this was really an excuse.
The new C.O. in the regiment to which Waugh officially belonged – the 2nd S.A.S. – found him too disruptive and difficult
a presence. Colonel Brian Franks, succeeding this C.O., found
himself feeling even more strongly that Waugh was not good
regimental officer material and further extended the leave.

Waugh, recognizing this as the rejection it was, gave in to
depression and spent much of this period at the Hyde Park over-
drinking, over-eating and over-socializing. Brian Franks writes
of Waugh:

> Little has been written about Waugh's impishness. When
> staying at the Hyde Park Hotel he changed round all the shoes
> left outside the bedrooms on his corridor. He was delighted
> with the subsequent confusion next morning.
>
> He telephoned one day to say that he would like to bring his
> daughter, Harriet, to tea. On arrival, he said that Harriet's
> greatest treat was caviar. It was provided. It is not difficult to
> guess who ate it.
>
> In his books he was careful not to make any character easily
> identifiable. An exception, perhaps, was in *Vile Bodies*, where
> 'Lottie Crump' and her hotel in Dover Street were clearly Rosa
> Lewis and the Cavendish.
>
> In an article published in the *Daily Mail* in 1930 he writes:
> 'Not long ago I published a novel in which a few pages were
> devoted to the description of an hotel. In order to avoid
> trouble I made it the most fantastic hotel I could devise. I

filled it with an impossible clientele, I invented an impossible proprietress, I gave it a fictitious address, I described its management as so eccentric and incompetent that no hotel could be run on their lines for a week without coming into the police or bankruptcy court. Here at least, I thought, I was safely in the realm of pure imagination.

'Imagine my surprise, therefore, when I received threatening letters from two irate old ladies in London, one in Newcastle and one in New York, all identifying themselves and their establishments with my invention!'

Rosa Lewis was surely one of the 'irate old ladies in London'. This, I suspect, was the start of Rosa's loathing of writers. She is quoted as saying, 'I won't 'ave that 'orrid little Waugh in 'ere ever again.'

Rather strangely, the Hyde Park Hotel had the idea of supplying the guests with shoe horns (best quality of course) with the name of the Hyde Park clearly embossed. It turned out to be quite a successful gimmick, many letters of appreciation arrived and many shoe horns disappeared. Waugh wrote: 'What do you think you are doing? Surely you know that no gentleman travels without a shoe horn!'

Waugh came to a private luncheon party at the Hyde Park. A fellow guest happened to be his publisher [Jack MacDougall]. He gave him a baleful look, turned to his host (me) and said, 'I suppose you will be asking your butcher next.'

When my company acquired the Cavendish and he learned it was to be rebuilt, he wrote as follows: 'Surely you know that any decent architect could preserve this façade with the front door for the guests and a back door for the tourists.'

Mary Shiffer said of Evelyn Waugh at this time:

He had nothing to do with his time except to find things to fill it with. He was often very rude and you could see he wanted to *do* something for the war. But they wouldn't let him in. Sometimes he would just sit in his room all day and wait for the phone to ring. Other times he would have crowds of people in his suite. But you could see he didn't like them – or most of them. He had it in for a man who talked on the radio

[Professor Joad on the 'Brains Trust', whom Waugh hated].
He used to go on about him – but he still listened to him.

In July 1944 Waugh thankfully went back into active service.
He left London with Major Randolph Churchill to join a British
Military Mission which was to help Tito's partisans in occupied
Yugoslavia. On 16 July he was involved in a plane crash with
Randolph Churchill, was flown to hospital in Italy, recuperated
in Corsica and returned to Yugoslavia in September. He then
worked with the mission in Croatia until early December and was
posted to Dubrovnik, where he became liaison officer between
the British troops and the Yugoslav authorities. He was then
expelled from Dubrovnik as a result of partisan pressure and in
February 1945 he returned to Italy. By March he was back in
London and his army career was over.

From the Hyde Park he wrote on Saturday, 31 March 1945:

Over a fortnight in England, mostly at the Hyde Park Hotel.
Expense enormous so that it seemed a great economy the day
before yesterday in living, eating and smoking. Comfort very
fair, and, it seems, better than a year ago. Good claret £2. 10s.
. . . . Rocket bombs fall two or three times a day within hearing
distance; one took out the windows of our sitting room on
Sunday morning, falling at Marble Arch. The war news is
consistently good. Everyone expects the end in a few weeks,
but without elation; all conditions expect worse from the
peace than they have had in the war. . . .

Waugh once came down into the wine cellars, where the
general manager of the hotel, together with his team of managers,
would use the war as an excuse to hold long, impromptu and
sometimes drunken parties. This meant that, apart from the free
use they made of the hotel wine, they also kept Jimmy and Mary
up well after their working hours had ended. The appearance of
Waugh certainly did not help. He immediately began to sample
some of the hotel's rarer wines, as well as the freshly imported
hogsheads.

Desperate to find a means of breaking up the party and getting
the semi-drunken Waugh back to his suite, Mary hit on the

devious plan of screaming her head off. Waugh, who was sampling a Medoc, did not seem to hear, but the manager looked at her with irritation in his glassy eyes. On being questioned Mary said she had seen a rat and then began to scream again, pointing to the dark shadow of the wine racks. Then, by some act of sympathetic magic, there was a scurrying sound and something detached itself from the darkness for a second and sped into a corner. Abruptly the party left, including Evelyn Waugh. But as he passed Mary, Waugh grinned, and she was convinced that he had seen through her ruse. She was also convinced that he sympathized with it.

The Second World War came to an end on Tuesday, 8 May 1945. The sense of anti-climax was shattering. The slow finish of the war, the mass of dust and insects that came away as Mary took down the blackout from her windows, the shabby war-worn furniture in the flat, her depleted wardrobe, the crumbling plaster and bomb-blasted windows, the still vital ration books – all seemed to make Mary's mood, always mercurial, depressed and stale.

The government did not help, and every public notice was grey and uninspired. None of their proclamations was designed to bring joy or a sense of fulfilment; they even broadcast the end of the war in a muddled way. Typical of such pronouncements was this desolate instruction given out by the Board of Trade on 7 May 1945: 'Until the end of May you may buy cotton bunting without coupons, as long as it is red, white or blue and does not cost more than one and three a square yard.' Equally drab was the broadcast statement that concluded six years of unrelenting war: 'It is understood that, in accordance with arrangements between the three great powers, an official announcement will be broadcast by the Prime Minister at three o'clock tomorrow.'

On the morning of V.E. Day, Mary listened on the radio to a cinema organ and later to Churchill's speech. Then, in the evening, Mary and Jimmy took a bus to the Mall and walked down it to Buckingham Palace. Mary described the scene:

I still felt tired and fed-up. Then, suddenly, the lights came up. It was all flood-lit and I felt better. I thought some magic would happen – and to be sure, after a while, it did. The balcony was covered in a crimson drape with a yellow and gold fringe to it. Everyone was very quiet. Some rockets went up and the whole crowd jumped – we thought we were being bombed again. Then the King and Queen came out on the balcony. The two princesses were with them. Then the cheering started and people started singing. I started crying. There was a bonfire in the Park. Later we went to see Big Ben all floodlit – and then the House of Commons and County Hall.

Walking by the bonfire near the lake, Mary saw her reflection in the rosy darkness of the water. She looked old and tired, pale after the mole-like existence of the war years. Later that night Mary and Jimmy went to a street party in Battersea. Once again there was a bonfire and attempts had been made to cook up 'treats' such as custard with some very strange ingredients. Luckily, there was plenty of drink to cover up the taste, and they danced to a record player mounted on the roof of a baker's van. The drink had its effect and soon emotion overtook the apathy. The celebration, although synthetic, was at least therapeutic.

By V.J. night – 14 August, however, the sense of anti-climax had increased. 'The war is over,' George VI broadcast, 'You know, I think, that those four words have for the Queen and myself the same significance, simple yet immense, that they have for you.' But for Mary they had no significance at all. She felt desperately tired – and her work at the Hyde Park seemed to have no purpose.

This attitude was largely caused by the extreme state of dilapidation that the once-grand hotel had fallen into. The ballroom and banqueting rooms were plaster-flaked, war-battered parodies of their former glory. The restaurant was in equally poor condition while, throughout the Hyde Park, carpets were threadbare, table linen was practically non-existent, cutlery, crockery and china were vastly depleted, tables and chairs went unpolished, and the once sumptuous foyer was stained, dirty and badly chipped. Hardly any of the window frames fitted – and the staff quarters were barely habitable.

Refurbishing was essential, but a new spirit was even more important. The state of the Hyde Park was similar to the state of the country – battered, lacking in morale, and desperately in need of a transfusion of adrenalin. Basil Bennett, now managing director of the hotel, realized that something had to be done instantly; somehow the Hyde Park had to be given new life-blood. He said as much to Mary one morning in the still-room.

'I need new blood too, sir,' she told him, rattling away at the antiquated coffee urn.

'We must get back to where we were before the war,' Bennett said desperately, wondering if Mary's attitude reflected that of the entire staff. She brightened slightly at this remark but returned a dampening reply.

'It's all gone. It won't be the same.'

'What's all gone?' Bennett tried to stifle his irritation.

'It won't be the same again,' Mary said doggedly.

'But we've got to make it the same – or even better.' Bennett found himself desperately appealing to her now. To him, she seemed the very roots of the old hotel; it was as if he was talking to the spirit of the place itself. He suddenly realized that if he could inspire this tired, prematurely aged servant, then he could revitalize the whole place. Bennett told Mary that the hotel needed the monarchy back; indeed the only way the Hyde Park could survive would be to win back royal custom. He then told her that he knew the very man who could do this.

After Bennett had left her, Mary Shiffer began to cut up brown bread for the sardine hors d'oeuvre that had replaced the smoked salmon. So much was the hotel part of her that this promise of renewal made her begin to come alive again. She looked around at the fading paintwork of the still-room. She remembered how she had first seen the hotel as a young girl when she was taken there by the redoubtable Captain Allen – a fairy-tale palace full of fairy-tale kings and queens. Now, unbelievably, perhaps it would be so again.

Chapter Ten

George and Elizabeth

1945-1952

BUT the royal glitter was not that easy to recapture. Bennett did, however, assemble a considerable team in which Mary, the un-promoted servant, was regarded as an essential figure. She reflected the past gloss of the hotel, and she had a legendary reputation, much inflated, of having been the confidante of Queen Mary, Valentino, Beaverbrook, Edward VIII and other notable figures. To Bennett, Mary Shiffer not only typified the old and distinguished world of the hotel, but she also pointed the way for the royal flagship to rebuild itself – by reverting to its former traditions.

At the same time, Bennett realized that to lean on tradition and an old servant was not enough. He needed a management team which was efficient, imaginative and, above all, well connected. It was these connections which would rebuild the Hyde Park's clientele, so the team would have to be carefully selected. Bennett came up with a brilliant combination. He made Colonel Brian Franks general manager, and a young man named Tom Sawyer manager. Both were old Etonians, and both had strong county family backgrounds. Franks then asked Bennett if he could add another member to the team, his old employee at the Mayfair, Massara, who came into the Hyde Park as catering manager. Together with Mary Shiffer and her traditionalism, they made a formidable team. Later Kinsman and Maroni were to join them. All shared in Bennett's determination to turn the Hyde Park into a grand hotel once more.

At the outset, however, the task seemed almost impossible. Franks told me:

The hotel was in a dreadful state. We had to rely totally on the black market for many kinds of food and the staff had slipped into many strange wartime habits. The old manager, for instance, could be seen cooking up his own kippers in the service lift and the wine-cellar seemed to have become a free social club. The heating was as idiosyncratic as some of the staff. Trucks of coal had to be taken down to the boilers which were like angry, unpredictable monsters. They were, in fact, boilers from an old battle ship and the boiler room was almost identical to its shipboard counterpart. About the only stable influence in the hotel seemed to have been Mary Shiffer – who had been a kind of maid-of-all-work in the Hyde Park since before the First World War. She had a legendary name but was not a character, thank God, like Rosa Lewis. Mary had a temper but otherwise was gentle and self-effacing. She was obviously wedded to the job and I had no idea she was wedded to the cellarman. I knew she came from an alarmingly poor background in Dublin but really I knew very little of her private life. I don't think she had any – particularly as she grew older. It was the hotel that was her life. She was very popular with the guests, particularly the few we still had in residence. The staff liked her too, despite the fact she treated them like erring children, calling all the Italian waiters Macaronis. The Hyde Park was her home and her personality was such that I can easily understand her receiving Royal confidences.

Massara also found the going rough in the run-down hotel, despite the fact that he knew he had achieved his ambition. He had finally made it; his dreams as a boy waiter had now come true. He remembers the Hyde Park in 1945 as:

full of rats with hardly any clients. Sir Nigel Balchin [the film director] was one of the residents throughout the war, mainly because he thought the hotel was so solidly built that it was

bomb proof. We were told that we had three months to pull
the place together. It was no easy job. Unbelievably there were
no serviettes – and all the plates were cracked – the few that
had survived the war years, that is. The staff were very old,
very set in the ways of the prewar days. When I asked if they
had any ice buckets they stared at me in bewilderment. Everyone was on the fiddle and I'm sure this is how most of the stuff
had disappeared. The hotel was a shell, and without any money,
we had to fill it – to bring it alive again. The only member of
staff with a spark of life in her was Mary Shiffer and we knew
we could depend on her. We knew Queen Mary remembered
her – and she had had some kind of relationship with
Edward VIII. She was certainly a fund of stories on the old
life. But we were only concerned with the new. Our objectives
were three – firstly to bring back the Monarchy; secondly to
bring back the very top aristocracy; thirdly to bring back the
debs – but twice as glamorously as before. Overall we were to
restore the Hyde Park to the height of fashion. As we tried to
lick the battered old place into shape I used to face every day
as a new fight. It was good – a glorious way to live.

The first new menu was on Victory Day, 8 June 1946. It was
fairly spartan:

LUNCHEON
Crème St Germain

———

Coquille de Turbot Mornay
or
Escalope Napolitaine
Petits Pois et Carottes à la Crème
Pommes Purée

———

Coupe Hélène

———

Algerian Wine en Carafe 15s. and 8s.

The team's first two objectives could be achieved by contacts,
despite the shabbiness of the hotel. But the debs needed glamour –

and this was not something that could be managed in the present decorative state of the hotel. But style they could produce. Massara had learned about style. For the debs of that time, style meant Tommy Kinsman.

Kinsman came from the same poverty-stricken background as Mary and Massara. He was one of six children; his father was a baker and he grew up in one of the poorest areas of Liverpool. Finding that baking was unprofitable, Kinsman's father then became a coal merchant and his son acted as his delivery boy, running a small hand-barrow between the coal yard and their customers' cellars. 'Four of us slept – two at the top, two at the bottom – in one bed. We were a happy, united family, although food shortages gave me rickets as a child.' Throughout Tommy Kinsman's life he has been marked by the after-effects of the disease. 'My hands permanently shake because of a damaged nerve in the brain – so much so that people assume I'm suffering from the effects of alcohol.'

When he left school, Kinsman sold chocolates in a pageboy uniform in a local cinema. Later he became a projectionist but left abruptly after burning 2,000 feet of film. Sacked, he acted in the traditional way for a Liverpool boy of that time – he ran away to sea. Throughout the 1914–18 War he worked as a cabin boy and coal shoveller. The Spanish 'flu, that had so vigorously attacked and decimated The Liberties, descended on one of his ships – and, like Mary, Kinsman had a lucky escape from it. Others were not so fortunate, and dead bodies littered the ship. The crew then spent most of their time on the macabre duty of stitching the bodies in canvas and burying them at sea.

Back home, Kinsman went on the dole until he was asked to be a banjoist. The problem was that he was unable to play the instrument. However, Arthur, the dance band leader who had suggested the idea, did not regard this inadequacy as a problem. He gave Tommy Kinsman his first piece of musical advice, 'I'll show you where to put your fingers and look convincing. Meanwhile I want you to stuff some old socks down the inside of the banjo so that no one can hear it!' This was Kinsman's musical debut and he made the most of the non-event. As a non-musician he travelled down with the band to the Bohemian Dance Hall near Mile End Station. 'I had to have a dress suit. The only one

I could afford was second-hand and this was designed for a six-foot man of about sixteen stone. I was five foot eight and weighed ten stone. But my sister cut down the tails and tucked in the sleeves and assured me I was fine!' Unfortunately the manager found this compromise unacceptable and accused Kinsman of 'deliberately looking like a comedian'. Later they found a better fitting dress suit in the market at Petticoat Lane.

Gradually Kinsman left non-banjo playing and with some difficulty mastered the saxophone. He also had to teach himself to read music. But this took years, and he learned the saxophone by chords alone. The next booking was at the Hammersmith Palais – a rowdy spot which the Prince of Wales and his brother, the Duke of Kent, would regularly look in to. But acceptance by society was not to arrive for a long while yet, and poverty once again hit him. For some time Kinsman survived in a bed-sitting room, paying half-a-crown a week rent. He could only afford the barest necessities, and a pennyworth of chips at night was often the largest meal he would have. Every day musicians met at Archer Street for work, and Kinsman was one of the few who were non-Jewish. As a result he missed out on all the big Jewish weddings and Barmitzvahs. Like Massara, however, Kinsman was determined to use his forceful personality to drag himself out of the everyday run of jobbing musicians. He decided the only way to do this would be to form his own band. He was now married, and he and his wife wrote hundreds of letters. Eventually bookings began to come in. By the early thirties Kinsman had developed an American style dance band known curiously as Thos. F. Kinsman and his London Frivolities Band. Gradually he became acceptable. Then the 'big-time' began. Kinsman became resident band leader at the fashionable Ciro's Club in Bond Street and now billed himself, appropriately enough, as Tommy Kinsman and his Ciro's Club Band. Next, he played at the Ritz as Kinsman and His Band. There, the Prince of Wales ensured his success in the mid-thirties by patronizing the band, enjoying and dancing its tangos, and inviting Kinsman to his table. Very suddenly Tommy Kinsman was 'in'. The Celebrité and other fashionable night-spots followed, and so did recording and radio contracts. The press lapped him up, particularly as he was fast becoming a debs' favourite and was playing for many of their public and private parties. Typical of press comments was the *Evening News* gossip column of 1932:

> The Prince of Wales never misses an opportunity to raise the standard of his dancing. . . . He had come with a small intimate party to the restaurant of one of those hotels that overlook the Green Park. . . . He danced three tangoes each of which lasted about thirty-five minutes! Of course the band went on playing as long as the Prince and his partner remained on the floor. Half-hour spells of tangoes three times running must be something of a record for the West End. Each tango lasts normally about four minutes.

Kinsman's musical style was well described by the *Torbay Herald* in 1936:

> Tommy Kinsman specialises in unearthing popular numbers of the past and arranging them in attractive pot-pourris. He believes that a band playing rhythm music should be easy to listen to, and the nature of his first broadcast indicates that he intends to live up to his signature tune 'Sweet Music'. His first programme included a favourite pot-pourri composed of 'Black Eyes', the Russian Gypsy song arranged as a foxtrot, 'The Peanut Vendor', 'Beautiful Spring' and other popular hits of the past.

Other Kinsman favourites, particularly with the debs, were 'Don't Do That to the Poor Pussy Cat', 'Sing me to Sleep with a Twilight Song', 'The Gift of Gladness', 'I Want to be Alone with Mary Brown', 'Tired Hands', 'There's a Rickety Rackety Shack', 'Dream Kisses', 'It's a Sin to Tell a Lie', 'Barbary Coast Blues', 'At the Close of a Long, Long Day' and 'A Feather in her Tyrolean Hat'.

By 1937 *Radio Pictorial* was saying: 'Tommy controls the destinies of considerably over a hundred musicians. He can put you in a three-piece band or one running to twenty pieces and he'll also come along and lead the band himself, if you insist, but that's liable to cost you a bit more.'

Massara knew that Kinsman was essential to restoring the fortunes of the Hyde Park and Mary thought he was right. 'Tommy was the debs' delight and we knew, if we had Tommy playing in the ballroom, we'd be back where we were. It wasn't just the debs who liked him – it was Royalty too. He played in a way that was very easy to dance to for them. Nothing too fast, nor too loud. And the tempo allowed for anyone with two left feet – which a lot of them had.'

What the new Hyde Park team wanted, however, was to test themselves out. Franks' contacts, Sawyer's suavity, Massara and Maroni's charisma, Tissot and Cavallo's cooking, Kinsman's atmosphere and Mary's tradition – all had to be proven to work in practice. Suddenly, the great opportunity came.

Lady Vyner, of distinguished stock (daughter of the Duke and Duchess of Richmond and Gordon, and bridesmaid to Queen Elizabeth), decided to hold her silver wedding party at the Hyde Park. As the silver wedding of the King and Queen was almost at the same time, the Vyners decided to invite them. The year was 1948 and the request sent the Hyde Park team into instant panic. In one way it was just what they wanted; in another they viewed the situation with mounting horror. The Hyde Park was still in a state of extreme decay and was in no condition to receive such distinguished and possibly critical guests. Although the occasion was to be a private one, Franks had no doubt that it would be heavily commented on in the press, principally because the King and Queen had not been into a hotel since the war – and had rarely been into one before.

The Vyners were surprised and a little alarmed by Massara's casualness. They did not realize that it was merely a cloak for his desperation. Lady Vyner told me, 'He was very vague – and foreign. He kept telling us to leave it all to him – food, flowers, band – everything. I kept reminding him that the King and Queen were going to be present. But he didn't bat an eyelid. He kept on telling us to leave it to him.'

Mary, who thought Massara 'a wonderful looking fellow with the women, but a real swankpot', was worried at first that he was not going to be able to pull it off. He worried her still further by several appearances he made in the still-room, looking anxious and flustered, trying to tot up an inadequate inventory of missing domestic items. Then he took an important decision. 'I realized there was no chance of doing anything else but making a dreadful mess of the occasion – unless I borrowed. But once I started checking on what I had to borrow – I realized it would be everything.'

Massara was exaggerating – but only slightly. He borrowed the china from an export order of Doultons, a loan that they made willingly enough, although they made the proviso that all breakages had to be paid for. He passed this information on to Mary but was rewarded only with a mouthful of Irish vitriol. She had taken exception to his condemnation of the war-battered Hyde Park, largely because she refused to accept that the cupboards of the once great hotel were bare. But Massara weathered Mary's temper, and swept on to make serviettes with his wife at home, to borrow waiters from every hotel in London, to get hold of white toilet rolls, which were at the time nearly unobtainable; he went to Harvey Nichols store in Knightsbridge to borrow rugs to cover the holes in the carpets and to Covent Garden to acquire fruit from mysterious sources there.

Mary put bowls of rose-water around the banqueting suite and helped arrange masses of flowers. She was nervous, particularly when Massara paraded everybody an hour before the royal couple were due to arrive and gave the staff a feverish set of instructions. He did not dare inspect the still-room but asked over and over again whether Mary had sufficient coffee for forty guests. Eventually she put Massara out of his misery by giving him a brusque reassurance. He then turned his attention to the commis waiters, the waiters, the wine waiters, the chef, the sous-chefs, the banqueting manager, the flower arrangers, the house detectives – and anyone else who could possibly ruin the evening.

Meanwhile Tommy Kinsman was also having his problems. Already aware that this was make-or-break rejuvenation night for the Hyde Park (as well as a vital booking for him), he was determined that nothing should go wrong musically. Accordingly, having been hired to play during dinner only, Kinsman sent Lady Vyner a list of light classical numbers that he thought would be a suitable background to the discreet champing of jaws. However, Lady Vyner was anxious that the party should be informal and she returned his programme with a request for the 'light classics' to be replaced by both nostalgic and modern dance tunes.

George VI was very much an unknown quantity to Mary. He had never been in the hotel before and all she knew was the image the popular papers had of him – a happy family man with a ready sense of humour. During the course of the next few years, however, she was to come to know him better, despite the fact that he never became a close confidant like his elder brother. But as she was such a familiar figure in any number of jobs in the hotel, he greeted her by name, passed the time of day and occasionally made a comment. But he regarded kingship very much as his father had. Mary said,

He was never like his brother, or the way I would imagine their grandfather, Edward VII, to be. He never wanted to be King but he grew into it. He was much like his father, quick to spot anything sloppy or out of place. That's why Massara was so careful over the Vyners' do. It was all the protocol that had to be observed – and if you didn't do it he'd go like ice. One of the first things I remember noticing about him was how smart and slim he was. He always walked round like a young-old man. He always looked controlled – as if he had learnt his part – and his part had become part of him. All of him. But he wasn't awkward with his children, who used to come into the Hyde Park a lot. The girls were taught to dance by Madame Vacani. Of course, he dinned into them all about dedication to duty – you could see that.

Mary approved of George VI because he was religious. Unlike his brother the Duke of Windsor, he regularly attended church, and although seen as a conservative churchman by many he was far from averse to church unity – and had a great respect for the Catholic archbishop, Cardinal Hinsley. He was also a Free-mason, at one point becoming Grand Master of the Middlesex province. But controlled and devout as he was, George VI loved dancing, and people, which is why, despite his reserve and attention to protocol, he found time to talk to Mary. Keith Middlemas says of him, 'He possessed the priceless gift of being interested in whoever he was talking to, and no one sitting next to him ever had to fear the chilling signs of royal boredom. He loved dancing and would often lead the conga at his daughters' parties.'

The best illustration of this was the Vyner party at the Hyde Park – Mary was to discover 'the man behind the king for the first time that night. Tommy Kinsman, having played throughout dinner, was wondering how long he would have to continue. Kinsman relates, 'I was wondering how many hours we would have to keep playing when a message arrived from the Queen to ask whether we knew a rather lurid party piece called "*Civilisation*". The song had recently come from America and started with the words "Bongo, bongo, bongo". Although I never dreamed the King and Queen would ask for it at a dinner party, I had the sheet music with me.' But worse was to follow. The royal party insisted that Kinsman sing it to them. But although he had taught himself to play some of the instruments in the band, Tommy Kinsman had not been able to teach himself to sing. Desperately, he turned to the band, but there were no volunteers. Blindly, realizing how much was at stake for the Hyde Park, Kinsman waved the sheet music at the King and Queen, imploring them to lead the singing.

It was at this point that Mary suddenly emerged from the still-room. With grim determination she went across to the royal couple and bowed. She told them that she knew the tune. With complete acceptance they made way for her and Mary joined a group surrounding the Queen, who held the lyrics up for all to see. Massara, Sawyer and Franks, standing at the back of the room, continued to sweat. There was no telling what the outcome of all this improvisation would be. But 'Bongo, Bongo, Bongo' won the day. George VI asked Lady Vyner if the carpets could be pulled up for dancing, and Lady Vyner asked Massara. Realizing this would expose all the holes, Massara agreed reluctantly. George VI, forgetting protocol in the excitement of an unexpected treat, helped him, dragging aside the Harvey Nichols mats and ignoring the mess below. Meanwhile, Mary, about to slip away, was asked by the Queen to stay. Soon the party really began. The Kinsman orchestra played foxtrots, waltzes, and eventually the royal favourite, the hokey-cokey.

The conga followed, and Mary found herself with her hands gripping the King's slim back as they circled the banqueting suite.

Later drinks were served and Mary returned to the still-room, where other members of staff greeted her with emotions ranging from awe to bewilderment to anger at her audacity. But she had been right. The evening was an assured success and the hotel she loved so much was back on its feet once more. But the evening was tinged with sadness when Mary later re-emerged from the still-room. She heard George VI saying to Tommy Kinsman, 'My brother was always very fond of Ciro's. Do you remember those tango competitions you had with him in the early hours when everyone had gone home? How pleased he was when he found a tango you didn't know. He was a great tango fan, my brother. And still is.' The melancholy in the King's voice saddened Mary as she returned again to the still-room. Brewing up more coffee, she realized that despite the rift between the two brothers they were still deeply attached to each other.

The King continued to reminisce with Kinsman. They talked about the thirties in Ciro's and the twenties at the Hammersmith Palais when, as Bertie and David, he and his brother used to come in to hear him play. The King remembered that his brother's favourite tune was 'I've Got the Navy Blues', and Kinsman reminded George that the Queen's favourite tune was 'Lady, Play your Mandolin'. Fascinated by this unknown preference, the King asked Kinsman for other royal favourites. He was told that Princess Margaret went for 'Honeybun' from *South Pacific*, the young Duke of Kent liked 'Willow, Weep for Me,' and Princess Alexandra always asked Kinsman to play 'Ain't Misbehavin'.

Perhaps the most embarrassing moment of the evening came for Kinsman when he found himself in a muddle over the dreaded protocol. But for once George VI let it pass, and indeed even encouraged a casualness that would have shocked him elsewhere. 'The Princess, I mean Her Royal Highness, the Princess Elizabeth . . .' Kinsman paused, having tied himself into knots. Then he said, 'It's awfully difficult, Your Majesty, to give them all their correct titles. Might I refer to them as your brother and daughters?'

'But of course,' replied the alarmingly accommodating King. 'That is just what I would like you to do.'

'Then, of course your wife . . .' Kinsman paused again and began to stutter. 'But I must call *her* Her Majesty the Queen.'

'No, no,' said the King, with a certain weariness in his voice. 'That is quite all right.'

Later George VI played the accordion (for the first time), and Mary was dragged out of the still-roo

5 a.m. This time the conga did not st

banqueting rooms but invaded the res

ing line bounced noisily about the H

the test had been passed – and her ow

had at last come alive again after its v

The royal hair-letting-down instan

the debs – on which much of the Hy

had been founded. By 1947 presentati

and there were 20,000 girls waiting to

numbers, the old style of presentat

garden parties were introduced. Dres

'Ladies: Day Dress with Hat. Gentl

Uniform or Lounge Suit.' *Queen* wr

were held during the war there are

applicants for presentation as there we

out parties littered the Hyde Park to th

even more each week. Despite rati

pigeon, venison and game sent in fro

market eggs, mayonnaise assisted by l

berries without cream. A deb's escort

It was rather a period of austerity, w
were just getting out of their cocoons. They had been very isolated because of the war and I think for the girls it must have been very traumatic to be introduced suddenly to such large parties. In London, they would be at hotels like Claridges, the Dorchester, the Savoy and the Hyde Park. In most cases there would be a dinner party first, and as there wasn't much meat you tended to get poultry. But at that time I hadn't known any different and though I could tell good wine from very bad wine, I couldn't do more than that. But you

were always reasonably well fed and given champagne to drink. It no longer seemed to have much to do with being a marriage market: I think that would be an over-simplification. But it did make the girls more sure of themselves after being cooped up at school, so that later they could pick out the sheep from the goats in potential matches. And it was not all that promiscuous. Of course there was always some girl who was meant to be sleeping around but I think hardly anyone actually did. Certainly I never came across it.

Kinsman played for all the parties at the Hyde Park, and each deb who was 'coming out' autographed his drum. He often wondered why he was so popular, and feels it might be explained by the deb 'who told me it was because I stuck to melody and to dancing tempo. She said even a corpse could dance to my music.'

To give an example of the Hyde Park fare in 1947, this dinner was served to the Transjordan Legation:

Filet de Sole Jeanette

Pintadeau Poelé Mascotte
Petits Pois
Pommes Rissolées
Salade

Pêche Melba

Café

Economic, but unstinting, was therefore the general policy. Mary pointed out,

Colonel Franks used to do the customers all right but the staff sometimes went hungry. Like young Sawyer [the Hotel's Manager] for instance – he used to be always scrounging for grub. I was serving in the directors' dining room again – now the men were back from the war to be waiters. The chef used to insist all the left-overs were brought back to the kitchen – but I managed to knock off bits for young Sawyer. They were still having even better food than the guests – with whitebait, oysters, smoked salmon, plovers' eggs, quails and partridge.

The years between 1948 and 1950 passed uneventfully. George VI used the hotel frequently for a variety of different functions but he never was to let his hair down again, at least not at the Hyde Park.

Evelyn Waugh continued to buzz waspishly around the hotel, using it as his London base and occasionally lunching in the grill room with his wife Laura or Basil Bennett. Normally Waugh ate at his club, and merely slept at the Hyde Park. Both Mary and Charlie Vyse, the chief valet, have the same memory of him at this period: 'He used to carry an old fashioned ear trumpet around with him but he certainly wasn't deaf. Or not deaf enough for that. He used to enjoy making people repeat remarks to him. Then he would bellow back at them. It was a joke. His kind of joke. Not that many people found it funny.' Vyse remembers him 'lying in bed with a cigar. Once I put the wrong shoes out for him. One belonged to the gentleman next door. I apologized and changed them over. But he wouldn't wait – and I saw him going off to White's in his carpet slippers.'

Mary had only the briefest acquaintance with the Queen.

She was a warm person, at her best with her family. She used to come into the hotel for some of the debs' dances but she wasn't right for that kind of company. But she felt it was her duty to be there – you could see that. She once told me something the King always used to say, 'We're not a family. We're a firm.' Her best friend was Lady Vyner and you could see she was a woman who had close friends. She wasn't withdrawn, like Queen Mary, but I knew she was at her happiest at Royal Lodge – their family home at Windsor.

By 1949 Mary was sixty. The fact surprised her. It seemed that the time had slipped away. There had been many highlights at the Hyde Park, but hardly any in her private life – such as it was, away from the hotel. She and Jimmy still went back to Dublin every year but they no longer visited The Liberties. Instead they went to her sister's house in a bleak suburb near the airport,

Mary no longer felt the need to draw energy from the old days of her childhood. Her longing for a family of her own had not diminished but she had accepted it and was able to live with it. The Liberties, with its still teeming hordes of children, only tended to bring that longing back.

But there was another reason for avoiding the area. The previous year her father had died and the funeral procession had been held there. She found it difficult to grieve although her Catholic traditionalism dictated that she should. Michael had become a sober-sided, rather self-pitying old man in his retirement. With her mother, he had occasionally come to England and, in a sense, Mary had felt brusquely sorry for him. But she could not forget his self-indulgences, the way he treated her mother, the drunkenness and the beatings. All these horrors of her childhood returned every time she saw him. As for Michael, he seemed to regret his former extravagances. He had become very pious, went regularly to mass, and prayed feverishly for mercy on his damned soul. His confessions were the longest on record, and many a priest had reason to dread Michael Dooley's appearances in the confessional. 'They used to take sandwiches in with them, he was so long. Once my mother told me he had been on his knees all day. I thought at the time – God have mercy on the priests.'

The funeral was medieval. In 1948 The Liberties were as battered and noisy as ever. Nor had they changed much from Mary's childhood days. Michael had saved a good deal of money for his funeral and it was stage-managed with considerable style. The hearse was drawn by four black horses, each with a black plume on its head. The hearse itself was in Gothic style, and its polished jet blackness gleamed in the pallid light of an early spring afternoon. The driver and his mate wore tall black hats and long silver-blue coats. The coffin was taken from the house and loaded on to the hearse. Then the hearse and the mourners drove to The Liberties. Once inside the narrow network of streets the mourners formed up and walked behind the slow-stepping horses with their sombre cargo. Michael Dooley was going to meet his Saviour. His last words had been to the priest as he plucked helplessly at the sweaty sheets, 'I have sinned, Father – sinned and bound for hellfire. My soul is damned, Father.' No amount of priestly reassurance would satisfy him, and he died tormented and apprehensive. Perhaps he's in the pit already, thought Mary as she walked behind her father's coffin. Try as she could to dismiss the thought, the notion of her father in hell stayed with her. What had he really feared? Fire and brimstone? Sulphur? Boiling oil?

Later, in the graveyard, Michael Dooley was at last committed to rest. The roped coffin was lowered in the damp earth: 'For as much as it hath pleased Almighty God of his great mercy to take unto himself the soul of our dear brother departed, we therefore commit his body to the ground.'

It's all very well, thought Mary with sudden irreverence, but has Almighty God really taken him? Or was her father, as he had feared, already in hell? The gravediggers moved forward to spade the earth back on to the coffin. Gradually the pit filled.

'He was a good man,' said her mother as she walked away from the grave. Then she added firmly, 'in many ways.' As the family walked back through the streets of The Liberties they passed a bar near Engine Alley that had once been one of Michael's favourite drinking places.

'Let's go and have one for him,' said Elizabeth Dooley. As they all went inside, Mary, for some reason, glanced across the road. Under a lamp-post stood a man, hands in pockets, gazing vacantly ahead. He was bare-headed and seemed not to notice the rain that was falling. Then he turned and walked away. In the half-light Mary was sure he had horns.

Chapter Eleven

❦❦❦❦❦❦❦❦❦❦❦❦❦❦❦❦❦❦❦❦❦❦❦❦❦❦❦❦❦❦❦❦

The New Royals

❦❦❦❦❦❦❦❦❦❦❦❦❦❦❦❦❦❦❦❦❦❦❦❦❦❦❦❦❦❦❦❦

1952-1977

THE 1950s were the prime of the Hyde Park Hotel. They were ten golden years of debbery, of theatrical royal splendour, of distinguished visitors and of success. In its second heyday, the hotel was very much as Mary remembered it when she first arrived. Although most of the marbled halls were still covered with a disastrous wallpaper that was a hangover from prewar days, the foyer was aglitter with chandeliers and plumed with flowers. It seemed to Mary like a set for a Valentino film; indeed, it had not changed much since the idol strode across it. The liveried doorman still stood on the threshold and the hall-porter within.

Mary's private life was soon to be shattered by the death of her mother and the totally unexpected death of Jimmy. Mary remembered, 'I had never been so desperately happy – or so desperately sad – in such a short space of time. That ten years I had all the magic and all the grief that anyone in their lives could take.'

First came the magic: the Festival of Britain, with its pleasure gardens, its Skylon, the Dome of Discovery, the Festival Hall and so on symbolizing the end of the hungry forties. The country knew it was a turning point and reached forward expectantly. Politically the situation was not good. Ernest Bevin had recently died and Aneurin Bevan had resigned, leaving the ailing Labour

Government split and lacking in credibility. 'Fun, fantasy and colour' was the keynote to the Festival of Britain, and it was indeed a spectacular success. George VI opened the Festival on 3 May 1951 but was too ill to attend its closure in September. He had cancer, though he did not know it. Mary and Jimmy spent some of the happiest times of their lives wandering through the fun-fair in Battersea pleasure gardens, and they both joined in the community singing, led by Gracie Fields, that closed the Festival. There was hope in the air – hope that was soon to be crushed. For as much as the Festival symbolized a new age, in its death throes it also symbolized the banality of that new age. The gardens on the South Bank were removed, and the Festival Hall remained the only permanent building, as the National Theatre was not built as expected, and the site lay derelict for nine years until the hideous Shell complex was built on it, the final, mocking symbol of materialism.

In October 1951, the King, his health worsening, put pressure on Attlee to dissolve Parliament. After some dithering, Attlee went to the country and lost the election. The Conservatives swept in with a majority of 321 to Labour's 195. Churchill became Prime Minister and shortly afterwards moved to the Hyde Park Hotel for two weeks while his town house was being redecorated. He immediately came into conflict with Mary.

After Churchill had been in the Hyde Park for a week or so, he returned to the hotel very late one night, when a pea-soup fog blotted out London completely. He was returning from the House of Commons and it was almost 5 a.m. The fog was so thick and obtrusive that it seemed to swathe the marbled foyer, and even the sleepy receptionist looked like a wraith. As Churchill walked past him, the man nodded with monotonous respect. However, once in the lift, Churchill suddenly realized that he had a voracious appetite, although he knew that the breakfast chefs would not be on duty yet. With sudden decision, he returned to the ground floor and, walking swiftly past the surprised receptionist, headed down the service stairs.

In the kitchens he found Tissot, who had been working all night on some special delicacies for a banquet the next day. Churchill gave Tissot two cigars in exchange for sending him up some breakfast. Tissot willingly agreed, but as he departed

Churchill asked if he could have some coffee sent up at once. Tissot, realizing Mary had only just come on duty in the still-room, agreed more warily, not knowing what her mood was like that morning. Churchill, noticing his hesitation, said he would drop into the still-room himself and see if he could persuade 'another member of staff to oblige me'. Tissot tried to dissuade him, but Churchill, with his normal forcefulness, walked out of the kitchens, up the stairs, across the empty restaurant and into the still-room.

Mary was noisily setting up her equipment, and when she heard a voice asking if she could possibly oblige by producing some coffee she assumed that a member of the kitchen staff had come to ask a favour. This morning she was in no mood to grant favours, and she barked out words to the effect that there would be no coffee forthcoming at all. The voice persisted and Mary said, 'There's no bloody coffee and that's it.' She then turned and saw the familiar bulbous shape of Winston Churchill. He was uncharacteristically cowed, and his face had the look of a child deprived of a treat. Apologizing with garrulous profuseness, Mary produced the coffee, and Churchill drank it, still childlike, in the still-room.

Churchill must have remembered Mary. Two days later, she took coffee up to his suite, where she found him painting at an easel. Despite his very temporary stay, a large number of paintings covered the walls, some originals and some reproductions of his own paintings. He looked up as she put down the tray and smiled. 'I am allowed some coffee this time?' he queried. Awkwardly Mary attempted to make a quick exit but he forestalled her.

Churchill asked Mary to stand in the mid-morning light of one of the windows that overlooked Hyde Park. He told her that he would like to paint a picture of 'Irish features', but he was 'not a portraitist – merely a landscapist'. Embarrassed, Mary could think of nothing to say, but Churchill continued to look at her bone structure with technical interest. Then he asked her if she liked paintings and she replied that she had known only a few pictures – apart from religious ones – and that her idea of a beautiful landscape was Booterstown, with the tide going down over the pebbles and the sun glowing red on the horizon.

Churchill then asked Mary to look at his own paintings and

pick out her favourite. She saw reproductions of 'Winter Sun-shine', 'Blenheim Tapestries', 'The Goldfish Pool at Chartwell', 'The Cross in St Paul's Churchyard' and 'The Blue Room', as well as a number of other landscapes. Mary said that she liked 'The Blue Room' best, and also a painting that showed the curve of a Berkshire down surmounted with beeches. Mary later said, 'I liked his paintings – they were very direct and it seemed that he knew exactly what he was going to do from the beginning of the painting to the end. It didn't seem as if he had hesitated at all, and the way he painted seemed very much to be the way he was as a man – at least the kind of man we had come to know through the press in the Second World War.'

Professor Thomas Bodkin, Barber Professor of Fine Arts and Director of the Barber Institute of the University of Birmingham from 1935 to 1953, supports Mary's contention when he writes:

Knowing a great deal about Sir Winston Churchill as a man we expect to find his salient qualities reflected in his paintings. We are not disappointed in this expectation. A striking characteristic of his pictures is their quite extraordinary decisiveness. Each is a clear and forcible pronouncement. He does not niggle or retouch. His paint is laid once and for all with no apparent hesitation or afterthought. It is never fumbled or woolly in texture. Spaces are filled with obvious speed. His colours are bright, clean and well harmonised. His drawing makes factual statements, though these may not always be quite accurate in detail.

'Indeed,' said Mary, 'there was a hint of a mystery to some of the paintings and things were never quite what they seemed.' She was particularly interested in a canvas called the 'Golden Walls of the City of Marrakesh', although she cannot remember whether she saw this painting as a reproduction in the Hyde Park suite or elsewhere. The painting is drenched in tropical sunlight and guarded by a rank of slender palm trees, but in the bottom left-hand corner three dark motionless figures stand in an enigmatic group. 'I never knew whether they were pilgrims or priests,' said Mary, 'but they stayed in my mind, worrying away at it for many years.'

A few days before he died, George VI attended a service dinner in the Hyde Park. Mary was shocked by his appearance. 'He'd lost so much weight that his clothes hung on him. I couldn't believe that he was the same man I'd done the conga with only a few years before at Lady Vyner's party. His face was tired and grey – and his speech was very slow.'

On a bitterly cold January day the King saw Princess Elizabeth and the Duke of Edinburgh off on their tour to East Africa and then Australia. He stood waving on the tarmac in a gale. He must have realized instinctively that this might be the last time he saw his daughter. Her marriage to Philip Mountbatten had not been encouraged at first, but eventually full approval had been given. Nevertheless it left a void in the lives of both George and Elizabeth. The depth of this is made clear in a letter he wrote to Princess Elizabeth on her honeymoon: 'Your leaving us has left a great blank in our lives but do remember that your old house is still yours and do come back to it as much and as often as possible. I can see that you are sublimely happy with Philip, which is right, but don't forget us, is the wish of your everloving and devoted papa.'

On 5 February 1952 George VI died. The footman who was the last to see him was a regular visitor below stairs at the Hyde Park. He told Mary about the King's last day. It had been a traditional Sandringham day.

The footman told us the King had been shooting in the morning with Lord Fermoy. They had shot over the fields for six hours and they had been served a picnic lunch. The King shot nine hares and a pigeon. In the evening the King went out to look at his golden retriever which had a thorn in his paw. After dinner he listened to Princess Margaret playing the piano, finished a crossword and went to bed at about half-past ten. The footman took some cocoa up at eleven and saw the King in bed. He was reading a sports magazine. He said goodnight to the footman quite normally. In the morning the valet came with early morning tea. The valet went over to draw the curtains. Normally the King woke up when this happened but that morning he didn't stir. After a while the valet realized the King was dead.

The news reached the Duke of Edinburgh at Treetops in Kenya that morning and for an hour he kept the tragedy to himself until it had been confirmed. George, at fifty-six, was young to die, and his daughter, Elizabeth, was deeply shocked when her husband finally told her. They all knew he had been very ill, but somehow his death seemed unexpected. They flew back immediately, and the new Queen stepped out of the aircraft on the evening of 7 February to greet the Prime Minister and members of the Opposition, the Duke of Gloucester and Lord and Lady Mountbatten. Once again Mary Shiffer was to take up her front row position for yet another royal funeral – and coronation.

The Hyde Park was packed with visiting royalty for the coronation. The hotel had now been restored completely to its former glory and was as sumptuous as it had been in the twenties. Very few architectural alterations had been made, although Evelyn Waugh had described one of the newly decorated suites as an example of 'ingenious hideosity'. Mary still had her succession of humble jobs, Jimmy remained in the wine-cellar, and Massara capitalized on and consolidated his success. He had become one of London's 'characters' and thoroughly enjoyed his role. The press took him up and improved the image. The *Daily Express* gossip column said:

From pottering about in a tiny Italian village to catering for London debutantes – that is the story of Ronald J. Massara, catering manager at the Hyde Park Hotel.

Massara, 48, caters for 5,000 guests every week. He is in charge of the restaurant, banqueting, and grill at the tall hotel overlooking Hyde Park.

He spent his boyhood in Turin, worked in Budapest and Vienna before coming to London.

Most Exciting Moment: Catering for the Silver Wedding dinner of George VI and Queen Elizabeth in 1948. After the three-course meal, the King suggested they should dance and helped Massara roll back the carpet.

Funniest: When Sir Winston Churchill drank champagne, red wine, and more champagne – in that order – at a dinner party, and said 'If the wine is best vintage, it doesn't matter in which order you drink it.'

Later, William Hickey took him up again, comparing him with other contemporary restaurateurs: 'Massara ... a debonair man who darts about like a rather extravagant bird. And the odd thing about these distinguished restaurateurs is that nearly all come from the same area – villages around the Italian lakes.'

Mary liked Massara. He always treated her very well – and he knew he'd get a mouthful if he didn't.

He was a good businessman as well as a character. He acted out the part of a womanizer but in fact he was devoted to his wife and two sons. He was inclined to bully and some of the staff were afraid of him. But he was such an organizing genius that the hotel would have come to a full stop if he left. But perhaps his main job was to be a personality – and he was certainly that. He treated all the nobs that came in as his own personal friends. And it worked. He had such a strong personality that they were flattered and liked to keep in with him.

This is borne out by Lady Vyner who told me, 'Massara was incredibly efficient. Everything was left to him to organize – and it all emerged perfectly afterwards.'

In fact organizing was Massara's great love. He thoroughly enjoyed activating the cogs of the great hotel, fighting battles with its managers and patronizing the guests. He told me:

I used to go back every two years to Alice Castello – I still drew strength from it. There I was just another Massara – amongst many. I would work on my uncle's fields as if nothing had happened. As if I'd never gone away – and the Hyde Park Hotel never existed. At lunchtime we'd have the garlic bread and wine, sitting in the heat of the fields. I was a boy again – and it was good to feel the earth beneath you – and not the deep-pile carpets of the hotel.

Massara's great gift was that he gave distinct personality to the hotel, and regular users like Sir Max Aitken and Giles the cartoonist genuinely liked him. Sir Max said: 'Massara gave the place a unique club atmosphere. He made it quite different from

any hotel in London by the sheer force of his personality.'
Cesare Maggi, the restaurant manager brought into the hotel by
Massara, said: 'He was interested in everybody's family, and
would always be asking after this Peer's daughter or that Lord's
son.'

Massara's finest hour came when one of the catering journals
wrote up a glowing tribute to him. Although it was published
in the mid-fifties, it is relevant to reproduce it at this point in the
Hyde Park's history as it describes so well the atmosphere
Massara had built up:

> On one of those golden Indian summer days with which this
> autumn has compensated us for June, we went to lunch at the
> Hyde Park Hotel. The enormous windows opening straight
> on to the Park made an almost theatrical backcloth to the
> spacious elegant rooms. Clear from the window, right to the
> horizon, under blue skies, the green of the Park turf and the
> autumn foliage of the trees were bathed in sunshine, like a vast
> framed picture.
>
> The Royal entrance to the Hotel lies on this side. Only for
> the monarch may it be opened up. Then the awning goes up
> and the red carpet is spread. Otherwise the rest of the world
> must enter from Knightsbridge. The hotel has a tradition of
> Royal usage ever since its beginning in 1892. It was built in
> the grand manner with spacious rooms lighted by dazzling
> chandeliers, elegantly panelled in the dovelike colours beloved
> by the French designers of that supremely elegant period. The
> huge mirrors reflect the subdued colours of the carpets and
> the brocades of the hangings.
>
> There is a perfect background for Royal occasions which
> have been legion. . . . It has become a tradition for daughters
> to follow their mothers in having their coming-out balls at the
> hotel and later on their wedding receptions. In the same way,
> fathers and sons continue to hold their Regimental and Public
> School functions there.
>
> The catering manager, Mr. R. J. Massara, is justly proud
> of the Royal connections of the hotel, and one of his most-
> prized possessions is the menu card in his sanctum from the
> Royal Silver Wedding Ball, signed for him by the late King

George, the Queen Mother, Queen Elizabeth and Princess Margaret.

Mr. R. J. Massara has the onerous task of running both restaurant and grillroom, as well as being responsible for the banqueting – which is quite an enterprise on its own. With the admirable and very necessary quality of being able to delegate authority, he leaves the charge of the restaurant to the imperturbable Mr. C. Maggi, and much of the banqueting to Mr. E. Osborne, who has eight wine-butlers under him. Mr. Osborne does not turn a hair at an order for 500 bottles of champagne – it is all in the day's work. Mr. Maggi takes visiting Royalty in his stride, having the gift of being always unobtrusively there when required and vanishing at will. I am sure if he had not been in his present position he would have been a diplomat – he has the air.

Mr. R. J. Massara is, of course, another diplomat. Born of an Italian father and a Scottish mother, he has all the best qualities of both races, and he needs them all in his job! He was 10 years at the Savoy with Santarelli; at the Ritz, in Paris, with Madame Ritz; in Vienna, at the Berkeley Hotel with Cavadini, and then at the Mayfair with Mr. Brian Franks, who was, at 24, the youngest manager of a premier London hotel. The war came to interrupt with five years' service, but when, afterwards, Mr. Franks took over at the Hyde Park Hotel, Mr. Massara happily joined him.

He brought with him the invaluable Mr. Maggi, whom he had long known from Claridges.

It was a formidable team and no wonder the hotel has excelled itself under such men.

On the day we visited the hotel, we were enjoying a pre-lunch dry sherry in one of the quiet lounges, when Mr. Brian Franks came over from a nearby table to greet us. For all his reserved and quiet manner, it is not difficult to discern in him the adventurous courage that moved him to be dropped behind the enemy lines for dramatic secret-agent activities during the war, emerging with a D.S.O. (and the determination, I am told, to lead a quiet life in future).

When we went to our table in the restaurant, it had so lovely a view over the Park that we exclaimed in pleasure, and were told that the Queen of Sweden, who was staying at the hotel, usually occupied it, but she was away on that occasion and they had thought we would appreciate it instead.

The view added to our pleasure while we enjoyed the Colchester natives, perfectly served and perfect in themselves. A tournedos followed accompanied by a delightful young Moselle, a Kanzemer Altenberg Spatlese 1953. The cheese trolley offered *embarras de richesse*, and notably a wonderful Brie on the straw which seemed just right for the moment, although one of us chose a fresh fruit salad from the equally tempting trolley of succulent sweets. A strong and aromatic coffee completed a notable meal.

Mary remembered the kind of guest list the Hyde Park had during this second heyday:

There was Otto Klemperer who always had the same suite on the seventh floor until he died. There were lots of royalty – the King of Italy, King Hussein (always looking very British somehow), the Danish Royal Family, the Crown Prince of Norway, the Grand Duke of Luxembourg – there were dozens of them. Then there was the aristocracy and I remember Lord Auckland, Lord Montagu of Beaulieu, Lady Louis Mountbatten and the Duke of Gloucester used to dine regularly at the Hyde Park. There was Field Marshal Slim and General Laycock and politicians like Lord Home, Edward Heath, Gaitskell, Rab Butler, Ian Smith and, of course, Churchill. But what I really remember about that part of the fifties was the way the hotel became so well known for celebrities. The kind of people you always see in V.I.P. airport lounges in films. And most of them were film stars too. Bette Davis used to stay, looking very smouldering. So did Lottie Lehmann. There was Claire Bloom, Anita Eckberg and Cary Grant. He looked exactly as he did on the screen – as if he'd been poured out of this very beautiful mould. He once asked me how I kept my skin so pink and white – I think he had an interest in the cosmetics business. I told him I used carbolic and he went away looking sad.

Then there was Elizabeth Taylor and Michael Wilding. I

hardly knew them but I did know John Wayne. He was very
crumpled and craggy and he always seemed to be smoking a
fag. I felt worried for him – he was that kind of man. He used
to sit in the still-room and quietly have a cup of coffee with me.
He didn't say much – but he seemed to want to get away from
people. Just like the Prince of Wales. Sir Malcolm Sargent was
another V.I.P. who regularly came in but the person I remember with the most affection was Lady Docker. She had a
kind of child-like wonder to her – as if she couldn't really
believe she was so grand. Sometimes she reminded me of
Queen Mary – she could be so regal and gracious. Then sometimes she reminded me of my own mother, singing and dancing
to the melodeon on those Friday nights in The Liberties. Not
that Lady Docker sang and danced to the melodeon – but I'm
sure you know what I mean. She had so much interest in
people like me – an old bit of furniture in a posh hotel. She
always spent time with me – as much time as she did with the
press really. Like me, Lady Docker loved a good time. If I'd
had the money I'd have done the same as she did. As it was I
was grateful to her for letting some of that – razzamatazz – rub
off on me. After she'd been in the still-room for a few minutes
I felt like dancing and singing. If I think of those early fifties
in the Hyde Park, I always think of Lady Docker. With great
affection.

But as yet the Hyde Park had not arrived at its final pinnacle
of achievement. Realizing that he now had the most glittering
clientele in Europe, the last of the grand hotels and a highly
personable staff, Colonel Franks decided to hold a ball the like of
which had not been seen outside Court circles since the turn of
the century. Seizing upon the anniversary of the Charge of the
Light Brigade, Franks launched preparations for the Balaclava
Ball.

Brian Franks used all his military contacts to create the
centenary ball. It was given by the five cavalry regiments which
took part in the short-lived but memorable Charge of the Light
Brigade. Mary laid out her traditional finger-bowls of rosewater
throughout the ballroom and banqueting rooms, and helped to
arrange the pink and white cyclamen, antirrhinums, carnations

and roses that, as the *Daily Telegraph* put it, 'took one back to more opulent times'. There were also banks of lilac and rare anemone-centred chrysanthemums. On the pillars, Massara had ordered floral representations of the emblems of the five cavalry regiments, worked in preserved flowers from France. They were provided free by descendants of our French allies in the Crimea. Meanwhile, the enemy, the Russians, contributed the recipe of a rare salmon dish for Tissot to produce. The kitchen also worked replicas of the regimental badges into the buffet dishes by using tomatoes, radishes and the whites and yolks of eggs. Mary remembered:

I walked around the rooms before the guests arrived: Everyone was running about putting final touches to the food, the decorations and the flowers. Massara was supervising every last detail. We were all terribly nervous. I was on cloakroom duty just like in the old Queen Mary days. The rooms were a rare sight. It was the kind of fairyland I'd dreamed about when I was a child in the slums of The Liberties. I said sòme day I'd escape from the dirt and the hunger and the beatings – and I dreamed when I escaped I'd end up in a world like this. But suddenly I wasn't happy any longer – I just felt guilty. I looked at all the richness around me and it seemed wicked. For the first time for years I felt homesick.

When the guests arrived all officers wore their full-dress uniform of dark blue tunics laced with silver or gold, tight trousers and hessian boots with rosettes. The Colonel of the 11th Hussars, Major-General Combe, wore the original tunic and slung jacket worn by the Earl of Cardigan who was in command of the Light Brigade's suicide charge. He also carried Cardigan's sword.

Just after ten the royal party arrived. The Kinsman orchestra was in full swing by then, and the Queen and the Queen Mother sought temporary respite in Mary's cloakroom.

I knew the Queen quite well by then [Mary told me]. I think she regarded her duties just as her father had – as a firm and its daily business. She was a proper queen – like the two before

her but without Queen Mary's shyness. . . . That night the
Queen was beautifully dressed. She wore a silver lace gown
with a blue riband and the Order of the Garter. She also had a
diamond tiara, necklace and earrings. The Queen Mother wore
a pink silk evening gown, and the Duke of Edinburgh looked
uncomfortable in the ceremonial uniform of the 8th Hussars.

The Queen inspected the guard of honour and then started the
dancing with Air-Marshal Sir John Baldwin, while Major-
General Combe partnered the Queen Mother. The Queen danced
most of the evening and the royal party left about 1 a.m. The
evening had been a great success; the Hyde Park had mounted
its most historic occasion. Franks was pleased to see his success
was sealed by the 'lead story' in the Court Circular for
26 November 1954. It read: 'Her Majesty and the Duke of
Edinburgh, accompanied by Queen Elizabeth, the Queen
Mother, were present this evening at the Balaclava Centenary
Ball at the Hyde Park Hotel.'

The new 'Elizabethan Age', as it was hopefully called in the
early fifties, was a boom time for the debs. Prices were relatively
low, food rationing ended in 1954, and the country's economic
situation was gradually improving. The debutante season was
becoming predominantly middle class and, as Margaret Pringle
writes in her book, *Dance Little Ladies*,

the catchment area was becoming wider and the number of
debutantes presented each year was rarely less than 1,000,
although not all went on to do a full season. In 1951, 877 were
presented, in 1953, 1,198, and after 1955 there were always
more than 1,300 – the peak year being 1958 when 1,441 made
their curtsey in a rush to get in before presentations were
finally abolished. The debutante had to be presented by a
married lady who herself had been presented.

However, social revolution was coming, the climate being set
by the publication of books like Kingsley Amis's *Lucky Jim*
(1954) and plays such as John Osborne's *Look Back in Anger*
(1956), and, 'now a divorced lady, provided she could prove she
was the innocent party, could make the presentation'.

'Princess Margaret', commented Mary, was the big draw for the debs' balls at the Hyde Park. If she was there the ball was "in".'

Tommy Kinsman's life was even more hectic in these boom years. Entries in his diary for one week read:

Monday
2.24 p.m. Train to King's Lynn
9 p.m.–3 a.m. Hunt Ball
Tuesday
7.31 a.m. Train to London
11 a.m. Waterloo Air Terminal
3 p.m. Arrived Glasgow to play at party for launching new Clan liner
Wednesday
Flew back to London
9 p.m.–2 a.m. Played at birthday party in Hyde Park Hotel
Thursday
Rehearsal for broadcast
9 p.m.–2.30 a.m. Ball at Dorchester
Friday
7.30 a.m.–11 a.m. Rehearsal and broadcast of *Music While You Work*
3.30 p.m. Train to Sparkford, Somerset, for Hunt Ball
Saturday
First train back to London
3.15 p.m. Train to Market Harborough to play at Hunt Ball
Played till 5 a.m. Sunday. Early train back to London

Kinsman told a magazine at the time, 'Not long ago I covered five gigs in one day. I began at a lunch at the Hyde Park Hotel, then went to a wedding reception in Knightsbridge, played at a cocktail dance at Stanhope Gate between 5 and 7, carried on to a military ball at Lord Burnham's place at Beaconsfield, and returned at 2.30 a.m. to the Royal Festival Hall to play at a hospital ball.'

Kinsman frequently had to split the band on royal occasions – as in the case of the Balaclava Ball. Whilst the Queen, the Duke of Edinburgh, the Queen Mother and Princess Margaret were at the

Hyde Park, Princess Alexandra and The Princess Royal went to
the '500' ball. Tommy Kinsman remembered: 'I had to try not
to be missed at either by the distinguished guests. I had a taxi
laid on all night. At the most opportune moments I dashed from
one hotel to the other. I travelled that road, back and forth,
eight times. And I was dead lucky. At both hotels I was told I
was there to lead the boys whenever the royal guests danced or
requested a number.'

Tommy Kinsman employed roughly the same musicians all
the time but on a free-lance basis:

I had an unwritten option on their services. Every Monday
morning my manager went down Archer Street, where all the
West End musicians met, gave the boys their cheques for the
previous week – and told them the duties for the next seven
days. Outside these dates they tried to lay on what they could –
be it broadcasting, filming, recording or teaching. But, providing I gave them 24 hours notice, any engagement with me
would take predominance.

'The debs' escorts', said Mary, 'were now mainly Guards
officers or young men who did something in the City.' One such
Guards officer was Mark Chinnery, who commented drily, 'It
was all a bit rowdy, with people behaving as they imagined
people did in *Vile Bodies*.' Indeed, Waugh, from his eyrie in the
Hyde Park, once told Mary, 'Sometimes I think I created these
people. God help me.'

Chinnery told Margaret Pringle:

A debs' escort frequently dined and danced for free. Around
1950, when I was at Oxford, I found myself going to parties
at Quaglinos and the Hyde Park [Quaglinos was also owned
by the Bennetts]. People were short of men and if a lady were
giving a dinner party before a dance, she would often be asked
to supply a couple of extra men. I remember the first dance I
went to was given by Lady Loyd for her daughter Chelsey at
the Hyde Park. I had a tail-coat but we didn't wear gloves, and
I know I was round the next morning at 11 with flowers for
my dinner party hostess and then I got invited to her dance.

But it wasn't like the old days when my mother was young and she could remember her cousin shuffling the pieces of cardboard on his groaning mantelpiece like a pack of cards, and you had to be positively repellent not to be invited to parties if you wore trousers.

Perhaps the best summary of the debutante season in the mid-fifties comes from a restrained article in *The Times* headed 'Brief Hour of Glory' and written by 'A Correspondent':

Once again the glad cry goes up, 'They're off!' and another posse of more-or-less 'finished' young women make their curtsey, attend a great many parties at which they meet the same people, and finally emerge, fitted to face the great cold world. The English are great students of Form where their twin passions, debutantes and racehorses, are concerned, and from now until the end of the Season we shall avidly follow the progress of the debs of 1956, read their comments and opinions, observe their stamina, speed and staying-power, speculate on their escorts, and cast our private votes for that minor modern mythological figure, ritually slain at the end of each summer, the Deb of the Year.

What a rum business it has become – a gavotte danced to the sound of Progressive Jazz, a formal pattern where Society and Commerce, Good Manners and Business Sense stealthily shake each other by the hand when nobody is looking. In the old days, the whole edifice of Coming Out was built on the sound foundation of a white dress, long gloves, and white ostrich feathers worn uncompromisingly at the back of the head. There was something reassuring about those feathers. If you could wear them at all, they were bound to look just right. But to-day, with afternoon presentation parties, there is no accepted uniform, and you must put your trust in Mummy and Hardy Amies. At present the popular bet seems to be a sort of sub-cocktail silk dress, worn with a small, modestly decorated head-hugger, guaranteed not to slip over the nose at the Debutante's Greatest Moment.

... The sun is warmer, Miss Constance Spry is in blossom, and the music of Tommy Kinsman is heard in the land. Soon now the names of a select few will become household words to us all, and a successor will be found to last year's favourite, the elegant and exotically named Miss Pearson Henry, who was such a figure in our lives. On the day of the first afternoon presentation party this Season, Kefauver had beaten Stevenson, bombs had been thrown in Famagusta, and Colonel-General Serov was winging his way to London. But the day was made memorable for me by a headline which, in spite of it all, said simply, 'Miss Cummings in a daisy hat goes to the Palace'. The debs are a great comfort.

Mary's feelings about the Seasons at the Hyde Park were mixed. 'It was all very glamorous but often the girls looked absolutely miserable. But it was when they behaved badly – sometimes like hooligans – that I really got cross.'

Certainly their behaviour was pretty crude. At one party the debs and their chinless escorts climbed through the ballroom windows to dance on the grass outside. Some used the fire escapes but some, exploded Mary, outraged, 'propped ladders up against the windows and went out that way'. The press comment, in the *Evening Standard*'s 'In London Last Night', underlined the fatigue as well as the banality of the occasion.

Some of the debutantes, however, left before midnight – among them Miss Patricia Rawlings. She said 'I've had so many late nights that I feel dead tired.' Others fought fatigue with pep pills: 'I haven't been to bed before five o'clock in the morning for 21 days,' said Miss Jacqueline Ansley. And Miss Tessa Kennedy, who stayed until the end of the dance, said, 'You just *have* to take pills. I take some to keep me awake; others to make me sleep. That's what the season does to you.'

'It was all such a shame', said Mary, 'at the Irish dance halls and clubs we danced our off-duty nights away. Just like the debs – except we knew how to enjoy ourselves without being vandals – or swallowing pills.'

Several officers of the 11th Hussars [wrote the *Evening Standard*], all in the plum-coloured trousers of their full dress uniform,

lost their spurs stamping to rock'n roll music at a regimental
ball at the Hyde Park Hotel. The spurs got kicked around the
floor. And finally bandleader Tommy Kinsman announced
'Please bring all loose spurs to me'. One officer at the ball was
Mr. Francis Newall. He was there with his father, Marshal of
the Royal Air Force Lord Newall. Said Mr. Newall towards
the end of the party, 'My spurs haven't come off once. It only
happens when you let them get heavily trodden on'.

'Once', said Mary, 'they threw fruit at Tommy. I threw it back
and caught one little miss right on her arse. I aimed even lower
at one of the escorts.' The *Manchester Evening Chronicle* preserved
the incident for posterity:

Oranges and lemons rained from the ballroom ceiling and a
'battle of fruit' raged at the Hyde Park, London, at a quarter
past five this morning after one of the gayest and most
spectacular coming out balls of the season. Hostesses Mrs.
Harriet Fane and Mrs. Robert Rivers-Bulkeley ducked to avoid
the flying fruit as Miss Carolyn Constable-Maxwell and Mr.
Billy Bromley-Davenport swung on the ends of a vast laurel
trellis, on which the fruit was suspended and which entwined
the ceiling.
    Soon debutantes and their escorts were playing football with
fallen oranges, lemons and apples among broken laurel leaves.
Others flung them in all directions – the chief target being
Tommy Kinsman's band. Lemons bounced off musicians'
heads during a furious Charleston.
    Said Mrs. Rivers-Bulkeley, who danced tirelessly for seven
hours, 'At least everyone seems to be enjoying themselves.'

Said Mary, 'It was a battle royal. Pity – because it was one of our
most lavish balls. There were 500 guests and Italian style decor –
mainly imitation marble plinths and statues made from painted
plywood. At the top of the stairs they had a tableau called
Invitation to the Dance. All the figures were made of coloured
metal foil and wire netting. They were set against a background
of silver trees and blue and green muslin as clouds.' The headlines in the *Evening Standard* the next day trumpeted:

THE DEBUTANTE PARTY ENDS IN A FRUIT BATTLE
AND TOMMY KINSMAN FINDS AN ORANGE IN HIS TROMBONE

And lemons featured in the next story:

COLONEL LLEWELLYN IS BEATEN BECAUSE OF A LAUGH
SO IT'S SUCCESS FOR BELGIUM IN THE LEMON DANCE

Dozens of lemons rolled all over the dance floor as international show jumpers and their partners competed in the
lemon dance – prize, a magnum of champagne – during a ball
at the Hyde Park Hotel last night.

Laughing crowds, including Miss Pat Smythe, Viscount
Knutsford, Earl Bathurst and Mr. Evelyn Rothschild, gathered
round to shout encouragement to the two couples remaining
in the finals – Colonel Harry Llewellyn dancing with Mrs.
William Hanson and Belgian show jumper Mr. George
Hemalsteems with Mme. Brigitte Shockaert.

Colonel Llewellyn struggled through a Charleston with a
lemon wedged between his eye and his partner's forehead.
Then he stumbled – the lemon fell – and the prize went to
Belgium.

'A shocking swindle,' he joked as he escorted his partner
back to their table. 'Someone made me laugh.'

Earlier younger guests at the ball – which was given for
competitors in the International Horse Show – requested a
Paul Jones. And the guests of honour, the Duke and Duchess
of Beaufort, joined in, energetically changing partners whenever the music stopped.

Then Colonel Vivian Dunn, Director of Music of the Royal
Marines, made a surprise appearance on the bandstand carrying
a violin. Dancers and friends applauded as he led Tommy
Kinsman's band with a flourish in a medley of tunes of the
Thirties. Requests poured in for popular jazz numbers but
Colonel Dunn turned them down. 'Jazz and the fiddle don't
really go together,' he said.

Hunting horns, noticeably silent during the evening, were
reserved for the last dance, where they provided a noisy
accompaniment to the Posthorn Gallop.

There was little need for Tommy Kinsman to advertise himself. *Vogue* said of him:

FOR A DANCE

Whether it is for a ball on the scale of one at Blenheim, or a simple hop for a hundred at home, have the best band you can afford and have whisky (and lots of it) both at the bar and at supper, as well as champagne. Nothing sends your most prized guests scampering off to the Satire Club or the Four Hundred, or just plain and simply, home, more quickly than a shortage of whisky. As for the band for the grand ball. Equally sought after is Tommy Kinsman (8 Rutland Gate, S.W.7. KNI 5453) who charges approximately £100 for an eight-man band from 10 p.m. to 3 a.m.

Meanwhile, the press was encouraging the debs to be even more 'outrageous':

As a debutante, you will find the competition hotter. Public relations men are 'out' this year, so make sure you do something spectacular at the first ball of the season, debag Tommy Kinsman, extract champagne corks with your teeth, drive your bubble-car into the fountain, wear an itsy-bitsy teeny-weeny yellow polka-dot bikini – *you* know the sort of thing. Daddy must spend at least a five-figure sum on your own party and Mummy must be ill in bed on the day and make a lot of snuffling utterances about how 'mis' she is at not being there but how Nanny will take good care of you. Cecil Beaton/ Oliver Messel *must* do the decor and Bobby Harvey should be playing somewhere down by the vegetable garden. Mr. Paul Getty should be on your right at dinner, thunderflashes should be handed out in the gents' cloakroom, and arrange for some valuable piece of jewellery belonging to a duchess to be stolen. (Regard this as a trump card.)

The press continued to be a boon to the Hyde Park throughout the debutante season – these are only a minute selection of the gossip columnists' coverage. Mary remembered each episode with mixed feelings. For instance, when guests took over the bandstand, Mary was very disapproving: 'I hate good music murdered – and they certainly did it. What got me was that the more the champagne flowed – the more rowdy they got. It was like a rugby scrum – and you can imagine the breakage bill.' The *Evening Standard* reported that:

Guests took over the bandstand at two o'clock this morning at the Hyde Park Hotel during one of the gayest dances of the autumn. The hostess Mrs. Edward des Graz invited Mr. Charles Gore and half a dozen others to play for Scottish dances.

Mr. Gore, sitting on the piano, swinging his legs, tucked a plastic signboard bearing the bandleader's name into his shirt front. Then he picked up a violin.

Double-bass player Mr. Tim Ritson wore white gloves. He said: 'My fingers get sore if I try to play without gloves.'

Bandleader Tommy Kinsman watched with amusement. 'They're not doing badly – and it gives me a rest.'

More than 700 people of all ages were at the ball. 'Its a 17–70 party,' said Mrs. des Graz.

Late supper and early breakfast were served concurrently in candle-lit rooms decorated with gladioli, white lilac, and mimosa flown from the South of France.

Mary relented however, when it came to the Charleston, a dance of which she was particularly fond. 'There was a Colonel Harvey who was a real pro – I wish I'd had the chance of dancing with him.' The *Evening Standard* reported:

I wondered what Colonel Bruce Harvey would have said. Earlier I had seen this tall, long-legged man stealing the Charleston honours at Lady des Voeux's party for her daughter Jane at the Hyde Park.

Colonel Harvey bounced around like a kangaroo. Afterwards I congratulated him on his performance. 'Well I should be able to Charleston,' he said. 'After all, I was one of the pioneers of it in London in 1924 when I returned from America.'

Colonel Harvey lives in the Isle of Mull. 'It's so peaceful,' he said. But on last night's evidence Colonel Harvey is a supporter of noise.

Cost was rarely commented on, although in the following description money was mentioned. Also the debs seemed to be going home earlier:

The days of the grand dusk-to-dawn dances are practically over, said Mr. Cecil Porter, a stockbroker, at a coming-out party at the Hyde Park Hotel.

The party, given for his daughter Victoria and Miss Rosamund Lee, daughter of industrialist Mr. Roger Lee, was a combined cocktail and buffet affair for 300 guests. It began at 6.30 and ended at 11 o'clock.

Said Mr. Porter: 'Last year just about saw the end of dusk-to-dawn dances. This year it is more fashionable to cut out dinner and end early – so that those who are tired can go home, and anyone who feels like it can go on to night clubs.'

And he added: 'It is also more economically advisable.' The cost of last night's dance? 'More than £1,000,' he said.

Two-thirds of the dance floor was carpeted to enable guests to 'sit out in comfort'. Tommy Kinsman, almost invisible through the throng of dancers, had dispensed with the bandstand to make more room.

Many of the debutantes – who included Lady Angela Cecil, Miss Susan Douglas and Miss Susan Wills – later formed small parties and went to night clubs.

Said Miss Elizabeth Thompson, a debutante two years ago, 'Eleven o'clock is a good time to end a dance. It makes the season so much less exhausting and it is fun to go to a night club afterwards for a change of atmosphere.' (*Evening Standard*)

Inevitably, the deb balls at the Hyde Park were peppered with younger members of the royal family, as reported in the *Evening Standard*:

The Duke of Kent and his sister Princess Alexandra went to the Hyde Park Hotel last night for the first big debutante dance of the season.

The dance was given by Lady Harcourt for her youngest stepdaughter, Virginia, and Miss Sally Snagge.

Lord and Lady Harcourt came from Washington specially for the party. Lord Harcourt is British Economic Minister there.

About 150 debutantes and their escorts were at the party. Parents and friends were allowed to join them at 11 o'clock – and 200 arrived.

The Duke and the Princess sat at separate tables – the Duke with Miss Harcourt and Lady Carey Coke; the Princess with Lord O'Neill and 1954 debutante Miss Elizabeth Abel Smith.

The Princess frequently asked bandleader Tommy Kinsman to play jazz tunes. Her favourite was 'The Darktown Strutters Ball'.

What did the debutantes think of the party? They said: 'The season has got off to a wonderful start tonight. Things are going to move this summer, especially with the new mambo dance.' But some of the debutantes' mothers were surprised at the way some of last night's escorts were dressed. Several men arrived wearing shabby Army overcoats over their evening dress. One wore suede shoes.

Dancing went on until five o'clock this morning. The Duke and Princess stayed until the end.

The next extract indicates how Kinsman was still the butt of 'ragging', and how vital it was for him – and his future bookings – to keep his temper. Mary was again incensed by the incident; she told me: 'It was amazing that Tommy kept his temper – I would have boxed their ears.' The *Evening Standard* reported:

In the heart of debutante-land a mammoth dance swung into the usual profusion of champagne, salmon and strawberries.

At the Hyde Park Hotel Miss Alice Sebag-Montefiore went through the process of a coming-out dance.

Undergraduates dotted the dance floor. 'Sixty per cent Cambridge,' announced Miss Sebag-Montefiore proudly.

'Where I went to school they didn't even teach me English,' said bandleader Tommy Kinsman as an undergraduate placed a lamp-shade on his head.

'1957,' said Mary, 'was the best year for the debs – they were in their prime. Henrietta Tiarks [now the Marchioness of Tavistock] was the deb of the year, and she used to be in on a lot of the Hyde Park parties.' At this time the Hyde Park would have been charging about £4,000 for each ball. The more economically minded, of course, shared the cost of the balls.

Presentation parties were finally ended in 1958 with an announcement towards the end of 1957 by the Lord Chamberlain. It read baldly:

> The Lord Chamberlain gives notice that there will be no Presentation Parties after 1958. The Queen proposes to hold additional Garden Parties in order that larger numbers may be invited to Buckingham Palace.
>
> For some time – in fact since 1954 – The Queen has had in mind the general pattern of official entertaining at Buckingham Palace, including the problem of Presentation Parties and certain anomalies to which they give rise. Her Majesty has felt reluctant to bring these to an end because of the pleasure they appear to give to a number of young people and the increasing applications for them. These applications have now risen until it has become necessary either to add to the number of these Parties or to seek some other solution.
>
> The Queen has decided that owing to her many engagements it would not be possible to increase the number of Presentation Parties. Her Majesty therefore proposes to hold (after next year), instead of Presentation Parties, additional Garden Parties, which will have the effect of increasing the number of persons invited to Buckingham Palace, both from the United Kingdom and from all other parts of the Commonwealth.
>
> In making these decisions The Queen has taken account of the increasing number of visitors from Commonwealth countries overseas who come to the United Kingdom, the large number of people who are presented to The Queen during Royal Tours and in the course of many other engagements, but who are not enrolled as having been officially presented, and the fact that the formal presentation of gentlemen, by means of Levées, has not been resumed since the war.

But, as Mary pointed out, 'The death of the debs was a very slow one; they petered out over the next fifteen years. I can't remember when it really began to fade away. There didn't seem to be any particular turning point. The dances just seemed to be less and less lavish. And there were fewer of them.'

The press, naturally, spent years writing the obituary of the Season – but obituary it was. And for those who did not snatch a husband during the Season, there was an obituary of another kind – a career. Usually something 'jolly' in dress designing or pottery. Then, quite suddenly, the 'failed' deb was simply never heard of again.

The bills were in any case becoming quite untenable in relation to current prices. A ball for 600 would cost £4,000 plus and a presentation dress was £80, while other aspects of the wardrobe, Ascot and cocktail dresses, could come to over £200. Also, bills for printed invitations worked out at approximately £80, while taxi and hire-car charges were astronomical. 'It was a good thing the Queen ended it all,' said Mary. 'It was out of date – and everyone was out of pocket.'

Mary's memory was crowded with dozens of epitaphs to the debs – and a few to their vacuous male companions. She remembered vividly the time when two fancy-dressed duellists had 'attacked' each other with swords, extracting tomato ketchup blood from pads inside their tunics. And the inevitable debagging of a young Guards officer. There were always as many people being humiliated as there were being smart. And as many lonely people as convivial. For years, Mary skivvied around the cream of the debutante balls, while her superiors, Franks and Massara, ensured that the Hyde Park became more and more fashionable. One of their ultimate accolades was the defensive article Robin Douglas-Home wrote in *Harpers Bazaar* in 1960, two years after the official presentations were ended:

The Suez Canal, Blue Streak, Strontium 90 . . . may all come and go, but The Season lives on for ever. Yes, the old annual bun-fight is once again splashing along its apparently impervious course. And this summer with a bigger splash than ever.

More champagne corks are popping, more swizzle-sticks are swizzling, more boiled shirts are crinkling, than have ever popped, swizzled and crinkled before. Ascot, Queen Charlotte's, The Fourth, Tommy Kinsman, the Hyde Park Hotel . . . all the old magic names on a myriad of twittering lips.

There is no doubt that the old order was reluctant to change – and still more reluctant to die.

One of the most haunting experiences Mary Shiffer had of a debutante Season in the fifties was during a party attended by Princess Margaret. It was very much a replica of dozens of other parties, and a shroud of tepid boredom was overcoming Mary. The same mid-fifties musical sounds, the same chatter – the Season was definitely beginning to pall. Because of all this Mary decided to walk down the passage to the servants' lavatory and while away the time for half an hour with a magazine. No one would miss her, there were plenty of staff about, and Massara, thankfully, was on holiday. Stepping out of the cream and gold corridor of the guests' section of the hotel into the dark brown corridor of the servants' section, Mary saw what she at first imagined to be a discarded heap of linen. On closer inspection she found it to be a crumpled white ball gown with an equally crumpled debutante inside it. She was crying soundlessly – and it seemed that she had been lying there for a long time. Mary paused – and then touched the girl's shadowed skin as if she were touching the flesh of a wounded bird. She remembered the beginning of the conversation vividly:

'You can't lie here, miss.'

There was no reply, no reaction except for a stiffening of the girl's body, a hopeless drawing away.

'I'm sorry, miss, you can't lie here.'

'Why not?' The voice was apathetic rather than challenging.

'These are the servants' quarters, miss.'

'So what?'

'To be sure – you can't stay here,' Mary's voice was suddenly warm and the girl responded to it with a series of hard, dry sobs. Involuntarily, Mary sat down and put her arm around her. Over and over again she asked the girl what the matter was, but however hard she tried she received more or less no response. Wondering what on earth she was going to do with this seemingly inconsolable child Mary began to feel a similar wave of despair.

At last the girl sat up. She looked angry and tragic. There was no hint of comedy to her misery, despite the fact that her smudged lipstick and running mascara made her look like a clown. Outside, as a swing door opened, faint bursts of the Kinsman band filtered through. He was playing 'Ain't Misbehavin'. Eventually the girl responded and told Mary that she just couldn't 'stand this bloody place any longer'.

Mary asked her if she had anyone to dance with and she reassured Mary that she had a partner, that she found him a damned bore, that she would be in a teaching job now if only Mummy hadn't told her that 'she'd break her heart if she didn't have a Season'. Mummy had had a lavish Season, apparently, also mainly centred on the Hyde Park. When she heard her name Mary dimly remembered the mother back in the twenties, floating languorously in a filmy dress, with a strangled voice and all the frenetic 'in' language of the times.

Mary tried to tell the disconsolate deb that 'it would soon be over', too late realizing that she sounded like a nursery governess. The girl returned her a bitter smile and went into a devastating tirade. She said that she'd got 'bloody months of it yet'. Every night was the same, and every night Tommy Kinsman seemed to be there too. So far, she'd been to eight different dances at the Hyde Park and the Season was still young. Her main complaint was the men: 'They talk about polo – and polo – and polo.' As for the girls, she said they spent half the time in the loo gossiping about the Season – and half the time on the dance floor, gossiping about the Season.

The strains of 'Ain't Misbehavin' filtered through again, and the deb yelled out to Mary that 'she wished someone would'. It was shortly after this that this spirited, if unpredictable, girl asked Mary if she could go below stairs and meet some people who were 'alive'. Mary turned away from her in embarrassment, and the girl was perceptive enough to realize immediately that she was being both patronizing and embarrassing. Nevertheless, although she approached Mary again in a gentler tone, she seemed determined to go through with the escapade. With sudden anger Mary pointed out that she was still on duty. But when the deb persisted, Mary looked at her watch – and discovered that her shift was over.

Mary never knew why she gave in. Perhaps it was because Massara was away – for his fury would have known no bounds if he had discovered what had happened. The girl told Mary that her name was Susan; beyond that Mary knew nothing about her. She did not speak about her background as she accompanied Mary to the still-room, where they had coffee, to the kitchen, where a surprised chef produced paella and chips, and to the cellar, where Jimmy produced the best claret. Continuously, almost feverishly, Susan questioned Mary about the running of the hotel, the jobs the staff did, Mary's own background, her home in Battersea, and so on. It was as if she was desperate to get a grip on reality, to tear herself away from the superficial world of the ballroom and her mother's ambition and Roger – her partner. Unfortunately Susan's fervour also applied itself to the wine. She quickly got drunk – and passed out in the cellar.

The problem was how to get her back into the ballroom without being seen. It was impossible – but it *would* be possible, somehow, to get her back to the servants' corridor. They tried to lift her, but she was too heavy for them. Cursing herself for getting involved in the first place, Mary went to fetch the brawniest of the chefs. Eventually she managed to persuade him to undertake the task.

In the semi-darkened corridors the three of them humped the soundly sleeping Susan back to the spot where Mary had originally found her. During the hazardous journey they had to duck first into a linen room, and second into the still-room, to avoid prowling managers. Finally Susan arrived at her destination and was dumped unceremoniously on a tatty horsehair sofa. Jimmy and the chef fled and Mary, feigning recent discovery, went up to the deputy banqueting manager and told him that 'she had found a young lady asleep in the staff corridor'. A few minutes later Mary had the grim satisfaction of seeing the chinless Roger scurry along to the rescue. She hung around to hear him wake his sleeping princess.

'Darling,' she heard him keep repeating, 'What on *earth* is the matter?' Eventually Susan came round and Mary heard her tell him to 'Fuck off out of it'.

'I liked her,' said Mary years later. 'She was really trapped – and it did her good to get drunk with us.'

In 1960 Mary was seventy-one, although she passed herself off to the management as sixty-one. She was terrified of retiring and desperate to keep on with the daily routine she had become so used to. Her mother had died in the last few years of the fifties. It had not been unexpected, and she had lived to a great old age. The funeral was in some ways very similar to her father's – but this time the grief was all too real.

Then, in 1960, Jimmy became ill. He had never been strong, his working life had been a hard and unhealthy one, and gathering bronchitis gave way to a coronary. For a while he had been confined to bed at home and then, because Mary had to earn for them both now, he was transferred to hospital. He quickly became worse, and then, quite suddenly, he died. Mary was completely shattered by his death. She had loved him deeply, despite their lack of home life and, worse still, their lack of children. Jimmy's sudden departure made her realize how totally dependent she was on the Hyde Park. Without the bustle and companionship of the hotel all she had was a couple of rooms in Battersea and a few old friends. Quite suddenly, Mary realized she was an old lady. It seemed incredible, as if her life at the hotel had been a few fleeting months. But it had not; she had been there for forty-four years. Her early life and her present life began to merge and all the old insecurity returned. She might have moved with the famous but now she was to be left destitute and forgotten. At all costs the management of the hotel must not find out about her age, and they must continue to find her useful.

At one of his regular Hyde Park polo parties, Prince Philip nodded to her and said, 'You're looking younger every day.' Mary nearly dropped a tray of glasses in her gratitude. At the back of her mind she realized it was only a way of being pleasant, but it gave her reassurance. If the Duke of Edinburgh thought she was still young enough to carry on, then who was Colonel Franks to question it?

On his deathbed Jimmy, his still boyish face set with the knowledge of death, had said to her, 'Go home now, Mary. Go home to your own people.' But she would not. For a start she no longer considered them her own people. Dublin had changed radically, most of her relatives and their children lived in the suburbs, and she felt she no longer had any association with any part of it. Jimmy had worried continuously over her as he gradually weakened. Over and over again he had pleaded with her to go back to Dublin, to live in at the hotel, to move in with one of her friends. Anything but return to the empty flat. But that was exactly where she wanted to go.

'It didn't matter,' she said. 'He thought I'd be lonely there. But I couldn't be – not with being surrounded with all our old stuff. He was there just as much as he was when he was alive. On Sunday, he was at mass with me. I was bored on my own – but never lonely. If I *had* gone back to Dublin I would have been lonely there all right. What Jimmy never understood was that London *was* my home. And always would be. Now.'

But the insecurity remained. If the hotel got rid of her she would have found time on her hands, and idleness was something that she knew would destroy her. She would be in a void and have no one to serve. After a lifetime of service it would be impossible to break the routine. Most of the staff of the hotel were well aware of her plight. Billy Bones, head barman in the Buttery Bar and inventor of the Hyde Park's most famous cocktail – the Clouded Moon – said, 'Mary was part of the tradition of the hotel. She had been very close to Queen Mary. I remember once my wife regularly meeting Queen Mary and her lady-in-waiting strolling in Kew Gardens. Somehow they got talking and Queen Mary told my wife how lonely she was now "she was on her own". That was just before the war. She often spoke about Mary – and how much she had enjoyed their talks.'

Charles Vyse, one of the few remaining valets, told me, 'In the sixties Mary was still part of the grand hotel system, a way of life that's dead now. There were two waiters and a relief on every floor, eight valets to every floor – and a clientele that ranged from prime minister to film star, from royalty to all the well-known aristocracy. I suppose they regarded Mary as part of the furniture, yet still saw her as an essential figure.'

John Insley, still *maître-chef de cuisine* at the Hyde Park, certainly regarded her as essential:

She used to come into the kitchens at about six in the morning and if the breakfast chef was late she'd start off the breakfasts.

She'd keep my office beautifully clean, see to all our laundry –
and so on. She wanted to be part of everyone. She really
needed to be. And we certainly needed her. She was a very
devout Catholic and ultra-respectable in one way. Yet when
she lost her temper no one was safe. Strangely, although she
had known so many celebrities, she never for one moment
gossiped about them – or even produced anecdotes about
them. She was the ultimate in discretion. It was the small
things she was so good at. In a hotel kitchen the temperature
soars – and so do tempers. But she always kept our fridge
stocked up with Vichy water or fruit juice so that we could
keep our thirsts under control!

Ginger Mason was an apprentice chef when Mary worked in the
kitchens and he had good reason to thank her.

As an apprentice chef you had to live in a hostel and work was
your life – it still is. The kitchens don't allow you much free
time – nor any opportunity to meet anyone else outside them.
I was very lonely at first but Mary mothered me like she
mothered all the young boys who came into the kitchen as
trainees. She never spoke about her private life – I didn't even
know she was married to the cellarman. I suppose we were her
replacement children – but what does it matter? In all the sweat
and heat of the kitchens, amidst all the lost tempers and impossible deadlines, she was like a rock of stability to us all. She
was always bringing us coffee, listening to our loneliness,
always feeding us goodies she'd lifted from the directors'
dining room. At first I thought she was an old dragon – and
in a way she was. She'd been there so long that she'd become
an institution. But we always knew how afraid she was – that
someday, sometime, she'd have to leave the hotel which really
seemed to be her home.

The sixties plodded on and Mary was seen to be ageing considerably. Mercifully, however, both Franks and Massara decided
to ignore it. She continued to function, though her shifts still
meant that she often left her Battersea flat at 4 a.m. to be at the
hotel by five.

People were ageing with me [said Mary], and just as unwillingly. Evelyn Waugh, for instance, fought against becoming old and ill – and lost. 'We're two old crocks together,' he once told me but I thought – speak for yourself. He used to go regularly every year to Colonel Franks' Christmas Banquet, when all the old wartime officers in the S.A.S. used to get together. The last time Mr Waugh was there he didn't eat anything. He just sat there looking – as if he was miles away. He didn't have anything to drink either. Then he asked me how I kept going. 'It's very tiring to keep going,' he said. I said that I had to and he looked away.

This account is borne out by Anne Fleming's account of the meal:

The last time he attended Brian Franks' Christmas luncheon at the Hyde Park Hotel, he had no appetite. We usually dined after the banquet, but on this occasion he was low in spirit and we stayed in his suite. The bathroom was without sponge or toothbrush, furnished only with aids to sleep. He wanted Laura, who had taken some of the children to the cinema and could not be found. I stayed with him until Laura's arrival was imminent, and was very sad to find him so changed.

Christopher Sykes, Waugh's biographer, strikes a similar, sombre chord:

It did seem to me that Evelyn had not long to live. I saw him only once more. Against his wish but in answer to appeals from Brian Franks and Bob Laycock, he attended the annual lunch at the Hyde Park in December 1965. He sat opposite me, next to Bob. He felt too ill to come down from his room before luncheon. He ate nothing. He drank nothing. He sat silent. I caught a glance from him which plainly said, 'You see my state.' After a quarter of an hour he left, leaning on the arm of a waiter. I never saw him again.

The last fifteen years of Mary's working life were more than ever centred on the hotel. Jimmy's death had left an aching void. Now, with both mother and husband dead, any semblance of a private life had gone. The Hyde Park was her life now, and there was nothing else. During the long, slow death of the Season, Princess Margaret and Princess Alexandra were the principal royals who used the hotel. The polo cocktail parties continued, and Mary remembered Prince Philip telling her that he had 'rigged up a gymnasium in Buckingham Palace with an electric horse and a padded wall' so that he could 'smash shots with my polo stick in comparative safety'. Prince Philip also had a penchant for the Hyde Park teas, which were of the old English variety and particularly sumptuous. 'He'd come in,' said Mary, 'like a little boy looking forward to his tea. And he certainly got through it. There was bread and butter and jam, scones, sandwiches, toast, all kind of cakes. It was a treat to see him tuck it all away.' The royal children also used to come into the hotel for tea, and soon Mary was to know the older two, Charles and Anne, very well. 'Charles was shy and never said much. But Anne was much more self-assured. I know she was meant to be a bit of a tomboy but she fitted into the Hyde Park like the most experienced of the debs. I only knew Andrew out of the younger two. They used to call him Andy and he was more noisy than Charles was at his age.'

Nonzio Nestola, hall porter at the Hyde Park, remembered Mary in her later years as 'one of the last of the old retainers', and head doorman, Harry Payne, said she was 'a perfect replica of the old days of the hotel'.

Mary had two final memories of the 1960s. 'Towards the end of the sixties the hotel was past its prime and was slipping back into the old weary days of the war. Its visitors were less well-known and royalty was not so obvious.' But one regular visitor to the hotel, who *had* been royalty but was now definitely 'ex', was King Umberto of Italy. Deposed by Mussolini, King Umberto still regarded himself as the rightful king and considered the current Italian government illegal. Exiled in Portugal, Umberto regularly came to the Hyde Park twice a year for shopping trips. 'If you caught him in a good mood,' Mary told me, 'he'd make you a knight. He made Nonzio one and he carries about a visiting card with it on. He gave him some land too – but when he'll get it is another matter. The King missed out on me – although I tried hard enough!'

In 1967 Kosygin, Chairman of the Council of Ministers of the U.S.S.R., came to the Hyde Park for a luncheon organized by the Confederation of British Industry. The menu was very lavish and represented the hotel's cuisine at its best. It read:

Vodka 'Stolichnaya'	Saumon Fumé d'Ecosse
	Crême de Lièvre
Château Cos d'Estournel, St Estèphe 1960	Filet de Boeuf Perigourdine
	Haricots Verts Frais au Beurre
	Pommes Nouvelles Persillées
	Soufflé Glacé Fleur d'Orange
	Timbale de Pêches au Bar-le-Duc
	Petits Fours
Remy Martin V.S.O.P. Grandes Liqueurs	Café

Mary remembered: 'I was working in the still-room and even in there we had Russian secret service men. They kept checking everything, even my coffee urn. I was furious; I kept asking them if they thought I was going to poison Kosygin. One of them spoke a little English, and he said that he had to consider every possibility.'

In the late sixties, the Bennetts decided to expand and bought Rosa Lewis's old Cavendish Hotel. Tom Sawyer was in charge of clearing it out, for it had stood empty for some years. He said, 'It was very eerie walking around the old place that had seen so much rackety history – so different from the Hyde Park. I knew Rosa was turning in her grave at the thought of the Bennetts buying the Cavendish. I found some old champagne in the basement and, even more spookily, a brocaded shoe in a corner that looked as if it had just been kicked off by its owner.' Mary commented, 'She definitely would have been furious. She thought we were a bunch of snobs at the Hyde Park, although there was no greater snob than her.'

While the Bennetts were in the process of demolishing the old

Cavendish Hotel, the group was taken over by Trust Houses, later to emerge as Trust Houses Forte.

One final below-stairs experience in the hotel brought Mary's extraordinarily long association with the Hyde Park to a close. She was now the only remaining member of the original postwar 'team' left – Massara had been promoted to being general manager of Quaglinos (another member of the Trust Houses Forte group), Brian Franks, Tissot and Cavallo had retired – and there was a temporary lull in the fortunes of the hotel. But, bearing in mind its traditions, Sir Charles Forte decided to capitalize on them. He would turn the Hyde Park into the flagship of his considerable European hotel fleet and engineer a third and even more glorious phase. Tourist coach parties had begun to infiltrate the marble halls since the beginning of the seventies, and the grand hotel atmosphere was beginning to fade. Determined to stem this, Sir Charles began to restore the marble, the grandiose symbol of the Hyde Park's earlier eras of élitism. And not only did he restore the marble but he also had more uncovered. Wallpaper and panelling were removed to show the glossy, veined texture in all its pale glory. Mary could see a third era of luxury gradually emerging. The Hyde Park, for the third time, was a grand hotel again, awaiting the depleted ranks of the crowned heads of Europe.

It was in 1976 that the kitchen crisis blew up – and, briefly, Mary felt needed again. A summer 'flu epidemic had taken its toll, not only of the general kitchen staff but of the top chefs as well. Despite this, a large banquet still had to be prepared on time. John Insley asked Mary to help. By this he had meant some pastoral work – like pouring out iced water or making coffee. He had forgotten Mary's personality. In the white hot urgency of checking on the arrival of meat, fish, vegetables and every other ingredient for the banquet, of preparing and cooking a ten-course dinner for two hundred, Insley still had time to notice, with alarm, exactly what Mary was doing. 'He needn't have worried,' she told me. 'I was glad to be useful again. It would have suited me if I'd dropped down dead on the job. After we'd finished, of course.'

Dropping down dead was just what Insley was afraid Mary might do. She seemed to be everywhere at once: working and shouting at the sous-chef; decorating a gâteau; slicing melon; making coffee; helping (and shouting at) one of the apprentices; clearing up dirty linen; making coffee again. Then, the crisis past and the banquet served, the staff sat around in the kitchen, exhausted and full of anti-climax. Suddenly, a grateful management sent down some champagne and the party started. It ended well after midnight with one of the Italian apprentices playing a concertina and Mary singing a ballad of The Liberties called 'The Three-Coloured Ribbon'. As she sang, she could see herself back in the kitchen in Engine Alley, her father in a rare good mood, her mother joyful and relaxed, her brothers and sisters dancing and fooling.

> *I had a true love, if ever a girl had one,*
> *I had a true love a brave lad was he,*
> *And one fine Easter Monday, with his gallant comrades,*
> *He started away for to make Ireland free.*
>
> *So all around my hat I wear a three-coloured ribbon,*
> *All round my hat until death comes to me,*
> *And if anybody's asking why I'm wearing that ribbon,*
> *Its all for my true love I ne'er more shall see.*

'Until death comes to me,' remembered Mary. 'I thought it had that night. After the party everyone went home – and I decided to sleep in the staff quarters. I just couldn't drag myself back to Battersea – I was too old and too drunk for the journey.'

It was 4 a.m. as Mary sat in the deserted kitchens. The breakfast shift would not be on for another hour and the clanging hubbub was temporarily ceased. The stillness was extraordinary. Then she saw them all, shadows amongst the shining steel. Queen Mary gave her a gentle, sad smile and sighed 'Poor David'. The Prince of Wales toasted her in whisky and winked at her. Clutching at his hand was Bridie. Her mother sat on Tissot's old wooden stool, while her father shouted out from within one of the ovens that he was roasting in hell. Valentino read her his poetry, sitting elegantly on a freezer, while Evelyn Waugh and Rosa Lewis noisily drank champagne leaning up against the griddle. Churchill drew her portrait in charcoal, sitting cross-legged on the floor. The Sultan of Zanzibar gave her fresh goat's milk in a chipped teacup. General Smuts stood above her, talking military tactics. The current royal family, dressed in tweeds and twinsets, drank tea and ate cucumber sandwiches around a chip fryer. The Tommy Kinsman orchestra played a samba from the fish counter, while Tissot, Cavallo and Massara sang,

> The struggle was ended, they brought me the story,
> The last whispered message he sent unto me.
> 'I was true to my land, love: I fought for her glory,
> And gave up my life to make Ireland free.'

As Mary drifted into deeper sleep she heard Jimmy telling her over and over to go home. 'No,' she said aloud as she awoke. 'This is home.' Shivering, she looked around the empty kitchens. A wave of despair settled over her. Soon she would have to go – not back to Ireland where she had nothing, but to Battersea where she had only a few memories. Her days at the Hyde Park were numbered, and she prayed that she might die now, where she sat, at the end of her glory and at the beginning of another phase in the hotel's. When she saw the kitchens peopled with her memories, Mary thought that death had really, so conveniently, come. But it had not, and as she stumbled stiffly towards the staff quarters she really understood what it meant to have a breaking heart. Unfortunately, she knew she could not die of it.

On her official seventieth birthday (in reality her eightieth), Mary had been given the usual retirement presents. But they allowed her to come back and work part-time until a bout of pneumonia put her in hospital. She recovered from this, and at eighty-five discovered that she finally had to accept the horrors of retirement. She found this almost impossible. It was so utterly depressing to stay cooped up in the tiny flat with its memories. But it was equally depressing to revisit the hotel and to find everyone busy at their jobs – except her.

It was at this point that the hotel management suggested to me that I might like to write the biography of this remarkable person. I met her – and instantly agreed. Mary seemed pleased, too, and I quickly saw that nostalgia could well act as a stimulus to her.

She never told me she was illiterate, although she firmly gave me to understand that she would prefer *me* to read the final manuscript to her. Mary began to relive her life with growing enthusiasm. But we had hardly started before continuous pain forced her back into hospital again, and it was there that the bulk of the work was done. .

Chapter Twelve

Childhood Revisited

1977

WE both unspeakingly accepted that there was very little time, and at St Stephen's Hospital in Chelsea we settled down to the task of recreating Mary's life. She would talk, I would prompt, and she only became irritable when she had misremembered something. Sometimes she would remember some episode of her life in the thirties, when it had actually occurred in the twenties. This made her very angry. Mary reminisced in the gloomy, off-white privacy of a cupboard-like television room. There were half a dozen vinyl-covered chairs, stained, empty ashtrays and the yawning, blank eye of the television. We used to sit close together, while Mary, a blanket drawn over her knees, tried to recall the details of everyday events.

Mary remained doggedly hospitable throughout the periods of interview. She asked the nurses to produce tea and would be careful to have her hair, nightdress and dressing gown always tidy and up to her own impeccable standards of cleanliness. Half-way through her memories, Mary was taken back to the Hyde Park for a special presentation for being the company's longest serving employee. She was keen to know how she would make the transition from car to foyer and she tested me out on this. I failed miserably by feebly suggesting that she might have to enter in a wheelchair. She certainly found walking enormously difficult, and used a wheelchair when going to another hospital for radium treatment. Mary was, however, adamant that she would only enter the hotel on foot. 'I'm certainly bloody well not going by wheelchair,' she told me angrily. 'And you make sure I don't. I'd feel such a fool after all these years.'

Somehow she made it, struggling in on the arm of a manager. Mary was given one of the luxurious suites to which she used to bring coffee. Here she presided over a tea for old friends. Tissot and Cavallo were there, retired now, and casting a critical eye over the chef's cakes. Later, an Irish band played and Sir Charles Forte presented Mary with a cheque, a colour television set and a large bouquet. A small dinner followed, and throughout the festivities Mary battled successfully to maintain the grand old serving lady image that was expected of her. She spoke to all the waiters, reprimanding them on this and that, told the current hotel manager of all the old (and possibly timeless) fiddles that she and the staff had instigated, and pointed out that the champagne was only a reasonable year. But by eleven she was exhausted and we helped her to her unfamiliar suite.

Next day, at the hospital, she told me, 'I enjoyed it – but I couldn't sleep a wink in that suite all night.' Mary had been thinking of the old days, lying in her luxurious bed and looking about the soft dove grey and white of the panelled walls. So, finally, the tables had been turned and she was ensconced in the soft other-worldliness of a guest room. Since coming in the back door with Captain Allen she had spent decades working as a minion. Now, in her late eighties and riddled with cancer, she was lying in state. Now was her brief hour of glory, and it was spent alone in the vastness of the ornate bed.

A few days later Mary began to deteriorate visibly. But she still talked to me and was unhappy if she was too ill to do so. Her greatest terror was for me to see her without her teeth, and this made the indignity of her end that much harder to bear. At this point Mary mainly talked about The Liberties; it was now closest to her. She was anxious for me to visit Engine Alley and was busy making arrangements with her Irish relatives so that I could go there with them. Every day it was as if she was about to go home: to the high narrow alleys with their stink of people and poverty and stout, to The Liberties of the 1890s – long before Mary ever imagined she would come to a grand hotel in London

and listen to the confidences of the leaders of the English nation –
with its handcarts, its scurrying bustle, the long evenings before
the fire waiting for the skillet to boil, or doing the family wash,
or nimbly avoiding her father's blows. It was as if her spirit was
yearning to filter through to The Liberties before it rose to its
God. At one point she was in the cathedral again, lighting a
candle for Bridie.

Then the cathedral burst into light and glory as the procession
slowly made its way from the shadows. The priests, acolytes,
servers and choirboys seemed like a medieval horde, striking a
strange combination of fear and reassurance in the hearts of their
flock. As her strength ran out, Mary saw Bridie sitting next to
her on the pew, diminutive and wraith-like. Mary found herself
sliding in time and would only occasionally surface to the everyday hospital life around her. This bewildered her, as if she was
tenuously living in two worlds. One moment she would be
racing down the Coombe as a young girl, the next she was
sitting up in her bed, clutching shakily at a cup of tea. 'Holy
Land,' she remembered. 'They called it the Holy Land.' But this
was not Israel but Coombe Street, which was called the Holy
Land because of its Jewish community. Then she dived back
into the past again and was playing handball in the streets with
the gang, or picking the orange lilies and blue irises that rioted
every summer in the garden of Elliott's the weavers, or buying
secondhand clothes off the stalls in the old Patrick Street market.

At one point in her delirium, Mary wandered back to The
Liberties at Christmas and the old children's chant beat
ephemerally in her head:

> *Christmas is coming and the goose is getting fat.*
> *Please put a penny in the old man's hat.*
> *If you haven't a penny, a ha'penny will do.*
> *If you haven't a ha'penny, God bless you.*

She recalled the cotton wool windows, cakes wrapped in silver
paper, glass-lidded biscuit tins, candied peel, raisins, currants and
cherries, the long red Christmas candles, and the·majesty of
Santa Claus with his sleigh and presents picked out in coloured
lights on the wall above McBirneys Shop on Aston Quay.

Shortly afterwards, screens were put round Mary's bed and I was told that she had only a matter of hours to live. In fact, she struggled on for two more days. The striking aspect of this period is that she insisted on checking the names of people she knew I had recently interviewed. She also insisted that the nurses propped her up in bed, and although she was almost unintelligible I tried to reassure her that the book was still progressing well. The very last time I saw her she was not able to rise – and merely lay gasping and rasping for air. I took her hand and she said, 'I helped them all – didn't I? I helped them all.' I told her that she undoubtedly had. I gave her the love of her remaining friends at the Hyde Park and she settled a little more peacefully.

By now she was sinking deeper into unconsciousness. I held her hand as she slipped further away. The last rites had been performed, her will had been made months ago, all her affairs were in order. I still sat there, the ordinary routine of the ward carrying on gently outside the screen. Then one final image of Mary appeared in my mind: she was standing in the still-room making coffee. Outside Tommy Kinsman's orchestra played; a lavish, exhausting function was at its height. Soon, one of the guests would find the frenetic gaiety too much to take. He or she would slip into the still-room for a few moments respite, which they found in the calm reassurance of Mary, to whom so many had confided when they found their own social position too difficult to maintain.

A week later I was walking in Ronald Massara's garden in the Kent cottage to which he had retired. He had not been able to spin out his active working life so long as Mary – much to his regret. After leaving the Hyde Park he had spent three years as general manager of Quaglinos, where he had cut a dashing, ageing but still romantic figure. Now, in his country cottage, he is restless, but finds solace in vigorously driving tractors on a local farm or sometimes, with the same determined energy, driving long-distance lorries.

In the rockery I was surprised to see a vast amount of marble. I asked him where it came from and he told me that he had brought it from a demolished lavatory and bathroom in the Hyde Park. It seemed appropriate that part at least of the marbled halls of the Hyde Park should find their resting place amongst the soil and flowers and creatures of the earth. Appropriate because that style of life is over now and its old servants and its palatial environment are part of history.

Leaning against an enormous piece of ex-Hyde Park marble, Massara said, 'Mary and I came from very similar backgrounds and although we ended up in very different situations we had one thing in common. Neither of us saw any shame in serving. All our lives we served people – and all our lives we drew strength from the past. Mary from The Liberties – and myself from Alice Castello. The past shaped our present.'

Mary Shiffer died a few hours after I had last seen her. She was eighty-eight. As the priest swung incense over her coffin, I heard again the cry of The Liberties:

> *Coal blocks, coal blocks,*
> *Eralamail, eralamail,*
> *Fresh fish, fresh fish,*
> *Coal blocks, coal blocks,*
> *Apples and oranges, oranges and apples,*
> *Coal blocks . . .*

Select Bibliography

Baily, Leslie, *B.B.C. Scrapbook Vol. 1 1896–1914*, Allen and Unwin.

Beaverbrook, Lord, *Men and Power*, Hutchinson.

Beaverbrook, Lord, *Politicians and The War 1914–1916*, Oldbourne.

Beckett, J. C., *The Making of Modern Ireland 1603–1923*, Faber.

Bestic, Alan, *The Importance of Being Irish*, Cassell.

Biggs-Davison, John, *The Hand is Red*, Johnson.

Borer, Mary Cathcart, *The British Hotel Through the Ages*, Lutterworth Press.

Bowyer, J. Bell, *The Secret Army*, Anthony Blond.

Contarini, Paolo, *The Savoy Was My Oyster*, Robert Hale.

Cooper, Derek, *The Bad Food Guide*, Routledge and Kegan Paul.

Cutforth, René, *Later Than We Thought*, David and Charles.

Davie, Michael, *The Diaries of Evelyn Waugh*, Weidenfeld and Nicolson.

Devlin, Bernadette, *The Price of My Soul*, André Deutsch.

Donaldson, Frances, *Edward VIII*, Weidenfeld and Nicolson.

Fanor, David, *G – For God Almighty*, Weidenfeld and Nicolson.

Fish, Robert, *The Point of No Return*, André Deutsch.

Fitzgerald, Redmond, *Cry Blood Cry Erin*, Barrie and Rockcliff.

Frischauer, Willi, *A Hotel is Like a Woman*, Leslie Frewin.

Gilbert, Martin, *Churchill: A Photographic Portrait*, Heinemann.

Gillespie, Elgy (Ed.), *The Liberties of Dublin*, O'Brien Press.

Gorman, Michael, *Ireland by The Irish*, Galley Press.

Graves, Robert and Hodge, Alan, *The Long Weekend*, Faber.

Gray, Robert and Olivier, Jane, *Edward VIII, The Man we Lost*, Compton Press.

Griffith, Richard, and Mayer, Arthur, *The Movies*, Spring Books.

Inglis, Brian, *Abdication*, Hodder and Stoughton.

Jenkins, Alan, *The Forties*, Heinemann.

Joyce, James, *The Dubliners*, Jonathan Cape.

Judd, Denis, *The House of Windsor*, Macdonald.

Kee, Robert, *The Green Flag*, Weidenfeld and Nicolson.

Kinross, Lord, *The Windsor Years*, Collins.

Laird, Dorothy, *Queen Elizabeth the Queen Mother*, Hodder and Stoughton.

Longford, Elizabeth, *The Royal House of Windsor*, Weidenfeld and Nicolson.

Longmate, Norman, *How We Lived Then*, Hutchinson.
Lyons, F. S. L., *Ireland Since The Famine*, Weidenfeld and Nicolson.
MacThomáis, Éamonn, *Gur Cake & Coal Blocks*, O'Brien Press.
Mansergh, Nicholas, *The Irish Question. 1840–1921*, Urwin University Books.
Marwick, Arthur, *Women at War 1914–1918*, Fontana.
Middlemas, Keith, *George VI*, Weidenfeld and Nicolson.
Montague-Smith, Patrick, *Royal Silver Jubilee*, Country Life Books.
Norman, Edward, *A History of Modern Ireland*, Allen Lane, The Penguin Press.
O'Brien, Conor Cruise, *States of Ireland*, Hutchinson.
O'Brien, Kate, *My Ireland*, Batsford.
O'Broin, Leon, *Dublin Castle and the 1916 Rising*, Helicon.
O'Callaghan, Sean, *Execution*, Frederick Muller.
O'Casey, Sean, *I Knock at the Door*, Macmillan.
O'Casey, Sean, *Pictures in the Hallway*, Macmillan.
O'Connor, Frank, *An Only Child*, Macmillan.
O'Faolain, Sean, *The Irish*, Pelican.
Pelling, Henry, *Winston Churchill*, Macmillan.
Perry, George, and Mason, Nicholas (Ed.), *Rule Britannia*, Times Newspapers.
Plunkett, James, *The Gems She Wore*, Hutchinson.
Pope-Hennessy, James, *Queen Mary 1867–1953*, George Allen and Unwin Ltd.
Pringle, Margaret, *Dance Little Lady*, Orbis.
Pryce-Jones, David (Ed.), *Evelyn Waugh and His World*, Weidenfeld and
    Nicolson.
Sherman, David, *World War I*, Octopus.
Shulman, Irving, *Valentino*, Leslie Frewin.
Stevenson, Frances (Ed. A. J. P. Taylor), *Lloyd George. A Diary*, Hutchinson.
Stewart, A. T. Q., *The Narrow Ground. Aspects of Ulster 1609–1969*, Faber.
Sykes, Christopher, *Evelyn Waugh*, Collins.
Symons, Julian, *Between the Wars*, Batsford.
Taylor, A. J. P., *Beaverbrook*, Hamish Hamilton.
Taylor, Derek, and Bush, David, *The Golden Age of British Hotels*, Northwood.
de Vere White, Terence, *Ireland*, Thames and Hudson.
de Vere White, Terence, *The Anglo-Irish*, Victor Gollancz.
Walker, Alexander, *Rudolph Valentino*, Elm Tree Books.
Wechsberg, Joseph, *Dining at the Pavilion*, Weidenfeld and Nicolson.
Wheeler-Bennett, John W., *King George VI. His Life and Reign*, Macmillan/
    St Martins Press.
Wilson, Sandy, *The Roaring Twenties*, Eyre Methuen.
Windsor, Duke of, *A King's Story*, Cassell.
Winter, Gordon, *The Golden Years. 1903–1913*, David and Charles.
Young, Kenneth, *Churchill and Beaverbrook*, Eyre and Spottiswoode.

All Futura Books are available at your bookshop or newsagent, or can be ordered from the following address:
Futura Books, Cash Sales Department,
P.O. Box 11, Falmouth, Cornwall.

Please send cheque or postal order (no currency), and allow 30p for postage and packing for the first book plus 15p for the second book and 12p for each additional book ordered up to a maximum charge of £1.29 in U.K.

Customers in Eire and B.F.P.O. please allow 30p for the first book, 15p for the second book plus 12p per copy for the next 7 books, thereafter 6p per book.

Overseas customers please allow 50p for postage and packing for the first book and 10p per copy for each additional book.